First Published in the United States of America
Fang Duff Kahn Publishers
611 Broadway, floor 4
New York, NY 10012
www.fangduffkahn.com

2009 2010 2011 2012 / 10 9 8 7 6 5 4 3 2 1

Editor: Gregory Mosher
Design: Ingrid Bromberg Kennedy, In-Grid Design
Printed in China through Asia Pacific Offset

978-0-7893-1864-0
Library of Congress Number: 2008936976

TABLE OF CONTENTS

I love movies. But I am no cinephile, and I often find myself at a loss when choosing a film to rent. Fortunately, I have friends who know films well, and I often ask them what I should watch—and that is the idea behind this book.

I asked both people I knew and many others in the film industry—people who are passionate and knowledge- able about film—to recommend a movie or a particular characteristic of a movie (performance, style, or theme) that they feel has been overlooked or underappreciated. I was delighted by their enthusiasm and eagerness to share their own little-known favorites. The short essays they wrote are personal as well as informative.

This book is not comprehensive, nor is it intended to be. It is, rather, a compilation of insights from a distinguished group of experts, including actors, direc- tors, producers, and critics. The result is a somewhat unpredictable collection of wonderful overlooked gems. Some of the selections may be familiar to you, but many, I suspect, are films you have never heard of.

I hope that you will discover some great films with this book, and that you will be inspired to search for your own cinema secrets.

I would like to thank all the writers—as well as The Film Foundation—for their thoughtful contribu- tions, generosity, and their willingness to share their love of film.

ROBERT KAHN
New York City, September 2008

MOVIES A-Z

A

Accident
1967, Joseph Losey

SCREENPLAY: Harold Pinter; based on the novel
by Nicholas Mosley
CAST: Dirk Bogarde, Stanley Baker, Jacqueline Sassard,
Michael York, Vivien Merchant, Delphine Seyrig, Alexander Knox,
Freddie Jones
U.K.

Accident was directed by Joseph Losey, the not-quite-but-almost-forgotten genius of British cinema. Losey took the gritty social realism of British movies in the early '60s and decisively shifted it toward a poetic voice: seductively soft, dangerously ambiguous, and threateningly gorgeous. No wonder Harold Pinter (who has a stunning cameo) was a perfect collaborator. Like Joseph Conrad and Henry James, Losey was a foreigner bewitched by the possibilities of English understatement, and in *Accident*, the huge stretches between utterances yawn so wide as to pull actors deep down into a place where they flail in tragic helplessness.

The cast (Dirk Bogarde, Michael York, Stanley Baker, Delphine Seyrig, and Pinter's first wife, Vivien Merchant) is infallibly pitch-perfect; in the poisoned garden of *Accident*, they have to be. Ostensibly it's the story of an Oxford undergraduate who falls for an Austrian student, and of his tutor's attempts to undo the relationship without quite having the conviction to replace him. Nothing happens for a very long time, and yet *everything* happens: raw envy, drunken backchat, pathetic delusions, thwarted silky desire—collisions so tiny they're heard as a menacing tinkle, yet so deafening and catastrophic they drown us in terror. And through it all, a true screen star called Oxford University shines, never so beautifully or tragically shot.

SIMON SCHAMA
Professor of art history and history, writer/presenter for the BBC and PBS, and writer

RECOMMENDED VIEWING: Other films directed by Joseph Losey: *The Servant* (with Sarah Miles, James Fox, and Dirk Bogarde), see p. 209; *The Go-Between* (with Edward Fox and Julie Christie).

An Actor's Revenge (Yukinojo henge)
1963, Kon Ichikawa

SCREENPLAY: Daisuke Itô, Teinosuke Kinugasa, and Natto Wada; based on a newspaper serial by Otokichi Mikami
CAST: Kazuo Hasegawa, Fujiko Yamamoto, Ayako Wakao, Ganjiro Nakamura, Raizô Ichikawa
JAPAN; IN JAPANESE

If you like backstage stories and are a little sick of *All About Eve*, don't miss this extraordinarily beautiful paean to a bottomless pit of rage. Set in the nineteenth century, *An Actor's Revenge* is the story of Japan's greatest actor, Yukinojo (Kazuo Hasegawa), who, as the star of a traveling Kabuki troupe, plays all the female roles. During a performance he notices his nemesis in the audience. Yukinojo's realization—his spinning in shock, the way the paper snow catches fire on the footlights—makes you empathize with his bloodthirsty anger. Yukinojo then seduces his enemy's daughter—without ever dropping his female drag.

JOHN GUARE
Playwright

All the world's quite literally a stage in Ichikawa's *An Actor's Revenge*, a gender-bending, genre-breaking fantasia that Nicholas Ray, Susan Sontag, and scores of others have hailed as one of the most breathtaking widescreen spectacles ever made. In this elaborate old tearjerker, filmed twice before, an *oyama*, or Kabuki female impersonator, steps out of the theater and into the streets of Edo (nineteenth-century Tokyo) to wreak vengeance on the three scheming merchants who drove his parents to madness and suicide. Making his three-hundredth screen appearance is the paunchy matinee idol Kazuo Hasegawa, who reprises the dual roles of *oyama* and ruffian that he first popularized in Teinosuke Kinugasa's 1935 version. (With a dagger concealed in his fan, he is fluttering femininity and machismo all rolled into one.) Subterfuge is the name of his game, as it is Ichikawa's, who joyfully sends up a dizzying array of Eastern and Western styles, from Japanese rolling scrolls and erotic *ukiyo-e* woodblock prints to American slapstick comedies and comic strips; and from *shimpa*, the theatrical melodramas of the Meiji period, and *chambara*, prewar samurai swordfight flicks, to Elizabethan farce and Jacobean revenge tragedy.

JOSHUA SIEGEL
Assistant curator, Department of Film, Museum of Modern Art

NOTE: Kazuo Hasegawa, who specialized in playing women's roles, starred in the original version of *An Actor's Revenge*, filmed in 1935.

The Adventures of Buckaroo Banzai Across the 8th Dimension

1984, W. D. Richter

SCREENPLAY: Earl Mac Rauch
CAST: Peter Weller, John Lithgow, Ellen Barkin, Jeff Goldblum, Christopher Lloyd, Clancy Brown, Carl Lumbly, Vincent Schiavelli, Dan Hedaya
U.S.

Brilliant neurosurgeon, daredevil jet-car pilot, martial artist, particle physicist, rock star, and philosopher: Buckaroo Banzai is not your average movie hero, and *The Adventures of Buckaroo Banzai Across the 8th Dimension* is anything but your average movie. Directed by W. D. Richter, one of my favorite screenwriters (*Invasion of the Body Snatchers*, *Big Trouble in Little China*), the film lives by the axiom that any idea ever used before in a book or a movie is good enough to put in this one. And they're all in there, every single one: evil scientists, alien invasions, Cold War paranoia, sidekicks with names like Pinky Carruthers and Rawhide, villains with names like John Bigboote (pronounced "big-boo-tay"), and a beautiful girl named Penny Priddy who just happens to be the identical twin sister of our hero's murdered wife. This has *got* to be the wackiest film ever made.

Peter Weller plays Buckaroo, delivering his lines deadpan no matter how ridiculous they are. In a reflective moment, he tells a judgmental crowd in a bar, "Hey, don't be mean. We don't have to be mean because . . . remember, no matter where you go, there you are." The cast also includes Jeff Goldblum, Ellen Barkin, John Lithgow, and Christopher Lloyd, plus a slew of great character actors whose faces you'll recognize even if their names don't ring a bell. Packed with hidden jokes, it's the kind of movie that reveals itself more each time you see it—in part because it treats all the completely ridiculous things people do and say ("Buckaroo, President's on line 1. . . . Is everything okay with the alien space cloud from Planet 10, or should he just go ahead and destroy Russia?") as completely natural. No matter how many times you watch it, you'll always discover something new.

ADAM DURITZ
Songwriter

After Hours
1985, Martin Scorsese

SCREENPLAY: Joseph Minion
CAST: Griffin Dunne, Rosanna Arquette, Verna Bloom,
Thomas Chong, Linda Fiorentino, Teri Garr,
John Heard, Cheech Marin, Catherine O'Hara, Dick Miller,
Bronson Pinchot, Martin Scorsese (cameo)
U.S.

Set in New York in the 1980s, a late-night encounter
evolves into a dark, lunatic adventure when Paul (Griffin
Dunne) tries to pick up a girl (Rosanna Arquette) in a
coffee shop. Director Martin Scorsese perfectly captures
Paul's panic (he's a word processor who lives uptown) as
he ventures into the then-untamed industrial underbelly
of downtown, inhabited by drug dealers, punks, and
assorted thugs. He persuades a cabbie to take him into
the dark, cobblestoned streets, where his last twenty-
dollar bill flies out of the window. We can feel Paul's
desperation as he flees into the night; he doesn't know
where he is going but he knows he is in big, big trouble.

INA SALTZ
Design director

Against All Odds
1984, Taylor Hackford

SCREENPLAY: Eric Hughes
CAST: Rachel Ward, Jeff Bridges, James Woods, Alex Karras,
Jane Greer, Richard Widmark, Dorian Harewood,
Swoosie Kurtz, Saul Rubinek, Pat Corely, Bill McKinney
U.S.

The Need to Escape not only drives the action of many
movie stories, it can also drive us *to* the movies—
whether it's to fool loneliness with a love story, trick

boredom with a thriller, or duck the blues with a bright comedy. One of the best ways to take a two-hour vacation is with *Against All Odds*, director Taylor Hackford and writer Eric Hughes's loose remake of *Out of the Past*, a 1947 RKO film noir that starred Robert Mitchum, Jane Greer, and Kirk Douglas.

The story, now featuring Jeff Bridges, Rachel Ward, and James Woods, serves up some of the genre's standard characters—the weak-willed Handsome Man, the reptilian Nightclub Owner, the sultry Femme Fatale—in a story of corruption, murder, and betrayal interwoven with a couple of decent twists and a satisfying ending. But the plot is not why we're here.

Against All Odds may be the most sun-drenched film noir ever made. From its opening shots in Mexico, over the wonderfully languid guitar score of Michel Colombier and Larry Carlton, the screen shimmers in the heat like an airport tarmac in the tropics. The story moves from Los Angeles (featuring a Sunset Boulevard game of chicken between a Porsche and a Ferrari that's among the best car chase sequences ever filmed) to various locations in Mexico (including two weeks of sex, sand, and tequila in the beachfront shack of your dreams) and back to L.A. in a haze of brutal sun and turquoise waters with barely a breath of breeze.

The lust between Bridges and Ward is convincing, adding to the general humidity. The supporting performances are uniformly good, especially Saul Rubinek's sweaty turn as a duplicitous sports agent and Swoosie Kurtz as his pining assistant. And, in a nice tip of the hat to the original film, Jane Greer returns as the picture's viperish Mrs. Big.

In films of this kind, the characters are usually in dire need of money, guns, or a second chance. In *Against All*

Odds, everyone also needs a cold beer. And watching it, even on a long winter's night, so will you.

KEVIN WADE
Playwright and screenwriter

Turtle Soup

The Age of Innocence

1993, Martin Scorsese
SCREENPLAY: Jay Cocks and Martin Scorsese;
based on the novel by Edith Wharton
CAST: Daniel Day-Lewis, Michelle Pfeiffer, Winona Ryder,
Alexis Smith, Geraldine Chaplin, Mary Beth Hurt,
Alec McCowen, Richard E. Grant, Miriam Margolyes,
Robert Sean Leonard, Sian Phillips, Jonathan Pryce,
Michael Gough, Stuart Wilson, Joanne Woodward (narrator)
U.S.

As six meals were pivotal in *The Age of Innocence*, choosing the right food was crucial. I researched and prepared several meals and met with Mr. Scorsese to discuss menu options. He was particularly interested in turtle soup, a ubiquitous dish of the period. But because the soup is dark brown we thought filming the turtles—live—would be more picturesque.

There's a shop in Chinatown that sells live turtles, so I ordered two dozen. I picked them up the day before their scene was scheduled, but to my despair it was postponed for a week. The unused bathtub in my office became a very large turtle bowl. After a call to the vet, the turtles were put on a diet of dry cat food (tuna flavored) and lettuce. All but one made it to the location—a lovely old house with a great kitchen, extensive gardens, and a pond. After their scene, we set the turtles free. A fine reward, we thought, for their cameo role.

I recently came across an article in the *New York Times* about the house we had used as a location. Toward the end of the article, the groundskeeper mentioned an abundance of turtles on the property. Maybe I should send him a recipe for turtle soup.

RICK ELLIS
Food stylist, writer, and culinary historian

Aguirre: The Wrath of God

1973, Werner Herzog

SCREENPLAY: Werner Herzog
CAST: Klaus Kinski, Ruy Guerra, Del Negro, Helena Rojo,
Cecilia Rivera, Peter Berling, Daniel Ades
WEST GERMANY/PERU/MEXICO; IN GERMAN

I've always felt that Werner Herzog's audience was not large enough, and sadly, it seems to be shrinking. Most of Herzog's films are wonderful, and *Aguirre: The Wrath of God* stands out as one of his best. From its astounding opening images of a tiny line of conquistadors making their way down an impossibly steep Andean ridgeline through the clouds, to a dazzling 360-degree spinning track around the expedition's raft, *Aguirre* epitomizes Herzog's concern with what seemingly could not be recorded on film. It's as if he were trying to get at what is going on inside the characters' heads by showing us what they are looking at. One of the most noticeable aspects of Herzog's style involves startlingly long takes, whether of roiling, muddy rapids or barely moving jungle canopies, during which, as he put it, "Nature itself—something oblique and ferocious—gains an independent life." The effect is a kind of visually enforced concentration—an enormously mesmeric power, as well as a new kind of expressionism in film.

JIM SHEPARD
Writer

Ai no corrida

see *In the Realm of the Senses*, p. 216

Alice Doesn't Live Here Anymore
1974, Martin Scorsese

SCREENPLAY: Robert Getchell
CAST: Ellen Burstyn, Alfred Lutter, Billy Green Bush,
Diane Ladd, Kris Kristofferson, Harvey Keitel,
Jodie Foster, Lelia Goldoni, Vic Tayback, Valerie Curtin
U.S.

As he has in many of his films, director Martin Scorsese
explores issues of family in *Alice Doesn't Live Here
Anymore*. It's a tender, funny film about the journey of
a mother and son traveling across America. The film's
sense of the ordinary gives it a brilliant touch, and
Robert Getchell's deceptively simple script is wonderful.
It also features one of the best—and earliest—performances by Kris Kristofferson. Music plays an important
role, with a sound track that ranges from Dolly Parton to
Gershwin. The end result is a film that touches the heart.

TIM KITTLESON
Former Director, UCLA Film & Television Archive

Alice in the Cities
1974, Wim Wenders

SCREENPLAY: Wim Wenders
CAST: Rüdiger Vogler, Yella Röttlander, Lisa Kreuzer, Edda Köchl,
Chuck Berry
WEST GERMANY; B & W; IN GERMAN

Alice in the Cities is my favorite Wim Wenders film. It's
a beautiful story about a relationship between a journalist and a little girl who are trying to return to homes
they've already lost. Subtle, shattering performances
and an awesome score.

ALLISON ANDERS
Director, screenwriter, and professor

RECOMMENDED READING: Alexander Graf, *The Cinema of Wim Wenders: The Celluloid Highway*. Wallflower Press, 2002.

Amen.

2002, Costa-Gavras

SCREENPLAY: Costa-Gavras and Jean-Claude Grumberg; based on the play *The Deputy*, by Rolf Hochhuth
CAST: Ulrich Tukur, Mathieu Kassovitz, Ulrich Mühe, Michel Duchaussoy, Ion Caramitru, Marcel Iures, Friedrich von Thun, Antje Schmidt, Hanns Zischler
FRANCE/GERMANY/ROMANIA/U.S.; IN ENGLISH, FRENCH, AND ITALIAN

This extraordinary film came and went far too quickly. It's based on the true story of Kurt Gerstein, an accomplished scientist who was recruited by the SS during World War II.

Gerstein, played by Ulrich Tukur, is horrified when the Nazis expect him to expedite the extermination of the Jews; as he maintains his duties, he tries to alert the Allies and the pope. Gerstein meets Riccardo Fontana (Mathieu Kassovitz), a young, well-connected Jesuit priest who tries, unsuccessfully, to get the pope involved. Disillusioned, Fontana decides to help prisoners in a concentration camp, thereby sacrificing his own life. When Gerstein tries to rescue Fontana, he in turn loses his family and his freedom.

Costa-Gavras punctuates the film with shots of fast-moving trains en route to and from concentration camps, arriving packed and leaving empty. The power of these images stays with you long after the film has ended. Unlike any film I have seen before, *Amen.* exposes the Catholic Church's denial of the atrocities of the Holocaust. Gerstein made great sacrifices to help strangers, knowing full well that he was betraying his country and risking his life. The futility of Gerstein and Fontana's actions leaves you empty and disheartened. This is one of the most gut-wrenching films about the Holocaust.

DIANE NABATOFF
Producer

American Dream
1991, Barbara Kopple

U.S./U.K.; DOCUMENTARY

Barbara Kopple is one of the leading observers of American life, and *American Dream*—which documents the mid-'80s union strike at the Hormel plant in Austin, Minnesota—is one of her best films. As luck would have it, Kopple was filming at Hormel when a cut in salaries was announced during early negotiations with the labor union. The workers were fighting not only the management of Hormel but also their own international union. The twists and turns of the story and the emotional arc of the documentary are as strong as any found in fiction films.

MICHAEL C. DONALDSON
Former President, International Documentary Association, author, and lawyer

American Society of Cinematographers

Hidden on a side street just off Hollywood Boulevard stands one of the oldest buildings in Hollywood. Once the home of silent-film star Conway Tearle, it is now the clubhouse of the American Society of Cinematographers.

The ASC has quite a legacy. It is the oldest continuously operating motion-picture society in the world. Housed within these venerable walls is one of the finest collections of motion-picture cameras anywhere. Also, *American Cinematographer* magazine has been published here since 1920. The love of cinematography echoes through its halls, where pioneers, past and present, share their hopes and secrets with new generations of artists.

STEPHEN H. BURUM
Cinematographer

The Americanization of Emily
1964, Arthur Hiller

SCREENPLAY: Paddy Chayefsky; based on the novel
by William Bradford Huie
CAST: James Garner, Julie Andrews, Melvyn Douglas,
James Coburn, Joyce Grenfell, Edward Binns,
Liz Fraser, Keenan Wynn, William Windom, Judy Carne
U.S.; B & W

A particularly outstanding year for movies, 1964 saw the release of *Dr. Strangelove*, *Becket*, *Zorba the Greek*, *My Fair Lady*, and *Seance on a Wet Afternoon*. It was also the year Julie Andrews, star of Broadway's *My Fair Lady*, was awarded a best-actress Oscar for the slight *Mary Poppins*, no doubt because the studio stole her role as Eliza Doolittle, giving it to Audrey Hepburn, who moved her lips but did not sing.

My favorite film that year was *The Americanization of Emily*, adapted by Paddy Chayefsky and directed by Arthur Hiller. It, too, starred Julie Andrews, in her first serious role. When the movie opened to good reviews, it seemed to have everything, including a Frank Sinatra hit, "Emily," and an all-star cast featuring James Garner, James Coburn, Melvyn Douglas, Keenan Wynn, Judy Carne, and Edward Binns. But it was a box-office bust. Web sites report that *Mary Poppins* sold $102 million in tickets—an astonishing figure in 1964—while sales for *The Americanization of Emily* were so paltry they were not even recorded.

I laughed harder during *Dr. Strangelove*, but *The Americanization of Emily* was, for me, a more powerful, moral film. Garner plays Lt. Comm. Charles Madison, a cynical navy officer who does not want to fight in World War II and debates the merits of war with a war widow, Emily Barnham (Andrews). Lt. Madison is as certain in his abstract logic as Raskolnikov is in Dostoyevsky's *Crime and Punishment* when he rationalizes murder; Emily is just as certain that he is a coward. Then, as the movie unfolds, they begin to exchange roles and fall in love.

After *The Americanization of Emily* bombed at the box office, MGM did a rare thing and rereleased the movie under a new name, *Emily*. Their conviction is worth celebrating; movies now are mass-marketed to five thousand theaters, and if they don't sell enough popcorn, they quickly disappear. But the movie bombed again. Today, *The Americanization of Emily* is hard to find. Keep looking.

KEN AULETTA
Columnist, The New Yorker

Applause

see p. 174

B

Ball of Fire
1941, Howard Hawks

SCREENPLAY: Charles Brackett and Billy Wilder; story
by Billy Wilder and Thomas Monroe
CAST: Gary Cooper, Barbara Stanwyck, Oscar Homolka,
Henry Travers, S. Z. Sakall, Tully Marshall, Leonid Kinskey,
Richard Haydn, Aubrey Mather, Allen Jenkins,
Dana Andrews, Dan Duryea
U.S.; B & W

One of the first things people notice about *Ball of Fire*
is that it's *Snow White and the Seven Dwarves*, but in
reverse . . . kind of. The opening scene is of seven little old
men—well, eight, actually, and the eighth is the very tall
and quite virile Professor Bertram Potts, played by Gary
Cooper—marching through Central Park on their daily
constitutional. Potts is the fairy-tale prince who needs
to wake up and stop thinking of himself as one of the
dwarves. The men are all professors writing an exhaustive
encyclopedia; they have begun the volume on "saltpeter"
and "San Salvador," and, as it turns out, "slang" and "sex"
and "Sugarpuss O'Shea," the bespangled, decidedly un-
showy showgirl and moll played by Barbara Stanwyck.

At one point, as Sugarpuss is trying to convince
Potts that the wealth of her linguistic resources will
compensate for the impropriety of her presence in the
bachelors' house, she quizzes the professor: "Do you
know what this means—'I'll get you on the Ameche'?"
Of course he doesn't. "An Ameche is the telephone, on
account of he invented it." "Oh, no, he didn't," says
Potts. To which Sugarpuss insists, "Like, you know, in
the *movies*." (Don Ameche played the lead role in the
1939 film *The Story of Alexander Graham Bell*.) Billy

Wilder's original screenplay, written in German when he was in Paris, was called *From A to Z*. It's fun to imagine him and co-writer Charles Brackett not simply translating but Americanizing the story. One of the film's delights is hearing American speech through the ears of a nonnative speaker, and under the guise of the professors' ignorance, lots of extremely off-color jokes are made: e.g., Potts explaining to the old men the meaning of "puss" ("face") and "sugar" ("sweet to look at"). "Enough about etymology!" one of them says. "Was she blond or brunette?"

But my favorite set piece in the film has little to do with language. The club where Potts is introduced to Sugarpuss features Gene Krupa's band. The first song is "Drum Boogie," with several kick-ass solos and close-ups of Krupa looking like a movie star playing himself. But then comes the surprise. After the curtain call, Stanwyck asks, "What do you hepcats want now? More? More of the same? Okay, come on down here, Kru!" She starts directing people to move chairs, clear a table, and gather around. "What's cookin', Sug?" asks Krupa as she pulls him next to her. "'Match Boogie,' Kru!" What follows is a stripped-down version of the song we just heard, with Krupa playing a matchbox with two wooden matchsticks and the audience accompanying sotto voce. The intimacy is extraordinary, the photography shimmers. Within a two-year period, Greg Toland, the cinematographer, also shot *The Grapes of Wrath*, *The Little Foxes*, and *Citizen Kane*. Twice, an extreme close-up of the matchbox reveals not only Krupa's delicate technique but also Stanwyck's face reflected—imperfectly, dreamily—in the black, glass tabletop. Gary Cooper's voice, always slightly off the beat, can be heard in the refrain. On the last beat, Krupa and Stanwyck, face-to-face, blow out the two tiny balls of fire that Krupa struck and lit on the previous beat. "Match Boogie" is an unforgettable matchmaking moment.

CASSANDRA CLEGHORN
Professor of English, Williams College

The Band Wagon
1953, Vincente Minnelli

SCREENPLAY: Adolph Green and Betty Comden
CAST: Fred Astaire, Cyd Charisse, Oscar Levant, Nanette Fabray, Jack Buchanan
U.S.

Vincente Minnelli's *The Band Wagon* is right up there with *All About Eve* as the real Broadway backstage story. It's as joyous as any '50s MGM musical, but more sophisticated than *Singin' in the Rain* or *An American in Paris*. The Faustian parody shot as a musical by a pretentious British director is hilarious, and the score includes two classic Dietz and Schwartz numbers, "Dancing in the Dark" and "That's Entertainment." Oscar Levant, who plays the writer Lester Marton, delivers my favorite procrastinating line ever: "Tell him I've gone to Tahiti to paint!"

WENDY WASSERSTEIN
Playwright

The Battle of Algiers
1965, Gillo Pontecorvo

SCREENPLAY: Gillo Pontecorvo and Franco Solinas
CAST: Jean Martin, Yacef Saadi, Brahim Haggiag, Samia Kerbash, Tommaso Neri
ALGERIA/ITALY; B & W; ITALIAN, FRENCH, ENGLISH, AND ARABIC

Billed as a "dramatic reenactment" of the struggle for Algerian independence, Gillo Pontecorvo's *The Battle of Algiers* is a stunning blend of fiction and nonfiction filmmaking techniques. Shot on location with both professional actors and amateurs, it's a work of startling realism that retains its vitality, urgency, and relevance nearly forty years after its release.

With the immediacy of a great filmmaker, Pontecorvo takes us deep inside Algiers to capture Algeria's revolutionary struggle against French colonial forces. His camera barrels with hurtling momentum through the narrow alleys, steep staircases, rooftops, and hideaways of the Casbah, deftly balancing the epic and the intimate. The grand scale of the revolutionary struggle emerges through the magnificently choreographed set pieces (the riots at the close of the film are equal in scale and execution to any contemporary Hollywood epic), while the personal stakes of those fighting for and against independence are revealed through finely wrought details. The story of Ali La Pointe, a young activist recruited into Algeria's National Liberation Front, provides our way into the revolutionary movement, but while Pontecorvo's sentiments are evident, he resists both caricature and glamorization. Both the French forces and the Front de Libération Nationale (FLN) rely on terrorism to achieve their respective goals, and the human cost of their struggle becomes terrifyingly clear as the film builds to its climax.

Although *The Battle of Algiers* ranks among the great films of the century, it seems to be known only by cineastes and critics. Yet it is a vital piece of filmmaking as relevant today as it was in 1965; modern audiences may find the film eerily prescient in its depiction of brutal military interrogations, random café bombings, and the formation of terrorist cells. While the colonial reach of the European powers is ever diminished, the costs and consequences of terrorist acts and the ideals at the root of those long-ago struggles (like human rights and self-determination) are the defining issues of our age.

The Battle of Algiers continues to inspire me. Each time I watch the film, and I watch it nearly every year, I discover something new.

BARBARA KOPPLE
Film producer and director

Baxter

1989, Jérôme Boivin

SCREENPLAY: Jacques Audiard and Jérôme Boivin;
based on the novel by Ken Greenhall
CAST: Lise Delamare, Jean Mercure, Jacques Spiesser,
Catherine Ferran, Jean-Paul Rousillon
FRANCE; IN FRENCH

If you like movies about cute dogs, you won't like *Baxter*. The title character is a bull terrier in search of the perfect master to obey, which he finds in the form of a perverse young boy with a fetish for Hitler and Maria Braun. This startlingly dark French comedy, narrated by the canine in a gravelly bass voice (*en français*), gives us a glimpse of what we humans look like from the point of view of man's best friend, and it's not a pretty picture. Jérôme Boivin's 1989 sleeper is a singular, subversive movie experience; you may never look at your pet the same way again.

DAVID ANSEN
Movie critic, Newsweek

Beat the Devil

1953, John Huston

SCREENPLAY: Truman Capote and John Huston; based on the novel by James Helvick

CAST: Humphrey Bogart, Jennifer Jones, Gina Lollobrigida, Robert Morley, Peter Lorre, Edward Underdown, Ivor Barnard, Marco Tulli, Bernard Lee
U.K./U.S./ITALY; B & W

The plot (in the loosest sense of the word) of *Beat the Devil* involves a seemingly random batch of wonderfully eccentric characters who cross paths in the Italian countryside while awaiting passage to British East Africa, where each has designs on a rich uranium find. This madcap adventure is all just a setup for the director, John Huston, and his wonderful cast to indulge in lots of offbeat humor. My guess is that if one were to compare the original script with the final movie, very few lines would match—but it's hard to argue with the results.

STANLEY F. BUCHTHAL
Producer and entrepreneur

Location Scout

Few people realize that not only is New York City the birthplace of filmmaking, but the Mayor's Office of Film, Theatre & Broadcasting was the first film commission in the country, founded by Mayor John Lindsay in 1966. It was the first of its kind to offer a free, one-stop permit that would expedite requests from production companies seeking to use public locations for film and television projects. The formula is so simple that it remains in use to this day and has been widely duplicated by locales across the globe. New York City has grown to become one of the world's largest international production centers, serving as host to hundreds of dramas, comedies, thrillers, and science fiction, period, and action films.

Unbeknownst to many film viewers, New York City is chosen not only for its unique locations but also for its elasticity as a double for other settings. Ron Howard's Academy Award–winning *A Beautiful Mind*, starring Russell Crowe, used three New York City colleges—

Bronx Community College, Manhattan College, and Union Theological Seminary—to stand in for the campuses of Harvard, MIT, and Princeton. Union Theological Seminary also caught the eye of director Michael Hoffman, who used the location to stand in for a fictional prep school in the Virginia countryside in his film *The Emperor's Club*.

Our prisons have also arrested the imagination of filmmakers. In Harold Ramis's *Analyze This* (starring Robert De Niro and Billy Crystal), Rikers Island becomes the Sing Sing Correctional Facility in Ossining, New York. Virtually all of the Louisiana jail scenes in Tim Robbins's *Dead Man Walking* (starring Susan Sarandon and Sean Penn) were shot in New York City's correctional facility system.

With hundreds of films shot in New York City every year, it's no secret that the city is constantly surprising us as an inspiration for new stories . . . and new locations.

KATHERINE OLIVER
*Commissioner, NYC Mayor's Office of Film,
Theatre & Broadcasting*

Bedazzled

1967, Stanley Donen

SCREENPLAY: Peter Cook and Dudley Moore
CAST: Peter Cook, Dudley Moore, Eleanor Bron, Raquel Welch, Alba, Robert Russell, Barry Humphries, Michael Bates
U.K.

Bedazzled is a mildly successful comedy from the '60s featuring the comedic genius of Dudley Moore and his then partner, Peter Cook. While it may seem a bit dated, it is well worth a look.

In this Faustian plot, Moore plays Stanley (The Loser) and Cook plays George (The Devil). As George grants Stanley's wishes, they encounter the Seven Deadly Sins. Lust is appropriately played by Raquel Welch. But the best and most memorable part of the

movie is the scene featuring a bevy of nuns on trampo-
lines. Not to be missed!

TIM KITTLESON
Former Director, UCLA Film & Television Archive

Berlin: Symphony of a Great City
1927, Walter Ruttmann

SCREENPLAY: Walter Ruttmann, Karl Freund, and Carl Mayer
GERMANY; B & W; DOCUMENTARY; SILENT

You may think you have little or no interest in watching
experimental films. And you may think you have little
or no interest in watching an eighty-two-year-old silent
documentary. Not long ago I operated under both of
these misapprehensions myself, and curing the first led
directly to the cure of the second.

I got to know Jeff Scher, an experimental filmmaker of some renown in the low-renown world of
experimental film, because he was the boyfriend (and
eventually the husband) of a friend of mine. When I
first sat down to watch his films a couple of years after
we'd met, I was a little anxious: what if I was bored or
confused or repelled by them? Instead, I experienced
something like the aesthetic-platonic version of that
stupid moment where the Guy sees the Girl without
glasses for the first time and sputters, "W-why, Miss
Johnson! You're—you're *beautiful*!" I won't try to
describe the films here. But they're all produced on
old-fashioned celluloid, they're all short (*Sid*, a comedy
starring a dog named Sid, is three minutes long; *Grand
Central*, a moody cinematic poem set in Grand Central
Station, runs fifteen minutes), and they're all gorgeous.
And unlike most art called "experimental," they're
gloom-free, pleasurable, even uplifting.

So once I realized Jeff was a kind of genius, I started relying on him for suggestions of movies to rent. And among the best of those was *Berlin: Symphony of a Great City*, a documentary made in 1927 by Walter Ruttmann. It's an amazingly rich, cinematically revolutionary, *Koyaanisqatsi*-esque day-in-the-life of a city, with black-and-white images quick-cut to the original score. And given the city and the moment—Berlin on the verge of the Nazi nightmare—the film seems all the more resonant and beautiful and sad.

KURT ANDERSEN
Novelist, essayist, and public radio host

RECOMMENDED VIEWING: Jeff Scher's short films, many of which can be seen online on the *New York Times* Blog page.

The Best of Everything
1959, Jean Negulesco

SCREENPLAY: Edith Sommer and Mann Rubin; based on the novel by Rona Jaffe
CAST: Hope Lange, Stephen Boyd, Joan Crawford, Louis Jourdan, Suzy Parker, Martha Hyer, Diane Baker, Brian Aherne, Robert Evans, Brett Halsey, Donald Harron
U.S.

There is nothing as relaxing as a good, cheesy soap opera, and they don't come any sudsier than the slick, tear-stained *The Best of Everything*, a delicious Working-Girls-in-New-York movie. This is a class-A chick flick, a chocolate-covered cherry of a movie. Such a guilty pleasure, in fact, that I swear I gain three pounds every time I watch it.

Hope Lange (I think of her as "Grace Kelly Lite") stars as Caroline, a prissy deb who Learns the Hard Way about men and careers, getting sleeker and more glamorous as the movie progresses. Diane Baker is corn-fed country gal April, who becomes . . . Someone Who's Had an Affair! Fashion–model–turned–actress Suzy Parker is tragic, loopy Gregg, who comes to a Bad End (spoiler: it involves a spike-heel shoe and is *not* to be believed). You can tell when Suzy is suffering emotional trauma, as the camera tilts kind of sideways. It's adorable. But the movie belongs to the great Joan Crawford as Amanda Farrow, the girls' nightmare of a boss. Playing the top editor of a publishing firm, Joan is at her Joaniest here: a cool, chic, unflappable shark. "Are you bringing your steno pad with you?" she asks Hope. "Or were you planning to beat it out on a native drum?" As someone in New York publishing, I can testify that there is still a creepy amount of accuracy to this film—I have worked for many an Amanda Farrow.

The glamour and tragedy and gorgeous frocks come fast and furious as our three heroines endure broken hearts, dashed dreams, and lush background music. Brian Aherne turns up as an aging, butt-pinching rogue; future producer Robert Evans is a smarmy playboy; and ooh-la-la Frenchman Louis Jourdan is Suzy Parker's bête noire. (Parker could easily have broken the wee Jourdan in two, but this plot twist is never explored.) This movie is the best antidote for a tough day at the office–especially if you, like me, work in the pink-collar jungle of Manhattan high-rises.

EVE GOLDEN
Writer

Big Deal on Madonna Street (I soliti ignoti)
1958, Mario Monicelli

SCREENPLAY: Agenore Incrocci, Suso Cecchi D'Amico, Mario Monicelli, and Furio Scarpelli

CAST: Vittorio Gassman, Renato Salvatori,
Memmo Carotenuto, Rosanna Rory, Carla Gravina,
Claudia Cardinale, Marcello Mastroianni, Totò
ITALY; B & W; IN ITALIAN

Big Deal on Madonna Street is a life-affirming heart-breaker of a movie filled with empty city streets, run-down apartments, and a gang of bungling thieves trying to survive in war-ravaged Rome. It's a black-and-white Italian film from the '50s that parodies hard-boiled American gangster movies and the earnestness of post-war Italian neorealism, starring a young cast that would go on to make cinema history.

The plot involves a group of street thugs who conspire to pull off the "big heist," which involves robbing a safe. Of course, nothing works out as planned. From the very beginning, everything goes wrong (except for love), but our sincere and charismatic bumblers persevere. An aborted car theft in the opening scene gives us a taste of what's to come, and the missteps continue as the gang comes together under the tutelage of the only real thief, a safecracker, played by the marvelous Totò. Vittorio Gassman plays a punch-drunk boxer, Marcello Mastroianni plays a photographer with a baby to look after, and Claudia Cardinale plays the luscious sister of an overprotective Sicilian who throws her—shouting—into another room every time the doorbell rings. There is slapstick humor, good intentions, and the ever-present danger of discovery and failure amid the camaraderie of the streets.

LOUISA ERMELINO
Writer

A Big Hand for a Little Lady
1966, Fielder Cook

SCREENPLAY: Sidney Carroll
CAST: Henry Fonda, Joanne Woodward, Jason Robards,
Paul Ford, Charles Bickford, Burgess Meredith, Kevin McCarthy,
Robert Middleton, John Qualen
U.S.

A small caper with a big ending, a Western version
of *The Sting,* Henry Fonda and Joanne Woodward make
A Big Hand for a Little Lady a masterpiece, with an
ending that will leave you banging the bar top.

ALBERT S. RUDDY
Producer

The Big Heat
1953, Fritz Lang

SCREENPLAY: Sydney Boehm; based on the novel by
William P. McGivern
CAST: Glenn Ford, Gloria Grahame, Jocelyn Brando,
Alexander Scourby, Lee Marvin, Jeanette Nolan, Peter Whitney,
Carolyn Jones
U.S.; B & W

True to its title, *The Big Heat* is *searing*—from its indict-
ment of big-city crime to the scalding coffee bubbling
on a hot plate, used as a most menacing weapon. It's
dark, too; the shadows are actually blacker in *The Big
Heat* (shot mostly at night), than in other film noirs,
making it perhaps the most "noirish" film of the genre.
And who better to star in such a dark film than the
glorious Gloria Grahame? She's intensely sexual, needy,
amoral, and fiercely determined to "blow the lid off
the garbage can" of city corruption, no matter what
sacrifices she must make. Glenn Ford matches her in his

portrayal of a good cop whose bitterness over the mob-arranged murder of his wife is about to corrupt him. The film is steeped in the paranoia of the McCarthy era, capturing what the early '50s must have been like. It's also full of surprises—more shocking, in fact, than any other film I've ever seen.

NEAL BAER
Executive producer and pediatrician

RECOMMENDED VIEWING: Other films with Gloria Grahame: *Crossfire*; *In a Lonely Place*, see p. 113 (Talk about paranoia. And with a great performance by Bogart.); *Human Desire*; and *Sudden Fear* (Gloria and Jack Palance make a swell duo out to kill Joan Crawford.)

The Big Lebowski
1998, Joel Coen

SCREENPLAY: Joel Coen and Ethan Coen
CAST: Jeff Bridges, John Goodman, Julianne Moore, Steve Buscemi, David Huddleston, Philip Seymour Hoffman, Tara Reid, Peter Stormare, Flea, John Turturro, David Thewlis, Sam Elliot, Ben Gazzara
U.S.

One needn't be a Pauline Kael wannabe, a *New Yorker* intern, or a Truffaut-quoting NYU film-schooler to know that the Coen brothers are among our era's wittiest filmmakers. But is it my imagination, or has the genius of *The Big Lebowski* slipped through the cracks? I saw and enjoyed the film in the theater (on opening day) but dismissed it as "a lesser Coen." It was fun maybe, but coming on the heels of the wood-chipper-sharp black humor of *Fargo*, it somehow registered as a disappointment. Until a colleague showed me his tattoo.

This colleague is no slouch; he's a successful movie producer and a man I respect. He rolled up his sleeve, and I saw, across his bicep, Jeff Bridges's final words in *The Big Lebowski*: "The Dude Abides." Tattooed across his arm. Permanently. I decided to give the movie another look.

The Big Lebowski is a Coen take on the L.A. detective story, with the gumshoe character replaced by the Dude, a hapless, aging hippie bowler. True to genre form, he's beaten up by bad guys, beaten up by cops, slipped a mickey by the rich thug, and seduced by the society dame, and he ends up essentially unchanged. But within this structure, the Coens subvert everything familiar. The "artists" care about nothing, the "nihilists" complain that things aren't fair, the rich heiress just wants to get pregnant, and the hot-tempered Polish Vietnam vet is Shomer Shabbos. The only sacred thing seems to be bowling (penance for *Fargo*'s Midwest bashing?), and those oiled lanes have never gleamed more radiantly than for Roger Deakins's camera. The cleverness, humor, and beauty are no surprise; these elements exist in every Coen brothers' movie. But Jeff Bridges's Dude pushes this film to another level. Like the rug that holds the room together, Bridges takes an archetypal character and makes him human enough to recognize and care about and yet doesn't rob him of his essential dudeness. When he says, "The Dude abides," I let my guard down. I believe the Coens are serious. It's a life lesson worthy of a tattoo. Or at least a nice embroidered throw pillow.

SAM HOFFMAN
Filmmaker

Big Trouble
1986, John Cassavetes

SCREENPLAY: Andrew Bergman (as Warren Bogle)

CAST: Peter Falk, Alan Arkin, Beverly D'Angelo, Charles Durning, Robert Stack, Paul Dooley, Valerie Curtin, Richard Libertini
U.S.

If you loved *The In-Laws*—the original, with Peter Falk and Alan Arkin—then you may know that many of the same people (including Falk, Arkin, and writer Andrew Bergman) reunited a few years later to make *Big Trouble*. It isn't really worth seeing, except for one three-minute scene that's as good as anything in *The In-Laws* and may be the best spit-take on film. It involves Falk insisting that Arkin try a new vintage of Norwegian sardine liqueur. You've got to see this for yourself.

KAREN SHEPARD
Professor, Williams College, and writer

Billy Liar
1963, John Schlesinger

SCREENPLAY: Keith Waterhouse and Willis Hall; based on the play by Keith Waterhouse and Willis Hall and on the novel by Keith Waterhouse (inspired by Thurber's *Walter Mitty*)
CAST: Tom Courtenay, Julie Christie, Wilfred Pickles, Mona Washbourne, Ethel Griffies, Finlay Currie, Helen Fraser, Leonard Rossiter, Rodney Bewes
U.K.; B & W

I've always believed that John Schlesinger's 1963 film *Billy Liar* is a seminal film that set the stage for its two stars, Tom Courtenay and Julie Christie (who later went on to star together in *Doctor Zhivago*). Further, it sparked the wave of incredible '60s British films. Surprisingly, few people have seen it, and fewer still have recognized its greatness. It's a simple story about the dreams of youth and the fantasies that go along with them, but ultimately it's about the courage to follow those dreams. Schlesinger's use of reality and fantasy, humor and pathos, creates the unique world seen through Billy's self-aggrandizing eyes. The remarkable performance by Courtenay, whose lies and fabrications catch up with him, culminates in a heartbreaking ending with the beautiful and all-too-real Julie Christie. The scene has always played in my mind as one of those rare moments when you scream out for the hero to make a different choice even though you understand why he does what he does. In my book, a moment like this is what filmmaking is all about.

TIM WILLIAMS
Head of production, GreeneStreet Films

Black Narcissus

1947, Michael Powell and Emeric Pressburger

SCREENPLAY: Michael Powell and Emeric Pressburger; based on the novel by Rumer Godden
CAST: Deborah Kerr, Sabu, David Farrar, Flora Robson, Esmond Knight, Jean Simmons, Kathleen Byron, Jenny Laird, Judith Furse, May Hallat, Eddie Whaley Jr., Shaun Noble
U.K.

When I was invited to recommend an underappreciated or overlooked film, I immediately thought of a scene from an art-house revival I attended long ago. I've never forgotten that scene, or the film, although I have not seen it since. The film, *Black Narcissus*, tells the story of an English Catholic nun, Sister Ruth, who travels with the Anglican Sisters to found a clinic and school in the Himalayas. There, she falls in love with Mr. Dean, the renegade English agent who serves as the convent's liaison to the natives.

The remarkable scene features Sister Ruth who, tormented by desire and jealousy, has begun a descent into madness. Her nun's habit abandoned, she is seen in her cell, wearing a provocative scarlet dress, peering into a mirror as she smears bright red lipstick on her lips. Crazed, she races down the mountainside to Mr. Dean's cottage, and declares her love. Sister Superior Clodagh, meanwhile, stands on the precipice of the mountain, ringing the convent's bell. Suddenly, from behind, we see Sister Ruth (who has joined Sister Clodagh) lose her footing and fall to her death. The film ends with the remaining sisters wending their way down the mountain as a gentle rain falls. This scene has been singled out as one of the most remarkable ever shot—a twelve-minute segment in which the music was written first and the actors then choreographed into it.

The visual beauty of the movie is probably its most astounding aspect. Cinematographer Jack Cardiff revealed that he was "not looking for a realistic setting but for a 'poetic evocation' of the Indian Himalayas." Cardiff shot the entire picture at the Pinewood Studios in England. "The mountains were three-ply cutouts. There was no modeling possible. All we could do was paint on it and it was a very ordinary sort of painting. . . . We used black-and-white backings and I suggested we color them by using pastel chalk—blue on the mountains, ochre in the foreground. Also, the set of the palace [the convent] was done with painted backings." Made more than a half century ago with these simple, primitive techniques, *Black Narcissus* remains unique in its beauty.

SHIRLEY LAURO
Playwright

Blind Chance (Przypadek)
1981, Krzysztof Kieslowski

SCREENPLAY: Krzysztof Kieslowski

CAST: Boguslaw Linda, Tadeusz Lomnicki, Zbigniew Zapasiewicz, Boguslawa Pawelec, Marzena Trybala, Jacek Borkowski, Jacek Sas-Uhrynowski, Adam Ferency, Monika Gozdzik, Zygmunt Hübner, Irena Byrska
POLAND; IN POLISH

In 1994 I had the privilege of interviewing Krzysztof Kieslowski, who was then promoting *Red*, the concluding film in the *Three Colors* trilogy, his magnum opus on freedom, responsibility, and fate. It would also be the last film of his career, as Kieslowski would abruptly retire from filmmaking shortly afterward, and then retire from life altogether on March 16, 1996, dying during heart surgery at the age of fifty-four.

He was as oblique and enigmatic as most of his movies but warmed up when I pointed out the unsettling irony of how the release of *Red*, which ends with a ferry disaster, coincided with similar, real-life disasters in the Baltic Sea and the English Channel. Such things happen to him all the time, he remarked. While making his second feature film, *Blind Chance*, for example, he was shooting a grisly autopsy scene. Later he learned his mother had died in an accident and was probably undergoing the same procedure, as he was shooting this scene.

Such brutal coincidence did not daunt him, however, and the finished film explores the themes that obsessed him throughout his life. Almost all of his later work is contained in this austere and difficult film; in a sense, it compresses the *Three Colors* trilogy into one film, a thorny triptych with more politics and less beauty, in which subtle nuances of choice and fate have enormous consequences on destiny.

Kieslowski said in the interview, "Chance exists in our lives all the time. We have some freedom, but it's all up to fate or destiny. You always hope that one day you will know why you live, and then as an old man you realize you don't know any more than when you were young. Wisdom is the process of being in agreement with fate."

And genius, if Kieslowski's career is any indication, is the ability to perceive the secret connections of destiny and render them into beauty. Death may have overcome Kieslowski's life and his art, but those who have been touched by either suspect that life might be a Kieslowski movie: a flurry of faces, images, music, coincidence, trauma, and love that snaps into meaning just before the final fade to black.

PETER KEOUGH
Film editor, Boston Phoenix

The Blue Angel (Der blaue Engel)
1930, Josef von Sternberg

SCREENPLAY: Robert Liebmann, Carl Zuckmayer, and Karl Vollmoeller; based on the novel *Professor Unrath*, by Heinrich Mann

CAST: Emil Jannings, Marlene Dietrich, Kurt Gerron, Rosa Valetti, Hans Albers

GERMANY; B & W; IN GERMAN AND ENGLISH

The Blue Angel, the first sound film in the German language, is compelling beyond its importance in cinema history. The contradictory real-life fates of its actors and the personal decisions they made in confronting Nazism make this classic film a disturbing reflection of the twentieth century's fiercest ironies. When *The Blue Angel* was released in 1930, it turned German decadence into legend. Marlene Dietrich's sexy (and slightly plump) Lola Lola is, obviously, historically the perfect siren to Emil Jannings's upright Professor Rath. Jannings was one of the film world's

greatest stars (in 1928, he won Hollywood's first
Academy Award for best actor). His thick accent ended
his American career when the "talkies" came in, and
he returned to Germany shortly before *The Blue Angel*
was conceived as a vehicle for him at the UFA Studios
in Berlin. In comparison to Jannings, Dietrich was
relatively unknown, although she had made other films
and appeared on stage. *The Blue Angel* was an immediate hit. Its success brought both the film's director,
Josef von Sternberg, and Dietrich to Hollywood, where
she quickly became a star of international magnitude,
an American citizen, and a highly public Nazi oppo-
nent. Even decades after the war, she was suspect in
Germany for her premature antifascism. Jannings,
his star status secure in Europe, took the opposite
path. He joined the Nazi cause as one of its most
esteemed cultural figures, appeared in numerous anti-
Semitic films, and became one of Goebbels's preemi-
nent state-sponsored artists. (An ironic note: Jannings's
father was American, and his mother may have been
Jewish.) Jannings never transcended his Nazi identity
after World War II and lived in obscurity until his death
in 1950.

In tragic contrast to the Aryan German who emi-
grated was the one who stayed: another member of
The Blue Angel's cast, Kurt Gerron. A popular Berlin
actor and director (he played Tiger Brown in the original stage production of Bertolt Brecht's *The Threepenny
Opera*), Gerron has an important supporting role in
The Blue Angel: a magician who runs the sleazy cabaret
troupe into which Professor Rath descends. Gerron
was Jewish. Banned from working in German films and
plays after 1933, he fled to Holland. He found theater
work in Amsterdam, but after the Nazi invasion of
the Netherlands, he was arrested by the SS, survived transfer

to a secondary concentration camp, and in 1944 was forced to direct one of the most grotesque and disturbing propaganda films of all time: *Der Führer schenkt den Juden eine Stadt* (*The Fuhrer Gives a City to the Jews*). This pseudo documentary of the Theresienstadt concentration camp (a "transit camp" maintained in part for illusory Red Cross inspections) was designed to bolster hatred anew: to show war-deprived Germans that their deported Jewish neighbors were, thanks to Hitler's good care, living well and in safety. The film shows clean dormitories, a library, neatly tended vegetable gardens, and a camp orchestra. Although actually filmed at Theresienstadt, the sites were "enhanced" for the camera. The "amenities" we see were cleaned or custom-built prior to film production and removed or demolished immediately afterward. Once the film was completed, Gerron, his wife, and many of those who worked on the film were transferred to Auschwitz, the final destination for most of the camp's inmates. Gerron was killed in an Auschwitz gas chamber on October 28, 1944.

A fourth actor of note in *The Blue Angel* also deserves mention: Rosa Valetti, one of the true stars of Berlin cabaret, appears here in the minor role of Gerron's wife. She is seen only briefly "onstage" in *The Blue Angel*, but what a world of seedy backroom performance she conjures!

ROBERT MARX
Essayist, producer, and foundation director

Broken Blossoms

see p. 173

Peter Hyams Double Bill

Busting
1974, Peter Hyams
SCREENPLAY: Peter Hyams
CAST: Elliot Gould, Robert Blake, Allen Garfield,
Antonio Fargas, Michael Lerner, Sid Haig, Cornelia Sharpe
U.S.

Capricorn One
1978, Peter Hyams
SCREENPLAY: Peter Hyams
CAST: Elliot Gould, James Brolin, Brenda Vaccaro,
Sam Waterston, O. J. Simpson, Hal Holbrook, Karen Black,
Telly Savalas, David Huddleston, David Doyle, Lee Bryant,
Denise Nicholas, Robert Walden
U.S.

I am a great admirer of *Capricorn One*, director Peter
Hyams's 1978 conspiracy thriller about an aborted—and
subsequently faked—NASA mission to Mars. So when I
came across a VHS tape of Hyams's first film, *Busting*, in
my video store a few years ago, I rented it. At the time, I
liked it very much, but I thought I should give it a second
look before writing about it. I borrowed a 35 mm print of
the film from United Artists and screened it at a friend's
house in Beverly Hills for a group that included five directors, an actor, and a cinematographer. None had heard of
Busting before, and everyone except me hated it.

Nonetheless, I continue to find many exciting things in
this picture. Elliott Gould and Robert Blake play a pair of
cops who are beaten down by a corrupt law-enforcement
system. They move down the ladder of the vice department
until they are working undercover in a public bathroom,
which they treat as their office. The two characters are
more or less interchangeable, and most of the interaction
between Gould and Blake feels improvised; they overlap
each other's wisecracks like a sad, failed comedy team. I
was caught off guard by the weird style of their partner-
ship. It's very '70s, but unique.

There is an interesting visual thread throughout the
film as well. The camera leads people down hallways, turns
corners as if through labyrinths, and occasionally loses sight
of characters for a second before they come around again.

I tried to argue the merits of this film, but I was met with gentle incomprehension. No one felt strongly enough about it to fight me, nor was I able to win any converts. I may have to stand alone on *Busting*. *Capricorn One*, on the other hand, I will defend relentlessly. I recommend a Hyams double bill with *Busting* on the B-side. If you don't make it through the second picture, at least you will enjoy (in *Capricorn One*) Telly Savalas flying upside down in a crop duster as he is being chased by helicopters; James Brolin fighting, killing, and *eating* a rattlesnake; and the incomparable slow-motion finale with Brolin and Gould (again) running through a cemetery to a waiting Hal Holbrook and Brenda Vaccaro. Sam Waterston, Karen Black, and O. J. Simpson also make appearances.

WES ANDERSON
Director

Bunny Lake Is Missing
1965, Otto Preminger

SCREENPLAY: John Mortimer and Penelope Mortimer; based on the novel by Marryam Modell (as Evelyn Piper)
CAST: Keir Dullea, Carol Lynley, Lucie Mannheim, Noël Coward, Martita Hunt, Anna Massey, Finlay Currie, Laurence Olivier, Clive Revill
U.K.; B & W

I'm the type who sits up past midnight watching a doubleheader of *Blonde Inspiration* and *The Adventures of Hajji Baba*. Underrated? Underappreciated? That's my regular viewing fare, and I've got an ongoing list of about three hundred titles. So what am I going to choose? Should it be the lovely piece of Americana *Stars in My Crown* or the harsh Korean War combat film *Men in War*? Maybe the hilarious genre spoof *What Did You Do in the War, Daddy?* Or *Man's Castle, Moonrise, The Tall T, Day of the Outlaw, Secret Beyond the Door, Sylvia Scarlett, Reckless Moment, Reign of Terror,*

My Son John, *The Man I Love*, *Summer Storm*, *Belle Le Grand* . . .

And the winner is . . . *Bunny Lake Is Missing*, the story of every mother's worst nightmare: a young woman drops her daughter off at a nursery school, and when she returns to pick her up, the child is not there, and no one has ever seen her (including, of course, the audience).

A great story, coolly directed by Otto Preminger in his signature objectified style and based on a carefully constructed script by John and Penelope Mortimer, *Bunny Lake* is designed as a puzzle, beginning with the opening credits by Saul Bass. Pieces of black construction paper are "torn" off the screen, each one revealing new information until only the paper-doll cutout of a child's body is left. As events in the plot unfold, viewers are invited to consider evidence, to make their own judgments, and then to reconsider and rejudge—and then to reconsider and rejudge again.

One by one, suspects turn up. First there is the hysterical unwed mother, Ann Lake (Carol Lynley), whose credibility is shaky. Then "her Stephen" (Keir Dullea) appears, blowing his stack, demanding attention, and giving the audience one of its first shake-ups. (Keir Dullea is Preminger's Norman Bates.) Stephen is not Ann's husband or boyfriend (as we are first led to believe) nor is he Bunny's father. He is Ann's brother, and suddenly their very close relationship becomes suspect.

The school is run by a collection of women who, each in turn, are frazzled, angry, uncommunicative, disinterested, or inclined to stomp out the door in a fit of pique. There is a dotty old lady (Martita Hunt) living in the attic over the school. She tape-records children's voices and has obviously gone way down the rabbit hole. She is topped by Sir Noël Coward in a bravura performance as a leering neighbor who collects African fertility masks. A doll-maker (Finlay Curie) seems to be a benign old man, but his is a world of detached little arms, legs, and heads with staring and unfocused eyes. You even start to wonder about the detective, played by Sir Laurence Olivier.

Preminger's camera never lies. It scrutinizes each character and probes every corner to reveal all possible clues. (The movie must be seen in its original, wide-screen format or letterboxed.) We are allowed plenty of time to look around and suspect everyone and everything we see. We start to wonder if Bunny is the product of an emotional imbalance, another of those imaginary kids à la Edward Albee's *Who's Afraid of Virginia Woolf?* or if she has been invented by siblings whose relationship may be incestuous. As each contradiction arises, the audience must deal with shifting suspicions. *Bunny Lake* is a film in which it is dangerous to make quick assumptions and impossible not to. Our objectivity is torn away like the pieces of paper in the credits as we unexpectedly experience a highly emotional, totally subjective, and frightening finale.

Critics of the day dismissed *Bunny Lake* as unworthy of Olivier's talent. Bosley Crother (always wrong in retrospect) called it "*Last Year at Marienbad* for non-intellectuals," and others dismissed its amazing mastery of objective filmmaking as "cold" and "uninvolving." However, it stands as a unique example of a movie that manages to make the audience believe they are there to solve a problem, only to shove them off a cliff and make them play a terrifying child's game of insanity.

At the very least, you have to say that it takes a lot of nerve to cast Sir Laurence Olivier and Sir Noël Coward along with Keir Dullea and Carole Lynley. And

when the Zombies enter the mix (appearing on a TV
set in a crowded pub) . . . well . . . let's say "underrated" and "underappreciated" don't even begin to
cover it.

JEANINE BASINGER
Corwin-Fuller Professor of Film Studies, Wesleyan University

Burden of Dreams
1982, Les Blank

Written by Michael Goodwin (narration)
With Werner Herzog, Klaus Kinski, Claudia Cardinale,
Jason Robards, Mick Jagger, Candace Laughlin (narrator)
U.S.; DOCUMENTARY; IN SPANISH, ENGLISH, AND GERMAN

In 1982 Werner Herzog set out to make a film,
Fitzcarraldo, about a man slowly going mad as he builds
an opera house deep in the Amazon jungle. Les Blank
went along to create a "making of" film. Needless to
say, the opera house did not turn out as planned and
neither did the movie. It's actually the documentary
that succeeds in telling the story of compulsion, obsession, shattered dreams, and the driving force of hope
and faith as no other film has. Herzog, incidentally,
would later make his own documentary, *My Best Fiend*,
detailing his stormy director-actor relationship with
Klaus Kinksi, the star of *Fitzcarraldo*.

MICHAEL C. DONALDSON
*Former President, International Documentary Association,
author, and lawyer*

Busting
see p. 42

C

Caged Heat

1974, Jonathan Demme

SCREENPLAY: Jonathan Demme

CAST: Juanita Brown, Roberta Collins, Erica Gavin, Ella Reid, Cheryl Smith, Barbara Steele, Lynda Gold, Warren Miller, Toby Carr Rafelson

U.S.

Caged Heat may belong to the women-in-prison genre, but here, women take action. They may wear bikinis, but unlike the traditional feminine image of the time (the hapless, passive female), they pick up machine guns and point them at men—forcing them to lower *their* pants. Women who break out suggest a positive, if militant, reaction to sexist victimization. Jonathan Demme displays impressive experimental style and technique in his directorial debut, especially in the razzle-dazzle escape sequence.

BETTE GORDON
Professor of Film, Columbia University, and director

RECOMMENDED VIEWING: *Johnny Guitar*, directed by Nicholas Ray (a 1954 Western that features a shoot-out between two women, Joan Crawford and Mercedes McCambridge), see p. 119.

The Cameraman

1928, Edward Sedgwick and Buster Keaton

SCREENPLAY: Clyde Bruckman (story) and Richard Schayer (titles)

CAST: Buster Keaton, Marceline Day, Harold Goodwin, Sidney Bracey, Harry Gribbon, Edward Brophy, Vernon Dent

U.S.; B & W; SILENT

History has given a bum rap to *The Cameraman*, Buster Keaton's penultimate silent comedy. Leonard Maltin's

movie guide calls it "a cut below his masterpieces," and
the late British historian David Shipman, who considered Keaton one of the greatest of auteurs, practically
dismisses it. One well-regarded Keaton study of the
'60s ignores it entirely.

Certainly, *The Cameraman* doesn't fit comfortably
in the Keaton canon. It was the first picture under his
infamous MGM contract, for which he gave up his own
studio and independence. But what injured its standing
above all was the appalling quality of existing prints.
If any one movie's reputation has been resurrected by
restoration, this is it.

After he falls in love with the beautiful Sally Richards
(Marceline Day), sidewalk tintype photographer
Luke Shannon (Keaton) attempts to become a bona
fide newsreel cameraman. That's plot enough for
a breathtaking barrage of gags and set pieces that
take the aspiring newsie from Yankee Stadium (for a
baseball game played entirely by himself) to Coney
Island (where he loses his oversize trunks in a very
public pool) to Chinatown (just in time to shoot a tong
war in progress). Though most of it was filmed on the
MGM lot in Culver City, California, *The Cameraman*
is truly one of the great New York movies. The year
it was released—1928—was a golden year for films set
and partially shot in New York; others included Harold
Lloyd's *Speedy*, King Vidor's *The Crowd*, and Paul
Fejos's *Lonesome*. Such freewheeling use of New York
in a Hollywood movie wouldn't be seen again until Jules
Dassin's *The Naked City*, exactly twenty years later.

The Cameraman reveals Keaton at the very top
of his form as actor, comedian, and filmmaker. The
credited director is his vaudeville chum and frequent
collaborator Eddie Sedgwick, but Keaton's hand is
visible in every frame, as it is in all his masterworks.

It's one of his richest films—a seamless construction of comedy, action, suspense, thrills, and romance. Most importantly, laugh for laugh, it's one of his funniest, though not all the laughs are Keaton's. For once, he was upstaged by his costar, a gifted monkey named Jocko (credited as Josephine by some sources), who may well be the same laugh-stealing simian in Harold Lloyd's *The Kid Brother*, released the previous year.

In his groundbreaking 1966 biography, *Keaton*, Rudi Blesh reported that *The Cameraman* remained in MGM's vaults as "a model of comedy writing, acting and directing." One executive quoted in the book claimed that every new comedian signed by the studio was required to study it.

So why has its reputation suffered? Because until recently it was hardly watchable. By the time the Keaton revival was in full swing in the late '60s, prints of *The Cameraman* were miserable dupes, several generations removed from the original negative (whatever happened to the original neg is still a mystery). The stunning visual sheen of late silent MGMs was completely gone. To make matters worse, at some point an anonymous saboteur added a cacophonous piano score that had nothing to do whatsoever with the action onscreen. I remember watching these old prints at revival-house screenings; audiences sat through them as stone-faced as Buster himself.

In 1990, looking for the ideal silent comedy to accompany a live orchestral score, I thought of *The Cameraman*. I wasn't crazy about using a movie that looked so bad, so I called Dick May, the head of film preservation for Turner Entertainment (now the guardian of the MGM library), hoping that better materials had turned up. May answered, "As a matter of fact, we just found the fine grain." For a film programmer this is like winning the lottery. (Fine grain is a positive image derived directly from the original camera negative).

A new 35 mm print from the restored negative was premiered at the Film Forum in New York, with music provided by Giordano's twelve-piece orchestra (quite a feat in a 180-seat theater; we would later repeat the show at New York's much larger Ziegfeld theater). Reel 1 was missing from the fine grain, so the first ten minutes had the poor quality of the dupe negative. This made the changeover to reel 2 even more dramatic. Within one scene, the movie changed from a dreary relic to a picture that was so alive, so vivid, that the audience gasped audibly with surprised delight. After that the laughs never stopped, building to a crescendo for the film's final gag. Since then, reel 1 has been replaced with improved footage blown up from a good-quality 16 mm original. But, I must admit, in some ways I was sorry to see the ten minutes of the dupe footage go, because they made the restored footage all the more exciting.

BRUCE GOLDSTEIN
Director of Repertory Programming, Film Forum

Forgotten Westerns

Little Big Horn
1951, Charles Marquis Warren
SCREENPLAY: Charles Marquis Warren
CAST: Lloyd Bridges, John Ireland, Marie Windsor, Reed Hadley, Jim Davis, Wally Cassell, Hugh O'Brian, King Donovan
U.S.; B & W

Canyon Passage
1946, Jacques Tourneur
SCREENPLAY: Ernest Pascal; based on the novel by Ernest Haycox
CAST: Dana Andrews, Brian Donlevy, Susan Hayward, Patricia Roc, Ward Bond, Hoagy Carmichael, Lloyd Bridges, Andy Devine
U.S.

Film history is filled with unrecognized, underappreciated, or forgotten Westerns. The genre was so popular that Westerns flowed out of the studios from the birth of movies right through the '60s—everything from lavish epics like *The Big Country* to cheap programmers like *Westward Ho!*, one of a slew of Z-movies John Wayne made during the '30s, between his first big role in Raoul Walsh's *The Big Trail* in 1930 and his breakthrough with John Ford in *Stagecoach* nine years later. There's King Vidor's *Billy the Kid*, made in 1930, a strikingly violent, unsentimental version of the outlaw's life with some interesting similarities to the gangster films being made during the same period. There's André De Toth's *Day of the Outlaw*, a moody, visually striking film with Robert Ryan. There's Edward Ludwig's *The Gun Hawk* from 1964, a beautifully crafted story of an old gun-fighter trying to keep a young kid from starting a criminal life. There's Nicholas Ray's flawed but affecting *True Story of Jesse James*, which has an unusual structure and a wonderful use of locations. Two films I've always loved from the genre are *Little Big Horn* and *Canyon Passage*.

Little Big Horn was the first film ever made by Charles Marquis Warren, who had been a Western novelist and went on to produce *Gunsmoke* and *Rawhide*; he also wrote *Little Big Horn*'s script. It's an exceptionally stark movie with a solid emotional core and a brutal minimalist power. Lt. John Haywood (John Ireland) and Capt. Phillip Donlin (Lloyd Bridges) lead a small party of cavalrymen on a search party through hostile territory in search of Col. Custer, to warn him about his probable fate at the hands of the Sioux. As that tension increases, the landscape becomes more ominous and threatening; one by one, the soldiers are picked off by Sioux hiding in the brush or behind rocks. It's quite a terrifying and physically immediate film, beautifully acted by Ireland and Bridges.

Canyon Passage was the first color film directed by the great Jacques Tourneur, and it's unusual in many ways. It takes place not in the desert, but in a small town in the lush mountain country in Oregon. As always with Tourneur, everything is very delicate—from the interactions of general-store proprietor Logan Stuart (Dana Andrews), local gambler George Camrose (Brian Donlevy), and his fiancée Lucy Overmire (Susan Hayward) to the overall mood and the lighting in every room. Tourneur once said that he spent less time worrying about the framing of a shot than about the lighting; he always wanted the light source to be realistic, as opposed to the way most period pieces of the time were lit. The film has a distinctive mood—serene but edgy—and it has an almost musical pace. It also has a lovely performance from Hoagy Carmichael, one of the greatest natural actors in movie history, and this is the picture where he sings one of his most beloved songs, "Ole Buttermilk Sky."

MARTIN SCORSESE
Director

Capricorn One

see p. 42

César

see p. 116

A Christmas Carol (Scrooge)

1951, Brian Desmond Hurst

SCREENPLAY: Noel Langley; based on the novella by Charles Dickens
CAST: Alastair Sim, Kathleen Harrison, Mervyn Johns, Hermione Baddeley, Michael Hordern, George Cole, Carol Marsh, Miles Malleson, Ernest Thesiger, Hattie Jacques, Peter Bull, Hugh Dempster, Clifford Mollison, Jack Warner
U.K.; B & W

Brian Desmond Hurst's film version of Dickens's *A Christmas Carol* is a worthy and faithful adaptation in the British tradition. But the particular reason to seek it out is Alastair Sim's extraordinary rendition of Scrooge's change of heart: giggling hysterically, singing madly, and moving with the uncoordinated energy of someone under the influence of a psychotropic substance. Sim finds a body language that makes Ebenezer's moral revolution altogether believable.

GEOFFREY O'BRIEN
Editor in chief, Library of America, and author

City Lights
1931, Charles Chaplin

SCREENPLAY: Charles Chaplin
CAST: Charles Chaplin, Virginia Cherrill, Florence Lee, Harry Myers, Hank Mann
U.S.; B & W; SILENT

The North Star of cinema. *City Lights* captures all the transfer emotions that a great film can express. A masterpiece of the heart, mind, and body.

TOM GRUENBERG
Founder and Co-CEO, Madstone Films

Best movie ever made.

TONY RANDALL
Actor

The Clock
see p. 174

Cologne: From the Diary of Ray and Esther
1939, Esther Dowidat and Raymond Dowidat

U.S.; B & W; SHORT; DOCUMENTARY; SILENT

Over the past eighty years amateur filmmakers have been on the front lines, documenting how we live and what we do. Now, decades later, these homemade films have taken on new value, revealing slices of America overlooked by professionals. One of my favorites is a fourteen-minute portrait of Cologne, a small town in

Minnesota, which was shot by a local doctor just before World War II. Cologne is a farming community so tiny that it gets only one sentence in the state's WPA Guide; not a lot happens in a place where cows outnumber people. Dr. Raymond Dowidat, *Cologne*'s filmmaker, knows everybody and uncovers interest in the commonplace. From workers in the grain elevator to drunks in the town saloon, he sees the town's best and worst with a doctor's understanding and distanced eye. The 16 mm silent film is narrated using diary entries written by his wife, and it gives the film a sardonic edge.

Cologne would have been lost if Dr. Dowidat's daughter had not donated it to the Minnesota Historical Society. Recognizing its value, the Society preserved it and included it on the Treasures from American Archives DVD set. In 2001 the Library of Congress named *Cologne* to the National Film Registry as a significant example of film Americana. We owe thanks to museums and libraries for saving one-of-a-kind films like this one.

ANNETTE MELVILLE
Director, National Film Preservation Foundation

NOTE: Cologne is included on Disk 1 of "Treasures from American Film Archives: 50 Preserved Films," produced by the National Film Preservation Foundation, distributed by Image Entertainment, 2005.

Como era gostoso o meu Francês

see *How Tasty Was My Little Frenchman*

Conan the Barbarian

1982, John Milius

SCREENPLAY: John Milius and Oliver Stone; based on the character created by Robert E. Howard

CAST: Arnold Schwarzenegger, James Earl Jones, Max von Sydow, Sandahl Bergman, Ben Davidson, Gerry Lopez, Mako, Valérie Quennessen, William Smith, Sven-Ole Thorsen, Cassandra Gaviola

U.S.

I was twelve years old when *Conan the Barbarian* was released in 1982. It had the greatest poster I had ever seen: Arnold Schwarzenegger holding a massive sword, with a scantily clad woman sitting at his feet. It promised a movie full of violence and gorgeous women, both of which were childhood fascinations of mine.

Conan the Barbarian is not your typical action movie. The plot actually makes sense. There's plenty of blood, guts, and sex, but it's not gratuitous. The dialogue (Oliver Stone co-wrote the script) is simple and realistic. The battle scenes are gorgeously shot and choreographed, and the musical score by Basil Poledouris is magnificent. Schwarzenegger is very reserved in his performance; stupid one-liners had not yet become his hallmark. He keeps his mouth shut for most of the movie and lets his muscles do the talking. The supporting cast is surprisingly good, including a menacing James Earl Jones as Thulsa and Max von Sydow as King Osric.

At the age of twelve, I adopted the motto of Conan as my own: "Crush your enemies, see them driven before you, and hear the lamentations of their women."

JAMES FREY
Writer

The Conformist (Il conformista)
1970, Bernardo Bertolucci

SCREENPLAY: Bernardo Bertolucci; based on the novel
Il conformista, by Alberto Moravia
CAST: Jean-Louis Trintignant, Stefania Sandrelli,
Gastone Moschin, Enzo Tarascio, Dominique Sanda,
Pierre Clémenti, Pasquale Fortunato
ITALY/FRANCE/WEST GERMANY; IN ITALIAN

While Bernardo Bertolucci's *The Conformist* is hardly
an overlooked film critically, it nevertheless seems to be
largely unknown today. It's as close to a perfect film as
I have ever seen. The confluence of Bertolucci's adaptation of Alberto Moravia's novel, Vittorio Storaro's
cinematography, Ferdinando Scarfiotti's production
design, Gitt Magrini's costume design, Georges
Delerue's music, and the young Bertolucci's direction is
sublime. Keep an eye out for a theatrical showing of the
film. Open yourself to romance, its eroticism, and its
heartbreak. The reward is unmatchable.

MARK JOHNSON
Producer

Vanilla Ice

Cool As Ice
1991, David Kellogg
SCREENPLAY: David Stenn
CAST: Vanilla Ice, Kristin Minter, Naomi Campbell, Candy Clark,
Dody Goodman, Michael Gross, Sydney Lassick
U.S.

Cool As Ice is a prized-to-the-moon generational fetish
object. This enormously pleasurable kitschfest, a 1991
vehicle slapped together to cash in on the dizzying popularity of pop rapper Vanilla Ice, cannot now be purchased
for less than twenty-five dollars on eBay. It has yet to
be released on DVD, so beat-up VHS copies circulate

nationwide, perhaps first placed on eBay by people hoping to recoup a buck on their unwanted, displaced videotapes. A gem in the bucket, *Cool As Ice* is feverishly bid upon by those yearning to own and hold its box with a picture of Vanilla Ice sitting astride a motorcycle, wearing a hilarious leather jacket covered with "cool" sayings like "Word Up." It speaks to beloved sense memories, much as Howdy Doody lunch boxes once spoke to an older crowd.

MATTHEW HOROVITZ
Television producer

The Cow (Gaav)
1969, Dariush Mehrjui

SCREENPLAY: Dariush Mehrjui and Gholam-Hossein Saedi; based on the play *Gaav*, by Gholam-Hossein Saedi
CAST: Ezzatolah Entezami, Mahmoud Dowlatabadi, Parviz Fanizadeh, Jamshid Mashayekhi, Ali Nassirian, Esmat Safavi, Khosrow Shojazadeh, Jafar Vali
IRAN; B & W; IN PERSIAN

Awarded the Jury Prize at the Venice Film Festival, Dariush Mehrjui's *Gaav* (*The Cow*) is considered by many to be the best film in the history of Iranian cinema. It was certainly the most inspiring for the next generation of filmmakers, and it remains as fresh and enjoyable today as it was back in the '70s. The plot—concerning a villager who attempts to revive his dearly beloved, dead cow by trying to become the cow himself—never gets old, and each frame is a carefully designed picture. It also features some of the greatest Iranian performances ever filmed, especially Ezzatolah Entezami in the role of Masht Hassan. *The Cow* is a classic, by any country's standards, and it's worth seeing many, many times.

FARROKH SOLTANI
Film critic, TehranAvenue.com

Creature Comforts
1989, Nick Park

SCREENPLAY: Nick Park
VOICE: Julie Sedgewick
U.K.; ANIMATION

Movies about animals are, of course, really stories about humans in disguise. In the pitch-perfect *Creature Comforts*, Nick Park complicates that mirroring by letting his Claymation animals speak about their zoo lives through the voices of actual Londoners. The result, both comic and sad, might be called the world's first Claymation documentary. "Sometimes you can't get out," says a bluish gorilla of a certain age, who has scratched a tally of her days on the cage walls. "You get stuck in for some reason, like I'm stuck in today, and then yes, you get bored and you get fed up with looking at the same four walls." Sure, "they try to make you comfortable," a jaguar explains from his perch on an artificial tree, but then you're served "food that looks like dog food, rather than food proper for a wild animal."

"Here you live in a very small place, with all the technological advances possible, you have everything sorted out, double-glazed, but you don't have space!" the jaguar continues, emphatically gesturing with his paws. "In Brazil we have space! We need to feel like we live, like we're part of the world, and not like a kind of a piece of object in a box."

Originally made for the BBC in 1989, *Creature Comforts* is available on an omnibus DVD that includes four other Claymation shorts from Park's Aardman Studios. Arguably Park's best film (it won an Academy Award for best animated short), *Creature Comforts* presents the shifting ironies that never allow viewers to grow complacent or secure. "Zoos are very important to animals," says a young polar bear on a family outing to the zoo. "They're a bit like nursing homes for poor animals." "I feel very secure," says a huge-eyed lemur, removing her eyeglasses to look at the camera. "Very secure and well looked-after, and I'm not worried about anything. I know whatever happens, they'll look after me. And put me where I ought to be."

SHAWN ROSENHEIM
Professor of Film and Literature, Williams College

Crime Wave

1954, André De Toth

SCREENPLAY: Crane Wilbur, Richard Wormer, and Bernard Gordon; based on the story "Criminals Mark," by John Hawkins and Ward Hawkins
CAST: Sterling Hayden, Gene Nelson, Phyllis Kirk, Ted de Corsia, Charles Bronson, Jay Novello, James Bell, Dub Taylor, Timothy Carey
U.S.; B & W

I have always been a fan of the underappreciated director André De Toth. His film *The Pitfall* first attracted my attention, and a little later his Western noir *Ramrod* sharpened it. But recently I got to see what I think is his cinematic masterpiece, *Crime Wave*. The exterior scenes shot at night in L.A., the performance by Sterling Hayden, the edge the movie has from beginning to end—it's a *policier* crime thriller that ranks among the best.

SAM POLLARD
Producer and film editor

The Crucible
1996, Nicholas Hytner

SCREENPLAY: Arthur Miller; based on the play by Arthur Miller
CAST: Daniel Day-Lewis, Winona Ryder, Paul Scofield, Joan Allen,
Bruce Davison, Rob Campbell, Jeffrey Jones, Peter Vaughan,
Karron Graves, Charlayne Woodard, George Gaynes
U.S.

In 1953, Arthur Miller's play *The Crucible* opened on
Broadway. Then, it took forty-three years, and countless attempts, for an American film version to be made.
Written by Miller himself, vibrantly directed by Nicholas
Hytner, and starring Daniel Day-Lewis, Winona Ryder,
and Joan Allen, the 1996 movie is electrifying, heartbreaking, and ennobling. Although Allen and Miller
were nominated for Academy Awards, the film was
largely overlooked by audiences and downplayed by the
press: Miller's allegory for the '50s Red Scare was dated,
and he had fallen out of fashion as a playwright. How
badly that criticism missed the point. The movie is a
riveting drama and brings a contemporary vitality and
cinematic flair to American melodrama. Ryder, according to Miller himself, gave the best performance as
Abby he had ever seen, and Daniel Day-Lewis's personi-
fication of a man unable to bear the compromise of his
name, even at the cost of his life, is unforgettable. And
for those who wonder about the danger of fanaticism of
any kind in our society, look closely at Paul Scofield's
Judge Danforth. In years to come, *The Crucible* will be
justly revered as a classic version of a classic.

TOM ROTHMAN
Chairman, Fox Filmed Entertainment

Crumb
see p. 102

D

Dance, Girl, Dance
1940, Dorothy Arzner

SCREENPLAY: Tess Slesinger and Frank Davis
CAST: Maureen O'Hara, Louis Hayward, Lucille Ball,
Virginia Field, Ralph Bellamy, Maria Ouspenskaya,
Mary Carlisle, Edward Brophy, Walter Abel, Harold Huber
U.S.; B & W

Dance, Girl, Dance is a film by Dorothy Arzner, one
of the first women directors. Starring Maureen O'Hara
(Judy) as ingénue to Lucille Ball's burlesque queen
(Bubbles), the film features intrigue, gambling raids,
song and dance, as well as high and low comedy. One
of my favorite moments is during a scene in which the
strap on Judy's top breaks during her burlesque act and
the audience cackles maliciously. She turns, stares at
the audience, and says with deliberate, wry cool, "Go
ahead and stare, I'm not ashamed. What do you think
we think of you up here with your silly smirks?" It's
a great speech that turns the tables on the burlesque
audience—and on the audience watching the film.

BETTE GORDON
Professor of Film, Columbia University, and director

Darling
1965, John Schlesinger

SCREENPLAY: Frederic Raphael
CAST: Laurence Harvey, Dirk Bogarde, Julie Christie,
José Luis de Villalonga, Roland Curram, Basil Henson,
Alex Scott, Pauline Yates
U.K.; B & W

From the opening credits, when a World Hunger
billboard is being repapered with a close-up of Julie
Christie's face, you know you are in for a cynical
look at life. Set in London in 1965, Christie plays Diana
Scott, a charming and frivolous model/actress who
hops from one doomed relationship to the next.

My favorite scene is Diana's vacation in Capri. While
considering an Italian prince's marriage proposal, she
goes off with her gay friend's lover. Cut to the next
morning and they have exchanged shirts—a good use
of costuming to further a story point.

Christie won an Academy Award, as did screenwriter Frederic Raphael and costume designer Julie
Harris. Christie starred in *Doctor Zhivago* the same
year and, oddly, in both revolutionary Russia and
Swinging London, Ms. Christie appears to be wearing
the same frosted lipstick.

SUSAN LYALL
Costume designer

Dastforoush

see *The Peddler*

Days of Being Wild

1991, Wong Kar-wai

SCREENPLAY: Wong Kar-wai
CAST: Leslie Cheung, Maggie Cheung, Andy Lau, Carina Lau,
Rebecca Pan, Jacky Cheung, Tony Leung
HONG KONG; IN CANTONESE, MANDARIN, AND ENGLISH

The passage of time is a central theme in Wong Kar-wai's
Days of Being Wild. Set in 1960, the film takes you to a
nostalgic world in which characters mourn lost moments
and missed opportunities. In the opening scene, Yuddy,
played by the charismatic Leslie Cheung (who took his

own life in 2003, ending his glorious career at the age of forty), attempts a pickup line. He insists that a young ticket clerk, played by Maggie Cheung, look at his watch for one full minute. She does and he tells her, "Because of you, I'll always remember this one minute."

Throughout the film, the presence of clocks reminds us that every minute is irretrievable. As he pursues women, Yuddy likes to tell a story in which he compares himself to a kind of bird without feet; it flies nonstop and sleeps in the wind when tired. This bird only lands once in its lifetime—on the day of its death.

The film sets the tone for later Wong films such as *Ashes of Time* (1994) and *In the Mood for Love* (2000). With its all-star cast, each at their best, *Days of Being Wild* invites you to tune your mood to a dreamy world in which what is lost is always the most precious.

LA FRANCES HUI
Senior Program Officer, Cultural Programs and Performing Arts, Asia Society

Dead Man
1995, Jim Jarmusch

SCREENPLAY: Jim Jarmusch
CAST: Johnny Depp, Gary Farmer, Lance Henriksen, Michael Wincott, Mili Avital, Iggy Pop, Crispin Glover, Eugene Byrd, Gabriel Byrne, John Hurt, Alfred Molina, Robert Mitchum, Billy Bob Thornton, Jared Harris
U.S./GERMANY/JAPAN; B & W

A sadly overlooked film, stunningly photographed by Robby Müller, *Dead Man* is an inspired take on the Western tradition. With brilliant performances by Johnny Depp, Billy Bob Thornton, and Mili Avital.

ANJELICA HUSTON
Actor

Dead of Night

*1945, Alberto Cavalcanti, Charles Crichton, Robert Hamer,
and Basil Dearden*

SCREENPLAY: John Baines and Angus MacPhail; stories
for each segment by John Baines, Angus MacPhail, H. G. Wells,
and E. F. Benson
CAST: Mervyn Johns, Roland Culver, Mary Merrall,
Googie Withers, Fredrick Valk, Anthony Baird, Sally Ann Howes,
Judy Kelly, Miles Malleson, Ralph Michael, Esme Percy,
Basil Radford, Naunton Wayne, Michael Redgrave,
Elisabeth Welch, Hartley Power
U.K.; B & W

I was twelve when I first saw *Dead of Night*, and with it
the uncanny made its abrupt entry into my psychic life.
The strange, dreamy underside of experience became
suddenly real, and I believed in its frightening and
inexplicable truths. I still do. The film, a dream within
a dream within which four very scary stories are told, is
probably best known for Michael Redgrave's role as a
crazed ventriloquist. I cannot be more specific without
ruining the film for those who have not seen it.

MARK STRAND
Poet

Deep End

1970, Jerzy Skolimowski

SCREENPLAY: Jerzy Skolimowski, Jerzy Gruza, and Boleslaw Sulik
CAST: Jane Asher, Diana Dors, John Moulder-Brown,
Christopher Sandford, Karl Michael Vogler
U.S./POLAND/WEST GERMANY

Set in a run-down London bathhouse in the late '60s, this
amazing Jerzy Skolimowski film is about a fifteen-year-old
boy's erotic obsession with his ideal woman, who works

alongside him at the baths. John Moulder-Brown is the boy, Jane Asher the older woman. The film is funnier and more surreal as the boy's obsession intensifies, culminating in a shocking ending in which fantasy and reality collide. This was the Polish director's first film in English (he later made the terrific *Moonlighting*, with Jeremy Irons), and while it may call to mind Polanski and Godard movies of the time, it has a visual style and a psychological perceptiveness all its own. *Deep End* came out in the U.S. in 1971, which happened to be one of the all-time great years for movies (*The Conformist*; *McCabe and Mrs. Miller*; *The Last Picture Show*; *Claire's Knee*; *Sunday, Bloody Sunday*; *A Clockwork Orange*; *The French Connection*; *Murmur of the Heart*; *Carnal Knowledge*; *Taking Off*; *Walkabout*; *The Garden of the Finzi-Continis*; *The Go-Between*; *Bananas*; and *The Sorrow and the Pity*). It's not hard to see why this beauty was overlooked, but it deserves a place right alongside its classic classmates.

DAVID ANSEN
Movie critic, Newsweek

Der blaue Engel
see *The Blue Angel*

Dirty Money
see *Un flic*

Dodsworth
1936, William Wyler

SCREENPLAY: Sidney Howard; based on the novel by Sinclair Lewis
CAST: Walter Huston, Ruth Chatterton, Paul Lukas, Mary Astor, David Niven, Gregory Gaye, Maria Ouspenskaya, Odette Myrtil, Spring Byington, Harlan Briggs, John Payne
U.S.; B & W

Despite an over-the-top performance by Ruth Chatterton, I've always felt that *Dodsworth* was one of the finest American movies. William Wyler's simplicity, Sidney Howard's language, and, above all, Walter Huston's and Mary Astor's performances result in one of the most mature and powerful movies in my memory. The glory and debasement that love can bring into one's life have never been explored so tellingly. In fact, because of our sentimentality about love, rarely do we consider its destructive power. *Dodsworth* plunges into this world unhesitatingly with art and power and subtlety. In my view, a *great* film.

SIDNEY LUMET
Director

Based on a novel by Sinclair Lewis, this 1930s movie has never received the attention it deserves. It was directed by the great William Wyler and stars the equally great Walter Huston, along with Ruth Chatterton, Mary Astor, and—briefly—David Niven. The story is about a self-made industrialist and his younger wife, who is fed up with her life in their dull Midwestern town. She persuades her husband to retire and take her on the grand tour of Europe. The movie is essentially about the unraveling of their marriage, but it also beautifully captures the romance of travel in the golden age, complete with sailings on liners like the *Queen Mary*, the *Aquitania*, and the *Rex*. Even though clearly not shot in Europe, the scenes evoking the Crillon in Paris, villas at Lake Geneva, the environs of Naples, and the snowy days in Vienna are thrilling.

WILLIAM SERTL
Travel editor

Drachenfutter
see *Dragon's Food*

Drácula (Spanish Dracula)
1931, George Melford and Enrique Tovar Avalos

SCREENPLAY: Garrett Fort, Baltasar Fernández Cué, and Dudley Murphy; based on the novel *Dracula*, by Bram Stoker
CAST: Carlos Villariás, Lupita Tovar, Eduardo Arozamena, Pablo Alvarez Rubio, Barry Norton, Carmen Guerrero
U.S.; B & W; IN SPANISH

If you made this up, nobody would believe you.

During the making of Universal's definitive vampire film, the studio was shooting a Spanish-language version simultaneously by night. The Spanish-speaking actors used the same sets, the same script, even the same marks. But rather than just reproducing Tod Browning's mise-en-scène, American director George Melford (who didn't speak Spanish) used his own eye. So it isn't a Gus Van Sant–style, shot-by-shot rendition. It doesn't even qualify as a remake, seeing as how neither came first. Plus it's a half hour longer, allowing for more melodrama, more atmosphere, and more plot, which makes the film more comprehensible or less mysterious, depending on how you want to look at it. In the English version, Bela Lugosi nailed the title role for the ages, but if he hadn't, we might well be talking instead about Carlos Villarías, whose Count is Christopher Lee by way of Fernando Rey. What the American Renfield does with a creepy giggle, his Latino counterpart achieves with a maniacal scream. And thanks to the less puritanical mores of the Hispanic market, Eva (Mina, in the American film) gets to say that a visit from Drácula made her feel like she had lost her virginity. She wears a lower neckline, too. Now, if only there were a Spanish *Freaks*.

HENRY GRIFFIN
Filmmaker

Dragon's Food (Drachenfutter)

1987, Jan Schütte

SCREENPLAY: Jan Schütte and Thomas Strittmatter
CAST: Bhasker Patel, Frank Oladeinde, Youngme Song, Wolf-Dietrich Sprenger, Buddy Uzzaman, Ulrich Wildgruber, Ric Young
SWITZERLAND/WEST GERMANY; B & W; IN GERMAN

Dragon's Food's bleak setting reeks of fear, uncertainty, and betrayal—all further heightened by the excellent black-and-white cinematography. It serves as a stark backdrop for a beautifully observed story of hope, determination, and friendship, written by Thomas Strittmatter and director Jan Schütte. Without a common language or background, Xiao (Ric Young) and Shehzad (Bhasker), against all odds, open a Chinese restaurant. The restaurant is not just a realization of their dreams of economic self-reliance and a motif of their courage, luck, and enterprise; it also represents an expression of their respective national and cultural identities, allowing each to regain some measure of personal dignity.

Dragon's Food (*Drachenfutter* in German, sometimes translated as *Dragon Chow*) is a brilliantly acted drama, and the heartbreaking twist at the end heightens the poignancy of the immigrants' lot. Pakistani social manners and body language are so acutely observed that only when the credits roll do we realize that the writers and the director are not Pakistani.

NABEEL SARWAR
Corporate lawyer

Dreamchild

1985, Gavin Millar

SCREENPLAY: Dennis Potter
CAST: Coral Browne, Ian Holm, Peter Gallagher, Nicola Cowper, Jane Asher, Amelia Shankley, Caris Corfman, Shane Rimmer
U.K.

The utterly original Dennis Potter (*The Singing Detective*) wrote this moving and wildly imaginative English film about Alice Hargreaves, the woman who was the model for Lewis Carroll's Alice. Here Alice is eighty years old (wonderfully played by Coral Browne) and heading to New York in 1931 for the centenary celebration of Carroll's birth. Her long-repressed memories carry her back to her childhood and to her relationship with Carroll (Ian Holm). Directed by Gavin Millar, *Dreamchild* leaps back and forth in time, with stops in Wonderland itself, as Alice comes to terms at long last with the meaning of the love Carroll felt for her when she was a child. Few people saw this movie when it came out in 1985; those who did fell in love with it.

DAVID ANSEN
Movie critic, Newsweek

Duck Soup

1933, Leo McCarey

SCREENPLAY: Bert Kalmar and Harry Ruby
CAST: Groucho Marx, Harpo Marx, Chico Marx, Zeppo Marx, Margaret Dumont, Raquel Torres, Louis Calhern, Edgar Kennedy, Leonid Kinskey, Charles Middleton
U.S.; B & W

Duck Soup was such a flop in 1933 that Paramount dropped its contract with the Marx Brothers. Set in

Freedonia, a mythical country that declares war on neighboring Sylvania for the hell of it, Leo McCarey's comedy holds nothing sacred and leaves nothing unscathed. But in 1933, the American economy was in collapse, democracy was faltering at home and abroad, and Hitler was on the rise in Germany—American audiences were simply not in the mood for a political satire.

Though *Duck Soup* was provocative enough to have been banned in Italy by Mussolini, Leo McCarey insisted that the only political message was "to kid dictators," and Groucho confided that "we didn't fight this war out of love for Freedonia, you know. We fought that war because we wanted to throw things."

JOSHUA SIEGEL
Assistant curator, Department of Film, Museum of Modern Art

E

East Is East
1999, Damien O'Donnell

SCREENPLAY: Ayub Khan-Din; based on the play
by Ayub Khan-Din
CAST: Om Puri, Linda Bassett, Jordan Routledge, Archie Panjabi,
Emil Marwa, Chris Bisson, Jimi Mistry, Raji James
U.K.; IN ENGLISH AND URDU

East Is East is a witty, poignant black comedy that examines a host of social issues through the prism of a large, lower-middle-class immigrant family coming of age in Manchester in the early '70s. A Pakistani father (Om Puri) discovers that his children (six sons and one daughter) are beyond his control. The "home culture" of the Pakistani father and the "foreign culture" of the British mother are usurped by a new world created by their children: a world where there are no easy answers, where neither Eastern nor Western social rules apply. Director Damien O'Donnell and screenwriter Ayub Khan-Din handle issues of family, mixed marriage, sexuality, race relations, and cultural clashes with sensitivity, making this film a must-see for those interested in understanding the Asian-diaspora phenomenon.

NABEEL SARWAR
Corporate lawyer

The East Is Red
1964, Wang Ping

PEOPLE'S REPUBLIC OF CHINA; DOCUMENTARY; IN MANDARIN

The East Is Red—not to be confused with the 1992 action film *Swordsman III: The East Is Red*—is a 1964 propaganda film that was produced for the fifteenth anniversary of the founding of the People's Republic of China. Named after a revolutionary song that became the Cultural Revolution's anthem, the film is a great musical spectacle reminiscent of Old Hollywood, but with the clear purpose of telling the story of twentieth-century Chinese history as seen through the eyes of Communism. In China, the film brainwashed us all with happy folk songs and dance.

CHEN SHI-ZHENG
Director, choreographer, singer, and actor

Eddie Bracken

Hail the Conquering Hero
1944, Preston Sturges
SCREENPLAY: Preston Sturges
CAST: Eddie Bracken, Ella Raines, William Demarest, Franklin Pangborn, Raymond Walburn
U.S.; B & W

The Miracle of Morgan's Creek
1944, Preston Sturges
SCREENPLAY: Preston Sturges
CAST: Eddie Bracken, Betty Hutton, William Demarest, Diana Lynn, Porter Hall, Jimmy Conlin, Almira Sessions, Brian Donlevy, Akim Tamiroff
U.S.; B & W

Was there ever a more hapless male lead than Eddie Bracken? He worked as a supporting actor well into the '90s, but for a couple years during World War II, the bumbling, adenoidal Bracken was a genuine star, thanks to the sly direction of Preston Sturges. In *The Miracle of Morgan's Creek* and *Hail the Conquering Hero*, Bracken's quavering voice and overdeveloped superego were used as subversive comic weapons. In *Miracle*, his Norval Jones pretends to escort Gertrude Kockenlocker (a wonderful Betty Hutton), while she's at a farewell party for departing soldiers. She wakes up married (she has the ring), pregnant, and clueless about her husband's identity. In *Hail*, the situation may be even worse; discharged from the marines for chronic hay fever, Bracken's Woodrow Lafayette Pershing

Truesmith returns home in shame, only to be mistaken for a battle-seasoned hero and thrust into a mayoral election against his will.

Both films are brilliantly scripted and make full use of William Demarest, Franklin Pangborn, and the rest of the Sturges's stock players. But more than anything, these films rely on Bracken's ability to manage tone. They require Bracken to be clumsy, sentimental, irritating, and impossibly naive—without losing the audience's sympathy. All of Sturges's work betrays enormous affection for the range of human foolishness, but in the films with Bracken, there is an underlying sweetness as well.

SHAWN ROSENHEIM
Professor of Film and Literature, Williams College

El espíritu de la colmena
see *The Spirit of the Beehive*, p. 216

El santo oficio (The Holy Office)
see p. 179

The Exploits of Elaine
1914, Louis J. Gasnier, George B. Seitz, and Leopold Wharton

SCREENPLAY: Charles W. Goddard and George B. Seitz
CAST: Pearl White, Arnold Day, Sheldon Lewis, Creighton Hale, Riley Hatch, Raymond Owens, Edwin Arden, Robin H. Townley, Floyd Buckley, M. W. Rale
U.S.; B & W; SILENT

I always regret that I was not in London on October 18, 1915. That may sound odd, because it would have been the middle of World War I. Certainly I wouldn't have wanted to be an adult then, but perhaps a child. On October 18, Pathé issued their second Pearl White serial, *The Exploits of Elaine*. For thirty-six successive weeks, I could have seen a different episode featuring that

master criminal, the Clutching Hand, plotting against
our heroes: the scientific detective, Craig Kennedy, and
every adolescent's dream girl, Elaine Dodge.

The Exploits of Elaine was one of the first serials
to realize the potential of science fiction in the action
melodrama. Many of the story ideas came from the
hand of George B. Seitz, who later became a well-
known Hollywood figure. In episode 9, the "death ray"
kills all who transgress its beam. Even more remarkable is episode 10, in which the heroine is actually
killed by the Clutching Hand's accomplices; luckily,
Craig Kennedy applies Professor Leduc's method of
electrical resuscitation and brings her back to life. In
episode 15, we meet the mysterious villain Wu Fang,
whose cryptic ring—the key to the whereabouts of the
Clutching Hand's fortune—falls into the hands of our
unfortunate heroine. Wu will do *anything* to get that
ring back, including cutting the tightrope between two
skyscrapers across which Craig Kennedy is chasing
him. Wu Fang is gone by episode 24, replaced by Lionel
Barrymore as Marcius del Mar, a foreign spy revealed
to be behind the theft (back in episode 17) of Craig
Kennedy's wonderful invention, a superforce torpedo
that will revolutionize the war. Marcius is still there
pulling the wool over poor Elaine's eyes in episode 28,
"The Submarine Harbor," and in subsequent episodes
with titles like "The Wireless Detective," "The Death
Cloud," and "The Life Chain."

To accompany the thrills and the ever-more-
outrageous scientific weapons, there would have been
a breathless pianist in the stalls pounding out music
like Ezra Read's "Fire! Fire!" and Alphons Czibulka's
"Hearts and Flowers." Best of all, each episode would
have been introduced with "Elaine, My Moving Picture
Queen," an original song written for the serial. How

could anyone resist a song whose last stanza is "Elaine, Elaine, please come down from the screen and be my moving-picture queen?"

By now I hope you are asking, "Where can I see this marvelous serial?" Alas, you can't—at least not in its entirety. Odd episodes exist in American-film archive collections. However, my philosophy as an archivist is that films are never lost—only temporarily mislaid. The first fourteen episodes were distributed in the States on 28 mm by the Pathéscope Company. The George Eastman House film archive has started a union list of films on 28 mm, which will include archive holdings and those in the hands of private collectors, and perhaps when this project is complete we will be able to see the first third of the serial in all its glory. Other episodes might be discovered in the National Archives of Canada collection or Bois D'Arcy, the French national film archive. Who knows—someone may even write the publishers of this book and tell them that they have the complete serial in their attic! I hope so. I really do want to see all thirty-six episodes.

DAVID FRANCIS
Former Chief of Motion Picture, Broadcasting, AMO Recorded Sound Division, The Library of Congress

F

Fail Safe
1964, Sidney Lumet

SCREENPLAY: Walter Bernstein; based on the novel
by Eugene Burdick and Harvey Wheeler
CAST: Dan O'Herlihy, Walter Matthau, Frank Overton, Ed Binns,
Fritz Weaver, Henry Fonda, Larry Hagman, Russell Collins,
Sorrell Booke
U.S.; B & W

Of all the atomic-scare movies—and there were
many in the late '50s and early '60s—*Fail Safe* was
the most horrifying. More than *On the Beach* or
Dr. Strangelove, it vividly shows how close we are to
the edge and how having a cool head in the hot
seat is our only security. The story centers on miscom-
munication due to a technical malfunction, which
causes American and Russian interceptors to shoot
down U.S. nuclear bomber planes before they reach
their targets. If the plot sounds like standard Cold
War paranoia, consider how unnervingly probable it
seemed in the wake of the Cuban Missile Crisis. The
film has brilliant performances by Walter Matthau
(as a cold-blooded, war-mongering Kissinger-esque
"professor"), Fritz Weaver (as a conflicted U.S. Air Force
officer who believes that the U.S. should indeed use
this opportunity for a preemptive strike), and a young
Larry Hagman (as a nervous translator locked in the
war room). But it's Henry Fonda, as the president, who
really holds things together. The resolution of *Fail Safe*
is decidedly un-Hollywood, but only in Hollywood
will you find a president of Fonda's quality: a straight-
shooting, even-tempered man of rare intelligence and

compassion. Who wouldn't feel safe with a guy like that at the country's helm?

STEVEN HELLER
Columnist, The New York Times Book Review, art director, and writer

Fanny

see p. 116

Fat City

1972, John Huston

SCREENPLAY: Leonard Gardner; based on the novel by Leonard Gardner
CAST: Stacy Keach, Jeff Bridges, Susan Tyrrell, Candy Clark, Nicholas Colasanto, Art Aragon, Curtis Cokes
U.S.

John Huston had already made some pretty good films (*The Maltese Falcon, Treasure of the Sierra Madre, The African Queen*) by the time he got to *Fat City*, his ballad of down-and-outers set in Stockton, California. In collusion with writer Leonard Gardner, designer Richard Sylbert (who clearly studied his Hopper paintings), and the great cinematographer Conrad Hall, Huston creates an extraordinarily moving film without much use for the director's usual best friend: a plot.

Redolent of Steinbeck's novels or *The Time of Your Life*, William Saroyan's barroom classic, *Fat City* reeks of its characters' physical and spiritual exhaustion. Hall's remarkable juxtapositions of California's glare and its darkest bars are a constant treat.

Huston's impending old age and illness hang over the film, but never intrude. As you'd expect from him, compassion for his characters never spills over into sentiment, and the film sneaks right up on you. See it in a theater if you can, if only for Hall's extraordinary nighttime work. Otherwise, pour yourself a stiff drink, turn out the lights, and surrender.

GREGORY MOSHER
Director, Arts Initiative at Columbia University, director, and producer

Federal Hill
1995, Michael Corrente

SCREENPLAY: Michael Corrente
CAST: Jason Andrews, Anthony DeSando, Libby Langdon, Michael Raynor, Nicholas Turturro, Frank Vincent
U.S.; B & W

Maybe it's an age thing, but having grown up on Bergman and Sturges, I've always been a sucker for black-and-white movies. Recently I came across a small black-and-white masterpiece called *Federal Hill*, a town-gown love story that takes place in director Michael Corrente's hometown of Providence, Rhode Island. Reportedly shot for eighty thousand dollars, *Federal Hill* is a visual feast, as compelling as *Raging Bull*. Performances by Nicholas Turturro, Anthony DeSando, and Libby Langdon are flawlessly relaxed, and Corrente's script is street-smart yet solidly structured. If you like Cassavetes, you'll love Corrente. Try to find the original, un-colorized director's version.

ISRAEL HOROVITZ
Playwright

F for Fake (Vérités et mensonges)
1975, Orson Welles

SCREENPLAY: Orson Welles and Oja Kodar
CAST: Orson Welles, Oja Kodar, Joseph Cotten, François Reichenbach, Elmyr de Hory, Clifford Irving, Laurence Harvey

FRANCE/IRAN/WEST GERMANY; DOCUMENTARY; IN ENGLISH
AND FRENCH

Resplendent in a black cape and black Fellini-esque hat, Welles is in top form as he hypnotizes us with his oracular, eye-of-the-hurricane narration and exquisitely timed direction in this part-documentary, part-fiction piece. Welles examines what is most likely the best modern true story of art and deception to date: the unbelievably intertwining lives of the prolific art forger Elmyr de Hory and his biographer, the American writer Clifford Irving, who himself was later the subject of scandal when he admitted to having faked an "authorized" biography of Howard Hughes.

The heart of the film takes place on the island of Ibiza in the early '70s, using priceless documentary footage that Welles procured from Frenchman François Reichenbach. There we see de Hory and Irving, cavorting in their aristocratic environment, unapologetically discussing the merits of fakery and the hypocrisy of the art world. De Hory, a Hungarian Holocaust survivor, made a fortune by copying such masters as Matisse, Modigliani, and Picasso. Hundreds of his forgeries were purchased by dealers, and many still hang in museums around the world today.

In staccato tones that keep the film feeling like a thriller, Welles interjects: "Value depends on opinion. Opinion depends on experts. Elmyr makes fools of experts, so who're the experts? Who're the fakers?"

Welles weaves in the story of his own life, telling us that as a struggling teenage artist he lied about being a famous New York actor in order to get his first job in London. Later, he reminds us, he became famous for delivering the "War of the Worlds" broadcast, a hoax. Many top reviewers ripped Welles's film apart when it came out in 1975, calling it derivative and pretentious.

But then, these critiques function as ironic postscript; they were making his point for him.

Although I think Welles could have done without the last seventeen minutes of the film, they're not enough to diminish its overall value as a provocative, timeless, genre-bending classic. Toward the end, Welles delivers the maxim that "art is the lie that helps us see the truth." But in *F for Fake*, he has gone one better. He has found the *art* in the truth.

JULIAN RUBINSTEIN
Writer and journalist

Mavericks: Welles and Cassavetes

F for Fake (Vérités et mensonges)
1975, Orson Welles
SCREENPLAY: Orson Welles and Oja Kodar
CAST: Orson Welles, Oja Kodar, Joseph Cotten,
François Reichenbach, Elmyr de Hory, Clifford Irving,
Laurence Harvey
FRANCE/IRAN/WEST GERMANY; DOCUMENTARY; IN ENGLISH
AND FRENCH

Shadows
1959, John Cassavetes
SCREENPLAY: John Cassavetes
CAST: Ben Carruthers, Lelia Goldoni, Hugh Hurd,
Anthony Ray, Rupert Crosse
U.S.; B & W

The filmmakers whose contributions have been most overlooked or underappreciated are those who, by design or circumstance, found themselves working outside the Hollywood system at a time when that system was practically the *only* way to get a film made and seen. Two of these filmmakers, Welles and Cassavetes, have names that are very well known, but in both cases they have achieved fame and recognition more through the force of their personalities and their appearances as actors in other people's movies than through their own films. Most of their best work as directors, in fact, has gone largely unseen.

Orson Welles was the first truly independent filmmaker of the modern age, though he preferred the word "maverick," saying that an independent was someone who simply couldn't get the financing, whereas a maverick "couldn't help himself, he was just built that way, needed to make films in a way and of a kind that would inevitably scare studios and financiers away." Although Welles's first film, *Citizen Kane*, has been hailed by many as the best film ever made, almost all of his other extraordinary films are rarely seen. There are few movies that can compare in imagination and creative craft to *The Magnificent Ambersons*, *The Lady from Shanghai*, or *Touch of Evil*, and few films based on Shakespeare's work have the infectious power of Welles's *Othello*, *Macbeth*, or *Chimes at Midnight* (based on Shakespeare's Falstaff from several of his plays). But the film that he considered his greatest accomplishment—as do I—is virtually unknown in the United States, never having had a commercial release. It is called *F for Fake* (see p. 72), and in addition to being an extraordinary contemplation—and personal confession—of the fraudulent role the artist plays in our society, it is also the single most inventive exploration of how a film can be made with no money. In fact, it was the movie that Welles hoped would free him forever from having to seek financing. The film was created almost entirely in the editing room, with much of its material being adapted from existing sources. Welles accomplished an artistic feat of great magnitude with *F for Fake*—and practically no one knows it.

In recent years, John Cassavetes has often been referred to as the "father" of the independent-film movement. But despite all that is being written about him, his films are practically never shown—with the possible exception of *A Woman Under the Influence,* a deeply affecting, brilliantly acted film. *Faces, Husbands,* and *Minnie and Moskowitz* all have a freshness and immediacy to them rarely found in American films—then or now. *The Killing of a Chinese Bookie, Love Streams,* and (most especially) *Opening Night* each capture a raw and desperate vision of human relationships unlike any other filmmaker's work. His first film, *Shadows*—virtually unseen due to its rough edges, technical lapses, and seemingly awkward performances—is perhaps the single most undervalued American film of real significance. Dealing with complex issues of race, sex, and identity with a vivid and easy honesty, it was made on the streets of New York in 1960 in grainy 16 mm with a rough script outline and a group of improvising actors and friends. With it, Cassevetes brought to the screen an unprecedented and uncompromising truthfulness about the way people actually behave and how they live their day-to-day lives.

HENRY JAGLOM
Writer and director

Fiddler on the Roof
1971, Norman Jewison

SCREENPLAY: Joseph Stein; based on the book of short stories *Tevye's Daughters* and the play *Tevye der Milkhiker*, by Sholom Aleichem
CAST: Topol, Norma Crane, Leonard Frey, Molly Picon, Rosalind Harris, Paul Mann, Michele Marsh, Neva Small, Paul Michael Glaser
U.S.

When was the last time you saw *Fiddler on the Roof*—the *movie*? If you're like most people, this masterpiece has been obscured, mutated, and diluted by countless high school and regional productions, not to mention by everyone and their brother at some time finding it necessary to launch into "Sunrise, Sunset" or "If I Were a Rich Man," accompanied not by an orchestra, but by facetiousness and alcohol. It's tragic how this film has been buried under the scab of popular culture that has formed around it; the dinner-theater kitsch too often associated with *Fiddler on the Roof* has about as much in common with director Norman Jewison's original work of art as a lounge Elvis has with the King during his Sun Records era, *Wings Greatest Hits* has with

Rubber Soul, or a Times Square blinking Jesus has with the real man from Galilee.

A semi-comic Broadway musical with Chagall-inspired scenery, famous for the bravado performance of the force of nature known as Zero Mostel—how the hell did Mr. Jewison (not Jewish!) turn *that* into a film that feels like the most entertaining documentary you've ever seen? A documentary that deals with pogroms and assimilation, foreshadows the Holocaust, *and* has catchy show tunes? Has a man ever so successfully channeled—or been possessed by—both Busby Berkeley *and* John Cassavetes? What a dybbuk! Jewison should have won Best Director of the *decade*—and we're talking about the '70s here. No one else has ever juggled so many diverse tones so effectively and made them feel all of a piece. A Death Star could have shown up during the dream sequence and we would have bought it.

Do yourself a favor: go rent this movie immediately and let its freshness and clarity wipe away all the *Fiddler* tchotchkes floating around your head. Now, if Jewison would only direct *Company*, another Hal Prince production, he could feel free to ascend to heaven.

DAVID BAR KATZ
Writer and director

Film as a Subversive Art

Amos Vogel, *Film as a Subversive Art*
D.A.P./C.T. Editions, 2005.

Find this book, consume it, and let it nourish you with filmic alternatives. When you open *Film as a Subversive Art*, you will find a compendium of the twentieth-century films that strive to provoke, enrich, and challenge through experimentation.

The book is broken down into chapters with titles such as "Weapons of Subversion," "The Assault on Montage," and "The Destruction of Time and Space." In each chapter you will find an overview and a list of films. As you read the descriptions of each film, you can sense the generosity of a sharp mind sharing and welcoming you to the restless world of the avant-garde.

Equal parts black-and-white film stills and text, *Film as a Subversive Art* presents a unique graphic narrative, both shocking and beautiful. Like Lotte Eisner's 1952 publication, *The Haunted Screen*, which was embraced by the German New Wave directors of the '70s, Vogel's book should be embraced as a manifesto for anyone who is bored by the current status quo of cinema.

DOUG AITKEN
Artist

Fire

1996, Deepa Mehta

SCREENPLAY: Deepa Mehta

CAST: Shabana Azmi, Nandita Das, Jaaved Jaaffery, Kulbhushan Kharbanda, Kushal Rekhi, Ranjit Chowdhry, Alice Poon, Ram Gopal Bajaj

INDIA/CANADA; IN ENGLISH AND HINDI

In 1996, the Indian director Deepa Mehta made the film *Fire*—the story of two women in arranged marriages, sharing a middle-class household in contemporary New Delhi. The film caused a scandal when it was released in India, only in part because it depicted the women's lesbian relationship. Protest against the film became so violent that the government ordered censors to make the film less offensive. They refused, and the film's rerelease was met with even more protest.

I was living in Calcutta at the time and, given the unruliness of the mostly male audiences, going to the movies there was difficult—and rumors of impending trouble persuaded me to stay home. It was a good thing because in one theater under siege, a fierce battle broke out between the counter-protesters and the reactionaries.

Calcutta has a largely unsuccessful but well-intentioned left-wing government. The Bengalis, who pride themselves on their high-spirited individuality and intelligence, have produced many great film directors, Satyajit Ray among them. Lest my admiration be taken for political sentimentality, it must be said that *Fire* is a good movie, as is *Earth*, the second film in the director's proposed quartet about the Partition of India in 1947. In 2000, Mehta was prevented from completing her next film, *Water*, when religious and secular conservatives attacked the set and crew in Benares.

SUSANNA MOORE
Writer

EDITORS NOTE: The filming of *Water* resumed in 2004 in Sri Lanka. A false title, *River Moon*, was used during production to divert attention.

Fireworks (Hana-bi)

1997, Takeshi Kitano

SCREENPLAY: Takeshi Kitano
CAST: Takeshi Kitano, Kayoko Kishimoto, Ren Osugi, Susumu Terejima, Tetsu Watanabe, Hakuryu, Yasuei Yakushiji, Taro Istumi, Kenichi Yajima, Makoto Ashikawa
JAPAN; IN JAPANESE

In *Fireworks*, a violent shooting shatters the world of two Japanese detectives. One is paralyzed, sending the other into a spiral of guilt and despair. The story alternates between one detective's search for redemption and his partner's search for meaning in his radically altered life.

Right from the opening confrontation—shot as a series of meticulously composed still-frames—it's clear that writer-director-actor Takeshi Kitano is willing to strip the story to its essence. He leaves out all but the most essential information while letting context seep in from the edges of the screen.

Kitano's austere approach can be disorienting at first, but it pays off with a compelling percussive rhythm: moments of lyrical beauty suddenly explode into violence before returning to scenes of quiet reflection. The tension is sustained by the unpredictable nature of these transitions; you never know what is coming next. Kitano's acting is all mood and impulse; his taciturn stare and occasional facial twitch are more than enough to convey the inner turmoil tearing his character apart.

The movie, which won the Golden Lion at the 1997 Venice Film Festival, plays out in nonlinear time and is layered with moments of humor and grace. This is not a film for those who prefer clarity and literalism, but for those who enjoy watching a filmmaker play with the limits of form and structure, searching for new ways to get under your skin.

ROBERT TYMCHYSHYN
Writer

The Front
1976, Martin Ritt

SCREENPLAY: Walter Bernstein
CAST: Woody Allen, Zero Mostel, Herschel Bernardi,
Michael Murphy, Andrea Marcovicci, Remak Ramsay,
Lloyd Gough, Joshua Shelley, Charles Kimbrough,
Josef Sommer, Danny Aiello
U.S.

In a rare appearance as the star of someone else's film, Woody Allen is pure comic joy. With a heartbreaking performance by Zero Mostel and an extraordinary script by Walter Bernstein.

JOHN PENOTTI
President, GreeneStreet Films

Funny Bones

1995, Peter Chelsom

SCREENPLAY: Peter Chelsom and Peter Flannery
CAST: Oliver Platt, Jerry Lewis, Lee Evans, Leslie Caron, Richard Griffiths, Oliver Reed, George Carl, Freddie Davies, Ian McNeice
U.K./U.S.; B & W

You've never seen anything quite like this astonishing, completely unpredictable comedy about comedy. Its hero is a failed Vegas stand-up (Oliver Platt) living in the shadow of his famous funnyman father (Jerry Lewis). To learn the tricks of the trade, Platt goes back to his birthplace in Blackpool, where he discovers a brilliant but unbalanced physical clown (Lee Evans) and some dark secrets from the past. This synopsis makes director Peter Chelsom's 1995 movie sound straightforward, yet it is anything but—it veers from piracy at sea to Leslie Caron in a Cleopatra costume to some of the wildest vaudeville acts you'll ever see. Evans is a sight to behold: he does with his body what Robin Williams does with his brain. *Funny Bones* is a high-wire act from start to finish, and quite unclassifiable: its U.S. distributor, Disney, hadn't a clue what do with it. But if ever a movie deserved a cult following, this one does.

DAVID ANSEN
Movie critic, Newsweek

G

Gaav

see *The Cow*

Galaxy Quest

1999, Dean Parisot

SCREENPLAY: David Howard and Robert Gordon
CAST: Tim Allen, Sigourney Weaver, Alan Rickman, Tony Shalhoub,
Sam Rockwell, Daryl Mitchell, Enrico Colantoni, Robin Sachs,
Patrick Breen, Missi Pyle
U.S.

Parody is the delicate art of the indelicate, the architecture of destruction, and the perpetual propping up of what one seems to be knocking down. Though fantasy novelists usually understand this completely, filmmakers are not often so clear-sighted. Sometimes the result is unintelligent, uninspired, and downright unfunny. *Galaxy Quest*, however, is parody's holy grail. It's an exciting adventure story that makes fun of adventure stories. And it gains credibility from its criticisms of the genre, just as the actors make us believe they're real people by their slightly over-the-top performances as actors.

Tim Allen plays a Shatner-esque TV star whose sci-fi series was canceled years ago, so his livelihood now depends upon sci-fi conventions and personal appearances. *Galaxy Quest* is the story of actors disconnected from their craft, scrambling for work, squabbling over stolen lines, and grieving lost opportunities. The television series may be gone, but the fans are forever, and some of them are space aliens seeking help from what they think are intrepid explorers. Science fiction comes up against science fact, actors play against reality, and fans who are aliens and fans who are human are entangled in a truth that is also a fiction.

If that sounds a little too philosophical for a *Star Trek* parody, the movie puts funny first and philosophy a long way second. Still, the fans are ridiculed and honored for their belief, while the actors are laughed at and lionized for their inspiration. No recent science-fiction film I can think of shows so clearly the reason for science-fiction films—the sheer glory of the vision of a universe waiting to be discovered for the pure joy of discovery. Admittedly, this transcendent realization occupies about three minutes of film time and is put in the hands of Tim Allen and Tony Shalhoub, but there's something oddly comforting about that.

ACE G. PILKINGTON
Professor of English, Dixie State College of Utah

Gamera 3: Revenge of Iris
1999, Shusuke Kaneko

SCREENPLAY: Kazunori Itô and Shusuke Kaneko
CAST: Shinobu Nakayama, Ai Maeda, Ayako Fujitani, Senri Yamasaki

JAPAN; IN JAPANESE

Gamera 3: Revenge of Isis (known to Japanese fans as *G3*) completes—at least for now—the turtle monster film series. More precisely, there are two *Gamera* series: the original, eight-film "Showa Era" series, directed by Noriaki Yuasa between 1965 and 1980, and the updated "Heisei Era" trilogy, directed by Shusuke Kaneko between 1995 and 1999. *G3* belongs to the later series, which boasts a redesigned Gamera and (naturally) significantly better visual effects.

So, is Gamera a good guy or not? We never know. The classic character oscillates between a bad destructive monster and a guardian of the Earth. In G3, he is clearly seen as an evil destroyer by young Ayana, an orphan girl whose family was killed by Gamera in a previous battle. Gamera kills a *lot* of innocent people in order to "protect" the Earth from other monsters, and in Ayana's eyes, such acts of mass destruction are never justified. And there is plenty of destruction in G3 as Gamera lays waste to various Japanese cities while battling a flock of flying, dinosaur-like creatures known as Gyaos. Gamera steps through the underground shopping mall in modern Sapporo, crushes buildings in downtown Shibuya, and destroys two exemplars of Japanese hypermodern architecture: the Tokyo Metropolitan Government Buildings and the newly renovated Kyoto Station. As a critic suggested when the film was released, this Gamera represents resentful, conservative middle-aged Japanese men who are determined to destroy nontraditional symbols.

Fittingly, young Ayana plays a vital role in the counterattack against Gamera by nurturing Isis, a powerful flying monster with multiple tentacles hatched from an egg found at an ancient religious site. The images of Iris soaring into the sky are breathtakingly beautiful, and the three-way air battle between Gamera, Isis, and the Japanese Self-Defense Force is spectacular.

HIKARI HORI
Visiting Professor, East Asian Languages and Cultures, Columbia University

Ganja and Hess
1972, Bill Gunn

SCREENPLAY: Bill Gunn

CAST: Marlene Clark, Duane Jones, Bill Gunn, Richard Harrow, Leonard Jackson, Mabel King, Candece Tarpley, Sam Waymon
U.S.

I had to go all the way to France to see *Ganja and Hess*. Bill Gunn was there, along with Bill Greaves and a number of emerging black independent filmmakers. It was the beginning of the "third wave" (students who came out of film schools in the late '60s and '70s)—if one thought of Spencer Williams, Oscar Micheaux, and others during that period as the first wave, and Ossie Davis, Gordon Parks, and Sidney Poitier as the second. If it weren't for his untimely death, Gunn would still be creating memorable works.

The success of *Ganja and Hess* was limited to Europe, and Gunn was hurt by the cold response he received in the U.S. It seemed to me that the film should have been embraced by American critics and audiences, because it is as eloquent a statement about black culture and myth as one will ever find in cinema. My friends and I were looking for a film that exemplified how black aesthetics and culture could be expressed effectively. *Ganja and Hess* set the bar and is a great example of work that reflects a collective consciousness while at the same time remaining uniquely Gunn's.

Although I haven't seen it in over two decades, I'm still inspired by my initial impression. In fact, I'm afraid to see it again; I want to remember it always as fresh and unexpected. This is important to me because *Ganja and Hess* validated the idea that for black cinema to have meaning, it has to incorporate one's roots, myths, and everything that we, as a people, experienced.

Everyone knows the hot young filmmakers of today, but if one wants to create something of importance one has to revisit an earlier generation of black filmmakers and spend a period of time studying films like *Ganja and Hess*. For me, Gunn was the one who laid the groundwork for what was possible.

CHARLES BURNETT
Filmmaker

Gattaca

1997, Andrew Niccol

SCREENPLAY: Andrew Niccol
CAST: Ethan Hawke, Uma Thurman, Jude Law, Gore Vidal, Xander Berkeley, Jayne Brook, Elias Koteas, Blair Underwood, Ernest Borgnine, Tony Shalhoub, Alan Arkin, Loren Dean
U.S.

The trouble with *Gattaca* was its timing: the movie was utterly buried by *Titanic* and *The Lost World: Jurassic Park*—lost in the shuffle of 1997.

It's too bad, because *Gattaca*, directed by Andrew Niccol (of *Truman Show* fame), is one of the few sci-fi movies where you can draw a straight line from today's trends back to every single futuristic detail in its frames. In *Gattaca*'s future world, your genes are your résumé, your blood sample is your ID card, and you're hired, married, and judged on the basis of your genetic code.

Perfect people get the best jobs. That's a problem for Vincent (Ethan Hawke), whose rebel parents gave birth to him naturally rather than choosing his genes in the lab like everyone else. As a result, he's a little on the short side, and his heart has an imperfection that predicts trouble. But his dream—to join the space program—burns so brightly that he's willing to undergo a risky genetic impersonation, using borrowed hair strands, skin cells, saliva, and urine samples that he buys from a genetically perfect counterpart (Jude Law).

Apart from the less successful murder-mystery sub-plot, the whole thing is understated, unpretentious, and utterly believable. It's one of those movies that pops back into your head months, even years later, as society continues to tumble along toward a future that looks more and more like *Gattaca*.

DAVID POGUE
Writer and columnist, New York Times

A Meager Existence

Nanook of the North
1922, Robert Flaherty
Written by Robert Flaherty
CAST: Nanook, Nyla, Cunayou, Al Lee, Comock
U.S.; B & W; DOCUMENTARY; SILENT

Man of Aran
1934, Robert Flaherty
Written by Robert Flaherty
CAST: Colman "Tiger" King, Maggie Dirrane, Michael Dillane
U.K.; B & W; DOCUMENTARY

The Gleaners and I (Les glaneurs et la glaneuse)
2000, Agnès Varda
Written by Agnès Varda
CAST: Bodan Litnanski, Agnès Varda, François Wertheimer
FRANCE; DOCUMENTARY; IN FRENCH

Robert J. Flaherty's *Nanook of the North* has often been called "the first documentary," but this is patently inaccurate. People were so fascinated by the initial concept of projected moving pictures that *all* of the first films were documentaries—man sleeping, train running, and so on. *Nanook* was the first full-length, narrated documentary, and for that reason alone, nobody who claims to be a cinephile should go to their grave without seeing it. This black-and-white documentary about Eskimo life in the Arctic Circle is a wondrous glimpse into a life as foreign to our own as possible. And there is a scene of Nanook tying up his kayak that is as funny in its simplistic acceptance of the harsh arctic conditions as anything you will ever see in a big-budget studio film.

If you like Flaherty's work in *Nanook of the North*, chances are you will also like *Man of Aran*. Like *Nanook*, it deals with a family eking out an existence, this time on a barren, godforsaken island off the coast of Scotland. But as this documentary teaches us, every place, even this one, is home to *someone*.

The Gleaners and I, by renowned French filmmaker Agnès Varda, takes another look at folks gathering and living and laughing and loving under the harshest of circumstances. Gleaners are people who forage for leftovers after crops have been harvested. It's a hard life, but one with all its attendant textures. Shot in Varda's native France, *The Gleaners and I* is one more example of the spirit soaring.

MICHAEL C. DONALDSON
Former President, International Documentary Association, author, and lawyer

Gettysburg
1993, Ronald F. Maxwell

SCREENPLAY: Ronald F. Maxwell; based on the novel *The Killer Angels*, by Michael Shaara
CAST: Tom Berenger, Martin Sheen, Stephen Lang, Jeff Daniels, Richard Jordan, Bo Brickman, James Lancaster, Patrick Stuart, Royce D. Applegate, Sam Elliot, C. Thomas Howell, Brian Mallon, Buck Taylor
U.S.

At four hours and fifteen minutes, *Gettysburg* is not for everyone. Certainly, if Civil War history holds no interest for you, don't see this movie. But if you like that sort of thing, then you may find this fascinating. Over a four-day period in the summer of 1863, the fate of the United States was decided near a small Pennsylvania town. *Gettysburg* examines the men and the events that conspired to make that decision.

The film deals mostly with high-ranking generals and colonels rather than with ordinary fighting men. On the Confederate side, it focuses on the relationship between two of the greatest generals in American history, Robert E. Lee (Martin Sheen) and James Longstreet (Tom Berenger), and how the one grievous error they made probably lost the war for the South. The movie's truly affecting Confederate story, however, is that of Gen. Lewis Armistead (Richard Jordan), who is torn apart because his best friend is leading the Union troops just across the valley.

The main Union story follows Col. Joshua Lawrence Chamberlain (Jeff Daniels), a rhetoric professor from Bowdoin College who finds himself commanding an already decimated regiment. Chamberlain knows that the Union force will collapse if his men fail to hold the line against the Confederates, who send wave after wave of soldiers up the hill known as Little Round Top. With few remaining troops and no ammunition, Col. Chamberlain executes an obscure textbook maneuver and wins the battle. This is one of my favorite moments in history: an unlikely hero with an unlikely plan that produces an unlikely victory.

Gettysburg has too many flaws (including its length) to be a truly great movie. But I've seen it three times and I've enjoyed it each time every bit as much as the last.

ADAM DURITZ
Songwriter

The Gleaners and I (Les glaneurs et la glaneuse)
see p. 93

The Gold Diggers of 1933
1933, Mervyn LeRoy

SCREENPLAY: Erwin S. Gelsey, James Seymour, David Boehm, and Ben Markson; based on the play by Avery Hopwood

CAST: Warren William, Joan Blondell, Aline MacMahon,
Ruby Keeler, Dick Powell, Guy Kibbee, Ned Sparks,
Ginger Rogers
U.S.; B & W

Everybody cheers for the return of the movie musical,
but no one seems to remember what a real movie musical is. Five years into the sound era, director Mervyn
LeRoy, choreographer Busby Berkeley, and Warner
Bros. produced *The Gold Diggers of 1933*, which remains
one of the overlooked classics of the genre. Unlike
more recent manifestations (*Moulin Rouge!*, *Chicago*)
that employ the short-attention-span, rapid-fire dynamics of MTV to chop the spectacle into ever-smaller bits,
Gold Diggers achieves that moment of transcendence
when the mundane shimmers into the magical, utopian
realm of song, spectacle, and dance. In the opening
number, the camera draws back from a glimmering
close-up of Fay's (Ginger Rogers) dazzling smile to
reveal her fully, albeit skimpily, adorned in glinting
strands of lucre. She's singing "We're in the Money,"
and the lyric becomes literal as the camera cranes and
the world unfolds into chains of dancers waving giant
coins. That is, until reality intrudes as bailiffs descend to
close down the show and a sheriff snatches the platter-
sized silver dollar covering Fay's crotch.

Berkeley's surreal, sumptuous, and polymorphously
perverse numbers offer pleasant distractions: a voy-
euristic baby on roller skates guides us through banked
bevies of cuties in "Petting in the Park," and the
warbly "Shadow Waltz" climaxes with undulating
rows of beauties playing glow-in-the-dark violins while
wearing diaphanous hoopskirts that look like beckoning
flowers—a real head-scratcher for any Freudians in
the audience.

But these elaborate diversions merely delay the inevitable return of "Forgotten Man" and other troubling truths looming behind the delightful trappings of the film: the misery, injustice, and dehumanization of the Depression. A surging requiem duet sung by Joan Blondell and astounding blues belter Etta Moten propels Berkeley's kaleidoscopic parade of wounded doughboys into the rain and their breadline legacy. The frivolous musical has, in the end, turned shockingly political and profound; "Remember My Forgotten Man" fuses the tragedy of real life and the transcendence of cinema into one of Hollywood's greatest triumphs.

PETER KEOUGH
Film editor, Boston Phoenix

The Good Fairy
see p. 174

The Great Escape
1963, John Sturges

SCREENPLAY: James Clavell and W. R. Burnett; based on the novel by Paul Brickhall
CAST: Steve McQueen, James Garner, Richard Attenborough, James Donald, Charles Bronson, Donald Pleasence, James Coburn, Gordon Jackson, John Leyton, Nigel Stock
U.S.

Take another look at *The Great Escape.* I love the way Steve McQueen is clearly wearing his own clothes: fab hip-hugging jeans and a wafer-thin post–James Dean leather bomber jacket. If there were any women in the movie they would be wearing something nice by Mary Quant and half a pound of pale blue eye shadow. And yet, in spite of its anachronisms and inaccuracies, the story has great power, and much of the acting is excellent. Particularly outstanding are James Garner as Lt. Hendley, the raffish bad guy who turns out to have a heart of pure American gold, and Donald Pleasence as Lt. Blythe, the mole-like master forger with unblinking eyes like saucers, doing enough blind acting for three films. Most people know three or four key scenes by heart . . . picking up the pin, the bit where Richard Attenborough blows it on the station platform, Charles Bronson freaking out when the tunnel collapses. It's like a Greek myth—fake but real. My father and I used to love watching it. He had spent time in a Stalag Luft himself, and he knew exactly how cold and dull and scary and hungry the real experience was. Now I watch it with my own son and try to explain to him what the war was all about, and why we fought the Germans, and why Steve McQueen's jeans are so very different from everyone else's . . .

ROGER MICHELL
Director

Gun Crazy
1950, Joseph H. Lewis

SCREENPLAY: Dalton Trumbo (as Millard Kaufman) and Mackinlay Kantor; based on the short story by Mackinlay Kantor
CAST: Peggy Cummins, John Dall, Berry Kroeger, Morris Carnovsky, Anabel Shaw, Harry Lewis, Nedrick Young, Russ Tamblyn
U.S.; B & W

Arguably the greatest B-movie ever made, this noir masterpiece is one of the earliest movies to connect the dots between sex, violence, and American culture's infatuation with guns ("Thrill Crazy . . . Kill Crazy . . . Gun Crazy," as the poster screamed). Co-written by then-blacklisted Dalton Trumbo under a pseudonym, the story centers on firearm-obsessed teen Bart Tare (played by little Rusty Tamblyn twelve years before *West Side Story*), who is sent to reform school for stealing a gun. After a stint in the army, where he further hones his skills, the adult Bart (John Dall, who appeared in Hitchcock's *Rope* the previous year) falls for a carnival sharpshooter named Laurie (Welsh-born Peggy Cummins, exuding hundred-proof eroticism), and the pair embarks on a deadly crime spree. This perverse portrait of the bond between the weak-willed Bart and the dominating Laurie ("We go together like guns and ammunition," he tells her), is stunningly executed by low-budget maestro director Joseph H. Lewis, whose remarkably sophisticated visual style is exemplified in the movie's pièce de résistance: a four-minute bank-robbery sequence filmed entirely from the backseat of a car—and shot in one continuous take. Like the rest of the movie, it's a breathless tour de force.

MICHAEL SCHEINFELD
Writer

RECOMMENDED VIEWING: Other films directed by Joseph H. Lewis: *My Name Is Julia Ross* (1945); *So Dark the Night* (1946); *My Undercover Man* (1949); *A Lady Without Passport* (1950); *The Big Combo* (1955); *The Halliday Brand* (1957).

H

Hail the Conquering Hero
see p. 72

Hana-bi
see *Fireworks*

Harlan County U.S.A.
see p. 102

The Heartbreak Kid
1972, Elaine May

SCREENPLAY: Neil Simon; based on the short story "A Change of Plan," by Bruce Jay Friedman
CAST: Charles Grodin, Cybill Shepherd, Jeannie Berlin, Audra Lindley, Eddie Albert, William Prince, Art Metrano
U.S.

If the Coen brothers' classic *Fargo* found the siblings getting even with their native Minnesota through a collection of shivering dimwits, a lesser-known satire made in 1972, *The Heartbreak Kid*, already had the state down cold—even though its makers had barely set foot there before the shoot began. "So whaddya wanna live in a dumb place like Minnesota for?" asks a New York salesman (Charles Grodin) of his blond object of desire (Cybill Shepherd) about a half hour into *The Heartbreak Kid*—hitting Minnesotans where we live while voicing the skepticism of nearly everyone else.

In May's ingeniously intuitive post-*Graduate* comedy, my homeland first appears as a whiteout, a blinding blur of snow, sun, sky, endless trees, and a big white mansion in the distance—the Wasp ice palace as seen by the protagonist from the window of a cab. Newlywed Lenny Cantrow has come out here in the wake of his claustrophobic honeymoon road trip from New York to Miami, where a brief encounter with seductive shiksa Kelly Corcoran (Shepherd) almost immediately compels him to drop his Jewish bride, Lila (Jeannie Berlin).

Reviewing *The Heartbreak Kid* in the *Village Voice* in late '72, critic Molly Haskell asserted that "the Wasps are treated with hardly a trace of the caricature lavished on the Jews." Similarly, the *New Yorker*'s Pauline Kael suggested in her otherwise rave review that "most of the Wasps in the film don't have the dimensions of the New York Jewish characters . . . There isn't enough dissonance in these people." Indeed not. But if the opposite of dissonance is conformity, might that not be part of the film's point?

With *The Heartbreak Kid*, May created a prescient allegory of what the "out-of-town" artist would face peddling her wares in Middle America: a place where Cybill Shepherd would be top-billed for an eye-candy role as the Other Woman, while Jeannie Berlin—May's own daughter—would be rewarded for her fearless performance with a quick descent into cinematic obscurity. Pretending to deliver a beauty contest, albeit framed by a (lively) Jewish wedding and a (stifling) Episcopal one, May answers the classic question "How will it play in Peoria?" Observing the triumphant and fully regressed Lenny at his second wedding reception, May gives the scene an added charge through her brilliantly improvised shooting style, in which the Wasps' slightly askance stares and the camera's sudden swish-pans serve as the perfect representation of Minnesota Nice—a vibe that's disorienting even to those of us who live here.

ROB NELSON
Film Critic

Hearts of Darkness: A Filmmaker's Apocalypse
see p. 137

Cinéma Vérité

Harlan County U.S.A.
1976, Barbara Kopple
CAST: Nimrod Workman, E. B. Allen, Bessie Lou Cornett, Jim Thomas
U.S.; DOCUMENTARY

Paris Is Burning
1990, Jennie Livingston
CAST: André Christian, Dorian Corey, Paris Duprée, Pepper Labeija, Willi Ninja
U.S.; DOCUMENTARY

Crumb
1994, Terry Zwigoff
CAST: Robert Crumb, Aline Kominsky, Charles Crumb, Maxon Crumb, Dana Crumb, Beatrice Crumb
U.S.; DOCUMENTARY

For years documentaries were deemed box-office poison. Today, critics and audiences alike are discovering that some of the most exciting, groundbreaking movies being made belong to a genre that once conjured up visions of the A/V monitor in junior high school, who dragged out a 16 mm projector to show films on driver safety.

It's a sea change that started in the 1950s with the development of portable, lightweight equipment that allowed filmmakers like D. A. Pennebaker, Richard Leacock, Robert Drew, Fredrick Wiseman, and Albert and David Maysles to create cinema verité. The officious voice-over narrator was sent to his death. A tiny crew (sometimes just a cinematographer and a soundperson) followed close on the heels of the subject to bring back footage that had a dynamic quality never before experienced. Think of a young John F. Kennedy giving out handbills on a snowy street to disinterested commuters in Drew's *Primary* or the now-legendary scene in Pennebaker's *Don't Look Back* of Bob Dylan torturing a reporter from *Time* magazine.

In the past thirty years many of the same filmmakers, joined by a new generation of documentarians, have made films that are classics of their kind. Barbara Kopple's *Harlan County U.S.A.*, made in 1976, was one of the first feature-length documentaries to be released theatrically. Her gritty, no-holds-barred look at the lives of striking Kentucky miners recorded poverty and exploitation, but it also told a profoundly moving story of resilience, courage, and fighting spirit. In 1990, Jennie Livingston's *Paris Is Burning*, a portrait of cross-dressing gay men who put on elaborate fashion shows for one another, was a breakthrough in its compassionate approach to a subject previously played for laughs or sensationalism. And in 1995, *Crumb*, Terry Zwigoff's portrait of underground cartoonist and dysfunctional family member R. Crumb, became a box-office success. The elusive Robert Crumb managed to open up to the camera while retaining his sense of mystery. His stories of a violent father and negligent mother are made all the more poignant when we meet his two deeply disturbed brothers, neither of whom had the inner resources to combat the traumas they sustained.

The best documentary films, interestingly enough, work much like their fiction-film brethren. They are inevitably inhabited by riveting characters, footage of whose activities the filmmaker shapes with an eye to narrative flow. Complete with dramatic climaxes and denouements, these films make us laugh, and they make us cry. And they get under our skin because the reality they illuminate on screen informs our lives long after the popcorn is gone and the lights have come up.

KAREN COOPER
Director, Film Forum

Hellzapoppin'

1941, H. C. Potter

SCREENPLAY: Nat Perrin and Warren Wilson; based on the play by Nat Perrin

CAST: Ole Olsen, Chic Johnson, Robert Paige, Jane Frazee, Martha Raye, Mischa Auer, Richard Lane, Elisha Cook Jr., Hugh Herbert, Shemp Howard

U.S.; B & W

"Any similarity between *Hellzapoppin'* and a motion picture is purely coincidental."
—Disclaimer at the opening of *Hellzapoppin'*

Hellzapoppin' is easily the strangest musical Hollywood ever produced, a self-conscious meta-movie lost on the road between *Tristram Shandy* and *Schizopolis*. For one thing, it opens in the projection booth, with the movie about to begin. Then the "real" picture opens with a musical number set in hell, where we meet Ole Olsen and Chic Johnson, the stage comedians whose eponymous, plotless Broadway revue inspired the movie. After a few gags, they storm through the brimstone onto the soundstage of their movie, *Hellzapoppin'*. They quarrel with the director and writer, who ultimately sell Olsen and Johnson on the idea that their picture, like all pictures, needs a love story. Then we're in a Long Island mansion, for the love story we've just been pitched. Olsen and Johnson wander through the hijinks like a pair of lost Marx brothers, periodically interacting with the filmmakers (conceiving the movie) and the projectionist (exhibiting and manipulating the completed results). If none of this makes any sense, you're starting to get it. But let me tell you about the best part. Slim Gaillard (the jive-talking guitarist famous for "The Flat Foot Floogie") and his partner, bassist Slam Stewart, dressed as deliverymen, stumble upon a cache of musical instruments. Slim plays the piano with the back of his fingers (one of his old vaudeville tricks; he could also play the guitar and tap-dance simultaneously), attracting jazz musicians from around the mansion, who pick up the other instruments and jam. They strike up a number that attracts the Harlem Congeroo Dancers (dressed like the help), who exploit the Lindy Hop for all it's worth. Suffice to say, it's the most breathtaking, gravity-defying musical number

I've ever seen. I'd take it over *Seven Brides for Seven Brothers*, over the Nicholas Brothers in *Stormy Weather*, you name it. Hands down.

HENRY GRIFFIN
Filmmaker

Hifazaat
see *In Custody*

The Hill
1965, Sidney Lumet

SCREENPLAY: Ray Rigby; based on the play by Ray Rigby and R. S. Allen
CAST: Sean Connery, Harry Andrews, Ian Bannen, Alfred Lynch, Ossie Davis, Roy Kinnear, Jack Watson, Ian Hendry, Michael Redgrave
U.K.; B & W

A rarely seen (or shown) film that I find extraordinary is *The Hill* by Sidney Lumet. Photographed and acted masterfully, it's brilliant and uncompromising. One of my favorite movies by an American director.

WOODY ALLEN
Director

The Holy Office
see *El santo oficio*, p. 179

The Hours and Times
1991, Christopher Münch

SCREENPLAY: Christopher Münch
CAST: David Angus, Ian Hart, Stephanie Pack, Robin McDonald, Sergio Moreno, Unity Grimwood
U.S.; B & W; SHORT

John Lennon and Beatles manager Brian Epstein took
a trip together to Barcelona in 1963. In this elegant,
haunting movie, the young director Christopher
Münch imagines what transpired between the brilliant,
working-class Lennon (Ian Hart) and the wealthy,
cultured, homosexual Epstein (David Angus), who
longed for him. The movie is only an hour long and
was shot in black and white on a shoestring budget in
a mere eight days, yet it has a gemlike sophistication,
delicacy, and intelligence almost never seen in American
independent movies. I was on the jury at the Sundance
Film Festival in 1991, when Münch's film was unveiled.
We all thought it was the best movie there, but because
of its length it wasn't eligible to receive the best-film
prize. We were tempted to break the rules but settled
for giving it a special jury prize. Such is the fate of fifty-
five-minute movies.

> DAVID ANSEN
> *Movie critic,* Newsweek

How Tasty Was My Little Frenchman
(Como era gostoso o meu francês)
1971, Nelson Pereira dos Santos

SCREENPLAY: Nelson Pereira dos Santos
CAST: Gabriel Archanjo, Arduíno Colassanti,
Manfredo Colassanti, Eduardo Imbassahy Filho, José Kléber,
Ana Maria Magalhães
BRAZIL; IN PORTUGUESE, TUPI, AND FRENCH

Imagine a film set in sixteenth-century Brazil in which
the characters speak an indigenous language unknown
to most Brazilians nowadays, and the protagonist, a
Frenchman captured by the native Tupinamba, is to
be festively cannibalized. *How Tasty Was My Little
Frenchman,* made by Brazilian filmmaker Nelson Pereira

dos Santos in 1971, is half comedy, half historical narrative. The story was presumably based on the journals of Hans Staden, who was held captive but managed to escape. Unlike him, the protagonist in this film ends up being devoured by the Tupinamba, but not before he experiences what it is like to live as a tribesman. While he awaits execution, the captive learns the tribe's customs and is allowed to participate in communal rituals. He is also given a wife, whom he grows fond of in spite of the fact that she will soon be eating his flesh. For the most part, the film focuses on this transitional period, a time when the threat of death is often overshadowed by the charm of the New World. But *How Tasty Was My Little Frenchman* neither romanticizes nor diminishes the indigenous culture. Rather, it celebrates—with a great sense of irony and a healthy dose of humor—the resistance against the European conqueror.

VINICIUS NAVARRO
Assistant Professor, Film Studies, Georgia Institute of Technology

RECOMMENDED READING: Richard Peña, "How Tasty Was My Little Frenchman," in *Brazilian Cinema*, by Randal Johnson and Robert Stam. Columbia University Press, 1995.

A Hollywood Primer

If you spend any time working in the movie business, sooner or later you learn there's a subtle game of one-upmanship that goes on. It's a sophisticated game that one plays in order to be perceived as an insider—and not at all dissimilar from the manner in which otherwise socialized packs of vicious jackals rip into one another's throats on the African veldt in order to establish dominance.

The object in Hollywood, however, is to establish your "cinematic bona fides" and stake out your position on the food chain (or car-valet return line). And as an added benefit—if that's how one terms "collateral damage"—you get to not only crush someone's ego but render their life, connections, and accomplishments utterly worthless. All of this, of course, is merely an adjunct to the old Hollywood ethos that "it's not enough for me to succeed; my friends must fail," but let's not get into that right now.

The ritual I'm describing here is often witnessed during meetings or at film-festival panels where the goal is always to reference the single most obscure Swedish, French, Japanese, or Spanish film possible. Better still if the film was never dubbed into English. Or, best of all, never even released. And if this doesn't work, simply invoke the "Buñuel." Almost no one I know in modern Hollywood has actually ever seen a film directed by Luis Buñuel, but it's always a conversation stopper. "I understand what Michael Bay is trying to accomplish, but Buñuel did it first."

On a more practical level, however, this game is played on a far more convivial and social setting—sort of like a steel-cage death match on a Bel Air tennis court—with hand grenades. To wit: if someone says they went to a movie premiere, you must immediately counter, "I saw a rough cut." (Note: Again, almost no one in Hollywood actually knows what a "rough cut" is, save, perhaps, Harvey Weinstein. But he's not telling.) If they claim to have seen a rough cut, you were on the set. If they were on the set, you read the first draft. And if they read—or wrote—the first draft, you had the idea fifteen years ago but passed on it because it wasn't commercial. Game, set, match.

We can now move on to the second inviolate rule—and ritual—in Hollywood: taking credit. In Hollywood, the basic social contract is that "I'll believe you're an actress if you believe I'm a producer." And this is followed closely by the notion that perception *is* reality: You're only as respected as the reputation you've managed to promote. Put another way: Failure is an orphan, but success has twenty-six coproducers. (Actually, success has twenty-six producers, eleven executive producers, twenty-two coproducers, one line-producer, four uncredited writers, the director, the leading man's manager, one extremely disgruntled original screenwriter who would have been much happier if they'd stuck to his original script . . . plus six German financial entities, each of which has a single-card animated logo at the beginning of the film.)

So what does all this mean, on a practical level? Simple: nobody knows for certain anyway. So if it ain't nailed down, take credit for it. No matter how specious or completely tangential your affiliation may have been with a film—"I once dated the director's mother's podiatrist's car detailer"—it is your moral right and social imperative to take credit for all of it. In my own career, I first learned about this back when I was working on the lot at Metro, in 1938. I'd just finished doing a two-week punch-up on *Oz* (my contribution: Tin Man—needs a heart) when David Selznick called in a panic. He had Rhett, he had Scarlett, he had the Civil War, but he didn't have an ending.

"What am I going to do?" he pleaded.

"Two words," I told him.

"What, what?" he cried.

"Atlanta burns."

Of course, being responsible for the success of *Gone with the Wind* is but one of the very small contributions I've made to the film business. (Note closely: false humility. Let the person you're trying to impress stand there slack-jawed in awe.)

I remember when I first got into the film business, through Charlie Chaplin. He was a real son of a bitch. Always complaining about one thing or another. And the day I showed up on the set—to serve him a subpoena, if I remember correctly, on some morals charge, I think—he was grousing about the caterer. "Yo, Charlie," I told him, "stop your whining. Dance with the dinner rolls if you have to. Eat your goddamned shoe."

In 1940, I told Jack Warner: "No. Ilse gets on the plane."

Orson Welles: "Why don't you try doing something with the sled?"

W. C. Fields: "You can't dance, you can't sing. Work the drink."

And when Billy Wilder and I. A. L. Diamond came down with a case of writer's block, I was always there for them. *Sunset Boulevard*? "Do it in flashback." *Some Like It Hot*? "Put 'em in drag." "No. Not *The Brownstone*. *The Apartment*."

Needless to say, I could go on. So I will:

When Hitch shot too much footage, I told him: "The shower scene? Use a lot of cuts."

Simpson and Bruckheimer? "Pummel the audience into submission with sound."

Woody Allen and Marshall Brickman? "Lobsters. Play the scene twice."

Spielberg? "Make it a shark."

Scorsese: "Shoot what you know."

Peckinpah: "Slow motion."

Of course, I wasn't always right. And in retrospect, I'm still not entirely convinced, but I suppose I can see where Jim Cameron was probably better off not doing the *Andrea Doria*.

The point I'm trying to make here—and I forget who said it originally, so I'll take full credit—is that movies are moments. Glimpses and scenes—Groucho and the boys in the stateroom, Bogie and Raines on the tarmac—are what linger in our memories.

For me, the real test of a film is when I say I'm going to watch five minutes—and two hours later, I'm still sitting there as the end credits roll:

Bridge Over the River Kwai. His Lady Eve. The Apartment. Pat and Mike. Thunderball, Dr. Strangelove, The Verdict, Notorious, The Professionals, The Sting. Annie Hall, Animal House, Heaven Can Wait, The African Queen. Rififi, Chinatown. The Man Who Would Be King. All About Eve, The Hustler. To Kill a Mockingbird.

And virtually anything with Fred MacMurray, Sean Connery, Spencer Tracy, Robert Mitchum, Jimmy Stewart, Burt Lancaster, or William Holden.

As I think back on my years in the film business, I suppose my greatest days were in the late '60s. I was working on the lot at Paramount. And one Friday, I stumbled back from lunch at Musso's to find a script on my desk from this new young director Coppola. (I'd been at lunch with Bill Goldman. He was having problems with an "oater"—a horse picture, as we used to call 'em. I told him: "Billy boy, you've got a shoot-'em-up. A cowboy picture. Nobody's buying 'em these days. But have you thought about doing it as a comedy?" Funny thing is, I never heard from Goldman again. No gift, no flowers, no fruit basket. And nothing—not so much as a word—from Redford or Newman. Not even a case of salad dressing at Christmas. Let me tell you: It's a tough business.)

It seems that young Francis was having trouble with a picture. It just wasn't coming together. He asked if I'd take a look. So I read the script over the weekend and called him Monday morning.

"Francis," I said, "It's genius. The script is amazing. A saga. You, this Puzo guy, and Bob Towne—if he goes for credit: statues at the show."

I heard him gasp. "But—"

"No, Francis," I interrupted. "Listen to me. You've got a chance to make one of the most beloved American movies of all time. A chance to imbue the American culture with characters and dialogue that will live forever.

"You've got the horse's head in the bed, the brother-in-law kicking out the windshield, the old man dying in the tomato patch. The wedding, the assassination of the police captain, the murder at the tollbooth.

"It's almost perfect," I told him.

"I know," he said quietly. "But how do I fix it?"

"Francis, that's simple," I said.

"Make them Italian."

BRUCE FEIRSTEIN
Writer

I

I Know Where I'm Going!

1945, Michael Powell and Emeric Pressburger

SCREENPLAY: Michael Powell and Emeric Pressburger

CAST: Wendy Hiller, Roger Livesey, George Carney, Pamela Brown, Walter Hudd, Finlay Currie, Petula Clark, Nancy Price

U.K.; B & W

In *I Know Where I'm Going!*, the blissful 1945 love story known as *IKWIG* to its cultists, the romantic and the pragmatist do not speak the same language of love. The romantic worries: can I love without being certain of love in return? The pragmatist worries: can I love without being certain of financial security? Yet they are powerfully, mystically, erotically drawn to each other. And they are literally thrown together on Scotland's Western Isles by inclement weather, gale-force winds, and whirlpools.

IKWIG was written and directed by Michael Powell and Emeric Pressburger, urbane expressionists responsible for decidedly un-British examples of British filmmaking (consider those feverish studies of vocation, *The Red Shoes*, about a ballerina, and *Black Narcissus*, about a nun). Roger Livesey plays the rugged romantic, a Scottish laird on an eight-day furlough from the navy. And Wendy Hiller plays the proud and pretentious pragmatist on her way to wed a much older man who, unbeknownst to her, is renting the laird's island castle— and his title—for the duration of World War II.

As the roiling Atlantic coast suggests their interior turbulence, Wendy gets close to what she wants and then uncertain that she wants it; the more the laird shares his Scottish customs and philosophy ("If I rent out my castle for three years, I can afford to live there for six—that's Highland economics"), the more he feels that he is doomed by island superstitions.

With the possible exception of *Local Hero*, which *IKWIG* influenced, no other movie makes such an eloquent argument for the transformational powers of a location. It's enough to make you believe that destination is destiny. And that curses are blessings in disguise.

CARRIE RICKEY
Film critic, The Philadelphia Inquirer

Il conformista
see *The Conformist*

Il gattopardo
see *The Leopard*

Il mio viaggio in Italia
see *My Voyage to Italy*

In a Lonely Place
1950, Nicholas Ray

SCREENPLAY: Andrew Solt; based on the novel
by Dorothy B. Hughes
CAST: Humphrey Bogart, Gloria Grahame, Frank Lovejoy,
Carl Benton Reid, Art Smith, Jeff Donnell, Martha Stewart,
Robert Warwick
U.S.; B & W

It has been a long while since I saw *In a Lonely Place*, directed by Nicholas Ray and starring Humphrey Bogart and Gloria Grahame, but I do remember thinking that it was Bogart's best performance. He plays a paranoid screenwriter given to violent outbursts of appalling intensity. Grahame, meanwhile, brings a sexiness to her role as the estranged lover of a real estate developer that—so far as I know—has never been surpassed and, come to think of it, probably never has been equaled. Film noir at its gloomy best.

MARK STRAND
Poet

In one of the darkest, sexiest pulp films of '50s Hollywood, Humphrey Bogart is Dixon Steele, a washed-up screenwriter whose fits of drunken rage make him the prime suspect in the murder of a hatcheck girl. His neighbor, played by the always-sultry Gloria Grahame, quietly fears becoming his next victim. *In a Lonely Place* can be counted among Nicholas Ray's finest and most deeply felt achievements; the coiled violence of Bogart's brilliant performance—his battles with inner demons and his bilious regard for the Hollywood dream factory—seems to be the director's own.

JOSHUA SIEGEL
Assistant curator, Department of Film, Museum of Modern Art

In Custody (Hifazaat)

1993, Ismail Merchant

SCREENPLAY: Anita Desai and Shahrukh Husain;
based on the novel *Hifazaat*, by Anita Desai
CAST: Shashi Kapoor, Shabana Azmi, Om Puri, Sushma Seth,
Neena Gupta, Tinnu Anand, Prayag Raj
U.K./INDIA; IN URDU AND HINDI

In Custody is Ismail Merchant's debut feature film. It is a beautifully made personal account of the director's love for the Urdu language. His despair at its decline is a sentiment reflected in the protagonist, Devan (Om Puri), an English professor in provincial India of the 1960s, who loves Urdu poetry. This was dangerous at the time, as India was intent on wiping out all traces of Muslim colonialism and repression. Devan is a Hindu, but his passion for the formal and elaborate Urdu verse is real and burns fiercely. This film looks beyond the faded decadence of the time, becoming a moving tribute to an era of grace and beauty.

NABEEL SARWAR
Corporate lawyer

The Innocent

see *L'Innocente*

The Innocents

1961, Jack Clayton

SCREENPLAY: William Archibald and Truman Capote; based on the novella *The Turn of the Screw*, by Henry James
CAST: Deborah Kerr, Peter Wyngarde, Megs Jenkins, Michael Redgrave, Martin Stephens, Pamela Franklin
U.K.; B & W

The Innocents is based on the great Henry James novella *The Turn of the Screw*, one of the most terrifying pieces of psychological horror in the English language. The adaptation to the screen is no less scary. The action all takes place in a huge, dimly lit English manor house during the latter part of the nineteenth century. There are vast gardens, a sinister lake, and *lots* of fog. There are also two children, the likes of whom you have never experienced, and what is arguably the best performance of Deborah Kerr's long career. As Miss Giddens, the young governess, Kerr walks a fine line between focused determination and obsession. Also contributing to the film's uniqueness is director Jack Clayton's decision to honor James's original premise: that which has poisoned this house, and the children, resides in the arena of the mind. This film will keep you on the edge of your seat.

TIM KITTLESON
Former Director, UCLA Film & Television Archive

In the Realm of the Senses (Ai no corrida)
see p. 216

I soliti ignoti
see *Big Deal on Madonna Street*

Marcel Pagnol Trilogy

Marius
1931, Alexander Korda and Marcel Pagnol
SCREENPLAY: Marcel Pagnol; based on the play by Marcel Pagnol
CAST: Raimu, Pierre Fresnay, Orane Demazis, Fernand Charpin, Alida Rouffe, Robert Vattier
FRANCE; B & W; IN FRENCH

Fanny
1932, Marc Allégret
SCREENPLAY: Marcel Pagnol; based on the play by Marcel Pagnol
CAST: Raimu, Pierre Fresnay, Orane Demazis, Fernand Charpin, Alida Rouffe, Robert Vattier
FRANCE; B & W; IN FRENCH

César
1936, Marcel Pagnol
SCREENPLAY: Marcel Pagnol; based on the play by Marcel Pagnol
CAST: Raimu, Pierre Fresnay, Orane Demazis, Fernand Charpin, André Fouché, Alida Rouffe, Robert Vattier
FRANCE; B & W; IN FRENCH

I first saw Marcel Pagnol's great trilogy, *Marius*, *Fanny*, and *César*, more than a half century ago in a small art theater in St. Louis. The trilogy maintains the miming characteristics of silent film; it was filmed between 1931 and 1936 when movies had barely learned to talk.

I recently watched all three again, and they were as good as ever. I am still fascinated by how skillfully Pagnol—who wrote all three films and directed the first and third—draws us into the lives of a dozen or so people he knew in Marseilles. Remarkably, they seem immediately familiar. Pagnol has a masterful ability to show us, through the lives of his characters, the universality of *everyone's* life: a bouillabaisse of humor, sadness, anger, joy, and everything in between.

LAWRENCE KAHN
Professor Emeritus of Pediatrics, Washington University

It's a Gift

1934, Norman Z. McLeod

SCREENPLAY: Jack Cunningham and W. C. Fields (story, as Charles Bogle); based on the play *The Comic Supplement*, by J. P. McEvoy

CAST: W. C. Fields, Kathleen Howard, Jean Rouverol, Julian Madison, Tommy Bupp, Baby LeRoy, Morgan Wallace, Guy Usher

U.S.; B & W

One of the greatest pleasures of my childhood, starting somewhere around the age of eight or nine, was watching late-afternoon television. This was in the 1950s, when local stations offered a panoply of classic movies. For that hour or two before supper, I was transfixed by vintage films and their distinctive actors, particularly by the comedies and especially by W. C. Fields. Today, Fields seems to be remembered mostly for amusing but strained comedies like *My Little Chickadee* or *Never Give a Sucker an Even Break*, but it was in his earlier films, such as *The Man on the Flying Trapeze*, *The Old Fashioned Way*, and *The Bank Dick*, that Fields was at his comedic best. My favorite? *It's a Gift*, a seventy-one-minute, gimlet-eyed view of domestic life.

The thin but serviceable plot of *It's a Gift* revolves around Harold (W. C. Fields) closing his doomed grocery store and setting out with his family for California, where he has purchased an orange grove. When they arrive, the property turns out to be a dust bowl with one scrawny tree. Sitting on the running board of his car and pondering his bad luck, Harold is saved by a developer, Harry, who needs the land for a proposed stadium. The rapid-fire negotiation between Harold and Harry features the following classic exchange:

HAROLD: *You're crazy.*
HARRY: *And* you're *drunk.*
HAROLD: *But tomorrow I'll be sober, and you'll still be crazy.*

It's a Gift has what the best of the Fields movies have: humor in the face of bleakness and humor in the face of triumph. In the Fields universe, the dark side of daily life is shown in all its tedium, children must be pandered to even though they are destructive devils, and one suffers winning and losing with equal nonchalance. Though cheerier than Beckett, it's a world the great playwright would have recognized. Fortunately for us, Fields provides a happy ending, one that, for the moment, convinces us that life is, in fact, a gift.

RICHARD LAVENSTEIN
Architect

J

Johnny Guitar
1954, Nicholas Ray

SCREENPLAY: Philip Yordan; based on the novel by Roy Chanslor
CAST: Joan Crawford, Sterling Hayden, Mercedes McCambridge, Scott Brady, Ward Bond, Ben Cooper, Ernest Borgnine, John Carradine, Royal Dano, Frank Ferguson, Paul Fix
U.S.

Joan Crawford saddles up in this deliriously stylized dream of a Western directed by Nicholas Ray. French critics of the time, including François Truffaut and Jean-Luc Godard, first recognized that this was much more than the simple Republic shoot-'em-up it appeared to be. Underneath its gloriously garish Trucolor exterior lie many things, including a lyrical love story, a feminist treatise, and an anti-McCarthyist allegory in chaps. The eternally cool Sterling Hayden—spouting lines like "I'm a stranger here myself" and "When you come right down to it, all a man really needs is a good smoke and a cup of coffee"—plays the titular six-string savior of pistol-packing saloon owner Crawford (all bulging eyes and neon red lipstick), who's framed for murder by a butch cattle queen who covets her land (an unforgettable Mercedes McCambridge). Brimming with surreal imagery, twisted sexual dynamics, and Freudian symbolism, this one-of-a-kind cult classic really puts the "opera" in "horse opera."

MICHAEL SCHEINFELD
Writer

RECOMMENDED VIEWING: Other films directed by Nicholas Ray: *They Live by Night* (1949); *In a Lonely Place* (1950), see p. 113; *The*

Lusty Men (1952); *Rebel Without a Cause* (1955); *Bigger Than Life* (1956); and *Run for Cover* (1955; reissued as *Colorado* in 1962).

Ju Dou

see p. 199

Just Tell Me What You Want

1980, Sidney Lumet

SCREENPLAY: Jay Presson Allen; based on the novel
by Jay Presson Allen
CAST: Ali MacGraw, Alan King, Myrna Loy, Keenan Wynn,
Tony Roberts, Peter Weller, Judy Kaye, Dina Merrill,
Joseph Maher, Michael Gross
U.S.

Sidney Lumet's *Just Tell Me What You Want*, written by Jay Presson Allen, is a very smart and unusual love story about two ambitious New Yorkers, Max Herschel (Alan King) and his girlfriend Bones Burton (Ali MacGraw). Watch for an extremely amusing scene, shot in Bergdorf Goodman, in which Bones catches up with Max (whom she's been fighting with), beats him with her handbag, and chases him into the street. I was lucky to be cast as Max's drunken wife, Connie, who raises hell. An overlooked gem.

> DINA MERRILL
> *Actress and Vice Chair, RKO Pictures*

K

Killer of Sheep
1977, Charles Burnett

SCREENPLAY: Charles Burnett
CAST: Henry Gayle Sanders, Kaycee Moore, Charles Bracy,
Angela Burnett, Eugene Cherry, Jack Drummond
U.S.; B & W

Killer of Sheep is writer Charles Burnett's documentary-like look at life in South Central Los Angeles in the '70s—pre-gangs, pre-crack, and pre-hip-hop. The film provides a unique look at a community in which everything appears to stand still but is actually on the brink of exploding. An air of tragic inevitability hangs over much of the movie, ultimately acted out in a breathtaking sequence, stunning in its simplicity, involving an engine block and a pickup truck. Heartbreaking and thought provoking—a truly unique film from the maker of *To Sleep with Anger*.

> CURTIS HANSON
> *Screenwriter, film director, and producer*

Kiss Me Deadly
1955, Robert Aldrich

SCREENPLAY: A. I. Bezzerides; based on the novel
by Mickey Spillane
CAST: Ralph Meeker, Albert Dekker, Paul Stewart, Juano
Hernandez, Wesley Addy, Marian Carr, Maxine Cooper,
Cloris Leachman, Gaby Rodgers, Nick Dennis, Jack Lambert,
Jack Elam
U.S.; B & W

I must admit that *Kiss Me Deadly* is one of my guilty pleasures. I view it just about every year and teach it in my classes in the directing program at UCLA, even though a few skeptics wonder why.

A low-budget, black-and-white independent film directed by legendary filmmaker Robert Aldrich in 1956, *Kiss Me Deadly* has attained cult status. If film noir subverts the hard-boiled detective genre by adding levels of perverse psychological conflict, *Kiss Me Deadly* subverts the noir genre by adding a level of tongue-in-cheek irony that calls into account the standard elements of noir—the femme fatale, the tough detective, the seamy side of Los Angeles life.

Based on a pulp novel by Mickey Spillane, *Kiss Me Deadly* tells the tale of a tough private detective named Mike Hammer (played by Ralph Meeker), who late one night stops his car to pick up a woman on the run. Wearing nothing but a trench coat, she's being pursued by ruthless killers who want something she has or knows. Hammer, a detective of scuzzy morals and sadistic methods, figures that it has to be big—and he wants a piece of it.

So begins the quest for the "great whatsit," taking us, in a loose-jointed series of episodes, through the dark underside of L.A. populated by a score of unforgettable secondary characters. Along the way we encounter murder, deception, seduction, and betrayal. But in the end, this know-it-all, streetwise pro turns out to know nothing at all. For when he finally finds and then opens the hot (both stolen and nuclear) treasure box, his greedy bumbling may trigger the end of the world—or at the very least, the end of Malibu.

The story can be appreciated entirely on its own terms as a deeply ironic noir drama pivoting around the theme of stolen nuclear materials—a relevant topic in the '50s as well as today. But there are deeper levels of meaning to the story that keeps me coming back to it again and again. Its core theme is decadence or, more specifically, American decadence. It's about a world so radically transformed by weapons of mass destruction that older and more traditional values have simply become irrelevant.

Pretty heavy stuff for a B-movie. There's more than meets the eye in *Kiss Me Deadly*. My guess is that after your first viewing, my guilty pleasure will become yours, too.

ROBERT ROSEN
Dean, UCLA School of Theater, Film, and Television

Kwaidan
1964, Kasaki Kobayashi

SCREENPLAY: Yôko Mizuki; based on traditional Japanese folktales "The Black Hair," "The Woman of the Snow," "Hoichi, the Earless," and "In a Cup of Tea"
CAST: Rentaro Mikuni, Michiyo Aratama, Misako Watanabe, Katsuo Nakamura, Takashi Shimura, Keiko Kishi, Tatsuya Nakadai
JAPAN; IN JAPANESE

A stylistic tour de force, this supernatural classic (consisting of four separate tales from a collection of Japanese ghost stories) won the Special Jury Prize at the 1965 Cannes Film Festival. A haunting film, *Kwaidan* will send chills down your spine.

Shot entirely on studio sets, the film evokes a theatricality that is rarely seen on screen. The vividly painted sky sometimes suggests blood, sometimes a void, and often appears to have a life of its own. Dark interior scenes are shot with theatrical lighting techniques to highlight characters' movements and accentuate the atmosphere, and the unnatural movements of the actors are reminiscent of those in Kabuki and Bunraku puppet theater.

In the tragic sea-battle sequence, one of the most haunting in the film, a staged battlefield is intercut with traditional paintings of war scenes. The seemingly slow-motion battle, accompanied by a piercing vocal score, is brought to a climax when men and women pledge to go down with their nation. One after another, women in brightly colored kimonos and men in battle gear plunge into the bloodstained sea for their final glory. Such stylized theatrics expand the scope of our imagination and allow the world of the supernatural to take over.

LA FRANCES HUI
Senior Program Officer, Cultural Programs and Performing Arts, Asia Society

RECOMMENDED READING: Lafcadio Hearn, *Kwaidan: Stories and Studies of Strange Things*, originally published in 1903.

L

La collectionneuse
1967, Eric Rohmer

SCREENPLAY: Eric Rohmer
CAST: Patrick Bauchau, Haydeé Politoff, Daniel Pommereulle,
Alain Jouffroy, Mijanou Bardot, Seymour Hertzberg
FRANCE; IN FRENCH

Patrick Bauchau, who plays Adrian, looks so great in
this movie: tall, lanky, long-haired, wearing an unbut-
toned shirt, black pants, black boots. Adrien takes
a vacation on the Riviera with his friend Daniel and he
wants to do absolutely nothing—even thinking is too
much. To his dismay, a stunning woman named Haydée
joins them. Adrien worries she'll be a distraction—
but a distraction he also craves. Bikini-clad Haydée is
amazing—and director Eric Rohmer gives us tantalizing
close-ups of her crotch, breasts, neck, and back.

In *La collectionneuse*, Rohmer reveals the discrep-
ancy between who we are and what we want to be.
We're left with a sense of longing and missed opportunities, reminding us of our maddening inability to
change course.

I think about this movie often. And for all its sadness, I wish I could climb inside it and live there.

NOAH BAUMBACH
Director

Lamerica
1994, Gianni Amelio

SCREENPLAY: Gianni Amelio, Andrea Porporati,
and Alessandro Sermoneta

CAST: Enrico Lo Verso, Michele Placido, Poro Milkani,
Carmelo Di Mazzarelli, Elida Janushi
FRANCE/ITALY; IN ITALIAN

Contemporary Italian director Gianni Amelio's work deserves far more recognition in the U.S. A direct filmic descendant of Antonioni and Olmi, Amelio depicts modern Italian life in complex, unsparing, yet touching stories that reveal a country torn apart by conflicts with its Adriatic neighbors, between the northern and southern regions, and between national laws and local traditions.

In Amelio's *Lamerica*, two Italian businessmen aim to make a killing in post-Communist Albania. When things go awry, one partner ditches the other. Without money or identification, he is forced to make his way back to Italy with Albanian asylum seekers. The film offers an unusual glimpse of Italy-as-promised-land for eager Eastern Europeans, drawing an interesting parallel to Italians' immigration to America in the early twentieth century.

MEGAN RATNER
Associate Editor, Bright Lights Film Journal

RECOMMENDED VIEWING: Other films directed by Gianni Amelio: *The Way We Laughed* (1998) and *Open Doors* (1990).

The Last Flight
see p. 173

Le Colonel Chabert
1994, Yves Angelo

SCREENPLAY: Jean Cosmos and Yves Angelo; based on the novella by Honoré de Balzac

CAST: Gérard Depardieu, Fanny Ardant, Fabrice Luchini, André Dussollier, Daniel Prévost, Olivier Saladin, Maxime Leroux, Claude Rich, Albert Delpy, Romane Bohringer, Julie Depardieu
FRANCE; IN FRENCH

The first two minutes of Yves Angelo's *Le Colonel Chabert* offer the greatest depiction of a pre-twentieth-century battle ever filmed—all the more so when the guns go quiet. In fact, the entire movie—a dramatization of the Balzac novella, set during the Bourbon restoration of 1814–30—is the most perfect evocation of a specific period I've ever encountered in the cinema, perhaps with the exception of Luchino Visconti's *The Leopard* (see p. 131). It also features the greatest performance in Gérard Depardieu's entire career, turning on a single extraordinary speech at the heart of the movie. What I would have given to see him deliver this to camera!

> SIMON SCHAMA
> *Professor of art history and history, writer/presenter for the BBC and PBS, and writer*

RECOMMENDED READING: Honoré de Balzac, *Le Colonel Chabert*, originally published in 1832; Honoré de Balzac, *La peau de chagrin*, originally published in 1831.

Legong: Dance of the Virgins
1935, Henri de la Falaise

SCREENPLAY: Henri de la Falaise and Gaston Glass
CAST: Goesti Poetoe Aloes, Goesti Bagus Mara, Njoman Saplak
U.S.; SHORT; SILENT

Paradise might be lost, but it can still be found in *Legong: Dance of the Virgins*, originally shot in 1933 in Bali and restored six decades later by the UCLA Film and Television Archive. The film—one of Hollywood's last silents—was codirected by Gaston Glass and Henri de la Falaise (Gloria Swanson's third, but not last, husband) and shot in two-process Technicolor by William Howard "Duke" Greene, who later won an Academy Award for his work on *Phantom of the Opera* (1943).

Made with an "all-native cast," *Legong* opens with the following enticement:

> *Out in the Dutch East Indies, just south of the equator,*
> *lies Bali—isle of perpetual summer. In this peopled*
> *paradise, untouched by civilization, lives a contented*
> *race who joyously worship their gods—to them life is a*
> *continuous feast—to them death holds no fear . . .*

Belonging to a genre of interwar travel films traditionally long on exoticism and short on plot (in this case, a doomed love triangle), *Legong* is bolstered by rare documentary footage filmed by the Americans and Europeans who, in the '20s and '30s, claimed Bali as their own: anthropologists Margaret Mead and Gregory Bateson, artist Walter Spies, composer/musician Colin McPhee, and dance ethnographer Beryl de Zoete. (Charlie Chaplin was just one of many luminaries to make his way to Bali.) This footage, plus a healthy, if cockeyed, dose of fantasy, was aimed at the first wave of mass tourism that swept the globe.

The original musical score—an overwrought rendition typical of the period—is replaced on the DVD by an ingenious new score that integrates traditional Balinese music with Western instrumentation. Composers Richard Marriott of Clubfoot Orchestra and I Made Subandi of Gamelan Sekar Jaya, collaborated on the composition of this propitious work, using three different gamelan ensembles for scenes featuring the island's dances and rituals, and Western instruments and motifs for the Hollywood-style plot. (The film is also available with its original score.)

In the reconstructed film, we see glimpses of real village life: cock fights (footage that had been cut by the British), bare maidens bathing in streams (cut by the Americans), elaborate cremation ceremonies, and crowded markets, all set against the lush backdrop of Bali's cascading rice fields.

The enchanting *legong* is, to this day, the island's best-known dance. But as a former resident of Bali, I find the footage of the power-charged *barong* to be the most compelling, especially in light of the sad and terrible bombings suffered by the island in 2002. The *barong* is a magical temple dance (not to be confused with the twice-daily tourist romp) in which a lion-like beast—the Barong—protects the village from Rangda, the witch of death and destruction. During the epic battle, villagers attack Rangda and, protected by the powers of the Barong, suffer no injury, even when—in trance—they turn their swords on themselves. The *barong* dance is performed in Bali to this day, invoking the balancing forces of nature. Each village has its own Barong spirit, and after the 2002 attack, as the entire island was immersed in ritual cleansing, the Barongs prowled about, shaking their manes against murderous forces. Today, as in the past, the Barong-versus-Rangda ritual engages the Balinese in the never-ending fight of good and evil, reminding us all of the redemptive powers of goodness and communal action.

SUZANNE CHARLÉ
Editor and writer

Le notti di Cabiria
see *Nights of Cabiria*

Léolo

1992, Jean-Claude Lauzon

SCREENPLAY: Jean-Claude Lauzon
CAST: Maxime Collin, Ginette Reno, Julien Guiomar,
Pierre Bourgault, Giuditta Del Vecchio, Denys Arcand,
Roland Blouin, Gilbert Sicotte (narrator)
CANADA/FRANCE; IN FRENCH

Though the film is barely a decade old, it's likely you
have never heard of *Léolo* or its writer-director, the
late Jean-Claude Lauzon. Considered by many to be the
most authentic filmmaker to come out of Canada, he
died at age forty-three, piloting a plane that crashed
in the remote and frozen wilderness twenty-four
hundred miles north of Montreal. He left behind just
two features: *Un zoo, la nuit* (*Night Zoo*), winner of
an unprecedented thirteen Genies, Canada's Oscars,
and *Léolo*, which must be seen despite its uncompro-
misingly poetic style and scenes too scabrous to be
easily described.

Profound, disturbing, and exhilarating, *Léolo* is a
memoir of the kind of brutal, destructive coming-of-
age that usually leaves its survivors without the ability
or the desire to remember. Yet Lauzon manages to
suffuse his story of the squalid desperation of a boy
growing up in his old Montreal neighborhood with
all-accepting warmth and humor. *Léolo* is a cry from
the heart of a brutalized poet, of a boy who escaped
by the merest chance, and you can't watch its intoxi-
cating images without *knowing* that even the worst
episodes—especially the worst episodes—really
happened. The film's brilliant sound track (using everything from Tom Waits and the Rolling Stones to music
from Arabia, Argentina, and Tibet) is yet another
element that pulls you deeper into Lauzon's very

particular and yet uncannily universal story. The wonder of *Léolo* is that Lauzon, in his passion to reveal his own personal truth, has ended up telling everyone else's as well.

KENNETH TURAN
Film critic, Los Angeles Times

The Leopard (Il gattopardo)
1963, Luchino Visconti

SCREENPLAY: Luchino Visconti, Suso Cecchi d'Amico, Pasquale Festa Campanile, Enrico Medioli, and Massimo Franciosa; based on the novel *Il gattopardo,* by Giuseppe Tomasi di Lampedusa
CAST: Burt Lancaster, Claudia Cardinale, Alain Delon, Paolo Stoppa, Rina Morelli, Romolo Valli, Pierre Clémenti, Ivo Garrani, Leslie French, Serge Reggiani
ITALY/FRANCE; AVAILABLE IN ITALIAN AND ENGLISH

Luchino Visconti's *The Leopard* is an immense masterpiece. To be appreciated fully, it needs to be seen uncut and in both the original Italian (with only Burt Lancaster dubbed) and the English-dubbed version (with Lancaster doing—brilliantly—his own lines).

SIMON SCHAMA
Professor of art history and history, writer/presenter for the BBC and PBS, and writer

RECOMMENDED READING: Giuseppe Tomasi di Lampedusa, *The Leopard,* originally published in 1958.

Les glaneurs et la glaneuse
see *The Gleaners and I,* p. 93

The Life and Death of Colonel Blimp

1945, Michael Powell and Emeric Pressburger

SCREENPLAY: Michael Powell and Emeric Pressburger; based on
the cartoon *Colonel Blimp*, created in 1934 by David Low for the
London *Evening Standard*
CAST: Roger Livesey, Deborah Kerr, Anton Walbrook, John Laurie,
James McKechnie, Neville Mapp
U.K.; IN ENGLISH, FRENCH, AND GERMAN

Michael Powell, an Englishman, and Emeric Pressburger,
a Hungarian refugee, formed the most creative production team in British history, collaborating on some
twenty films, of which *The Life and Death of Colonel
Blimp*, though less well known than *The Red Shoes*, was
arguably their masterpiece. Produced by their company,
The Archers, it takes off from Colonel Blimp, a character
then instantly recognizable to millions of Britons from a
daily cartoon in the *Evening Standard*. With a potbelly
and a walrus moustache, he represents everything Tory
and out-of-date, trumpeting his opinions on anything
and everything from his favorite haunt, the Turkish bath
(then more respectable than now). Conceived by the brilliant caricaturist David Low, Blimp was in his own way
a subversive engine: though Lord Beaverbrook's *Evening
Standard* was then, as now, a bastion of conservative
political sentiment, Low was allowed to satirize the very
positions their editorials were proclaiming.

The Powell-Pressburger Blimp is called Clive Wynne-
Candy, and impersonated by Roger Livesey. In one
long flashback, the film traces Candy's life and military
career from the Anglo-Boer War of 1899–1902 up to the
present (1942). He has retired from active duty and is now
a senior officer in the Home Guard (something like
the U.S. National Guard). When the film opens, Candy
has just issued orders for a military exercise—a simulated

declaration of war—to start at midnight. When Candy's subalterns outmaneuver his so-called rules, just as a real enemy might, we see Blimp as the crusty veteran left high and dry by the military realpolitik of the modern world. But in this moment, we begin to understand that there is more to the man than the features of Low's familiar caricature: this more complex variation of Blimp, both outmoded and endearing, offers an apt metaphor of his country, a metaphor that has remained relevant since its cinematic inception.

MURRAY BIGGS
Adjunct Associate Professor of English and Theater Studies, Yale University

Light Sleeper

1992, Paul Schrader

SCREENPLAY: Paul Schrader
CAST: Willem Dafoe, Susan Sarandon, Dana Delany, David Clennon, Mary Beth Hurt, Victor Garber, Jane Adams, Paul Jabara, David Spade
U.S.

Paul Schrader is truly in his element as his characters drift ominously through late-night New York in this underappreciated gem. Susan Sarandon is striking as the all-in-red spider lady who runs a tight drug operation, partly flirting, partly harassing the men around her. Her henchman (Willem Dafoe) cruises from score to score in a state of wary boredom, never sure when danger will strike, which it often does. While the film is strangely melancholic, its upbeat ending feels just right. Knowing performances by Sarandon, Dafoe, and Dana Delany give real heft to this dreamily atmospheric film.

WENDY KEYS
Former Executive Producer/Programming, Film Society of Lincoln Center

RECOMMENDED READING: Any book written by Paul Schrader:
Paul Schrader and Donald Richie, *A Hundred Years of Japanese
Film*. Kodansha International, 2005; Paul Schrader, *Paul Schrader:
Collected Screenplays Volume 1: Taxi Driver, American Gigolo,
Light Sleeper*. Faber & Faber, 2002; Paul Schrader, Kevin Jackson
(editor), *Schrader on Schrader* (Director on Directors series). Faber
& Faber, 1990; Paul Schrader, *Taxi Driver*. Faber & Faber, 2000.

Lily Festival (Yurisai)
2001, Sachi Hamano

SCREENPLAY: Kuninori Yamazaki; based on the novel *Yurisai*,
by Houko Momotani
CAST: Kazuko Yoshiyuki, Mickey Curtis, Utae Shoji,
Kazuko Shirakawa, Sanae Nakahara, Chisako Hara, Hisako Ôkata
JAPAN; IN JAPANESE

Sachi Hamano, the director of the award-winning
independent film *Lily Festival*, has had quite an unusual
career for a female director in Japan. She entered the
film industry in 1968 as an assistant director on low-
budget 35 mm pornographic movies, a genre called
"pink film" in Japan. Since 1971, she has directed
more than three hundred of these films, most of
them commercially successful both in theaters and on
home video. In particular, her early '90s series *Reverse
Massage Parlor*, in which workingwomen receive superb
service from good-looking young men, was an underground hit among women.

It is not unusual in Japan to find aspiring young
directors starting their careers in the adult film industry,
as the declining studios no longer offer them training or
secure directorship. Masayuki Suo, the director of *Shall
We Dance?*, is one well-known example. Hamano's first
nonporn independent feature film was 1998's *In Search
of a Lost Writer*, which aimed to re-create the life and

works of female novelist Midori Osaki. The film mobilized more than twelve thousand women supporters, fund-raisers, and feminist activists.

The award-winning *Lily Festival* is Hamano's second nonporn feature (though she continues to make pink films). Seven women, who range in age from sixty-nine to ninety-one, are the heroines of this story. When a man moves into their old-fashioned apartment building, a tremendous commotion ensues. Unlike the typically reticent Japanese man, this old fellow charms the women with graceful gestures and eloquent rhetoric. It all makes for a lively romantic comedy, reminiscent of—while also subverting—the Japanese classic text *The Tale of Genji*. It offers both a straightforward portrayal of elderly women's sexuality and desire and a sharp critique of society's treatment of those in the doubly discriminated position of "getting old" and "being a woman."

HIKARI HORI
*Visiting Professor, East Asian Languages and Cultures,
Columbia University*

RECOMMENDED VIEWING: *In Search of a Lost Writer* (1998), directed by Sachi Hamano.

L'Innocente (The Innocent)
1976, Luchino Visconti

SCREENPLAY: Suso Cecchi d'Amico, Luchino Visconti, and Enrico Medioli; based on the novel by Gabriele D'Annunzio
CAST: Giancarlo Giannini, Laura Antonelli, Jennifer O'Neill, Rina Morelli, Massimo Girotti, Didier Haudepin, Marie Dubois
ITALY/FRANCE; IN ITALIAN

L'Innocente was Luchino Visconti's last film, based on the novel by Gabriele D'Annunzio. It features Giancarlo Giannini and Laura Antonelli at the height of their careers, along with a fine showing by Jennifer O'Neill. The three have never looked more gorgeous. The plot concerns a lovers' triangle, played out in the aristocratic circles of Victorian Italy. Giannini's character raises the bar for double standards. All of this unfolds in a palette of lush color as well as stunningly beautiful composition—two of Visconti's greatest talents. This isn't a "happy" film, nor is it one of the director's best, but it does linger in my memory.

TIM KITTLESON
Former Director, UCLA Film & Television Archive

Liquid Sky

1982, Slava Tsukerman

SCREENPLAY: Slava Tsukerman, Anne Carlisle, and Nina V. Kerova
CAST: Anne Carlisle, Paula E. Sheppard, Susan Doukas,
Otto von Wernherr, Bob Brady, Elaine C. Grove, Stanley Knapp,
Jack Adalist
U.S.

I have shot several films in New York City and, while scouting for locations I have often seen tape marks that other productions have left behind—proof that most New York movies follow well-worn pathways. Not so in *Liquid Sky*, a low-budget film by Russian filmmaker Slava Tsukerman and cinematographer Yuri Neyman, a film that strikes out on its own with refreshing results. The story is set in New York and photographed brilliantly through the fresh eyes of an outsider. Check it out.

JOHN LINDLEY
Cinematographer

Little Big Horn

see p. 50

Behind the Scenes

Living in Oblivion

1995, Tom DiCillo

SCREENPLAY: Tom DiCillo

CAST: Steve Buscemi, Catherine Keener, Dermot Mulroney, Danielle von Zerneck, James LeGros, Rica Martens, Peter Dinklage, Hilary Gilford, Robert Wightman, Michael Griffiths, Matthew Grace

U.S.; B & W AND COLOR

Hearts of Darkness: A Filmmaker's Apocalypse

1991, Fax Bahr and George Hickenlooper

SCREENPLAY: Fax Bahr and George Hickenlooper

CAST: Francis Ford Coppola, Robert De Niro, Robert Duvall, Marlon Brando, Laurence Fishburne, Harrison Ford, Dennis Hopper, Martin Sheen, Frederic Forrest, George Lucas

U.S.; DOCUMENTARY

Lost in La Mancha

2002, Keith Fulton and Louis Pepe

SCREENPLAY: Keith Fulton and Louis Pepe

CAST: Johnny Depp, Vanessa Paradis, Jean Rochefort, Terry Gilliam, Jeff Bridges (narrator)

U.S./U.K.; DOCUMENTARY; IN ENGLISH, SPANISH, AND FRENCH

Burden of Dreams

1982, Les Blank

SCREENPLAY: Michael Goodwin (narration)

CAST: Werner Herzog, Klaus Kinski, Claudia Cardinale, Jason Robards, Mick Jagger, Candace Laughlin (narrator)

U.S.; DOCUMENTARY; IN SPANISH, ENGLISH, AND GERMAN

I recommend these four films to people who want to know what it's really like making movies. They are all filled to the brim with the unbelievable madness, creativity, and exasperated tenacity that it takes to live and work in the film industry.

Living in Oblivion stars four of the best indie actors around—Steve Buscemi, James LeGros, Catherine Keener, and Dermot Mulroney—and while it's true they're sending up the industry, when you see this film in the context of *Hearts of Darkness, Lost in La Mancha,* and *Burden of Dreams* (see p. 46)—three documentaries—it doesn't quite seem like a send-up at all. These films should be required viewing in all Filmmaking 101 classes.

ERIC STOLTZ
Actor

Living on Velvet
1935, Frank Borzage

SCREENPLAY: Jerry Wald and Julius J. Epstein
CAST: Kay Francis, Warren William, George Brent, Helen Lowell,
Henry O'Neill, Russell Hicks, Maude Turner Gordon,
Samuel S. Hinds, Edgar Kennedy
U.S.; B & W

Frank Borzage was, at one time, one of the most famous
directors in Hollywood. Today he's almost forgotten,
his name known only to film lovers and scholars. Why?
Probably because his pictures epitomize everything
we find "old-fashioned" about the Hollywood of the '20s,
'30s, and '40s: they're deeply romantic and firmly
rooted in the belief that love conquers all. In most films
of the period, that idea is a cliché, a device, or a pretext
for character exploration. But in a Borzage movie,
love really *does* conquer all, and it really *does* make the
world go 'round. When Borzage shows two people
in love—Charles Farrell and Janet Gaynor in *Seventh
Heaven*, Gary Cooper and Helen Hayes in *A Farewell to
Arms*, Spencer Tracy and Joan Crawford in *Mannequin*,
Dane Clark and Gail Russell in *Moonrise*—you feel as
if you've entered a sacred realm. He lets the action play
out in lovers' time, and every little physical and emotional detail feels precious. Borzage's cinema reminds me
of Renaissance painting: everything feels rounded,
perfectly aligned—sanctified.

In the mid-'30s, Borzage made two films at Warner
Bros., both with Kay Francis and George Brent. The better of the two is *Living on Velvet*, which is quite similar
to the Peter Weir picture *Fearless*. Brent plays Terry, an
aviator who survives a plane crash only to live in a kind
of dream state, untouched by emotion. Francis plays
Amy, the woman who loves him; she knows that he

hasn't really started to feel the terror of this experience, that he hasn't had a catharsis, and that he could crack at any moment. At the heart of the movie are these extraordinary exchanges between Terry and Amy; they are incredibly powerful, and they give you a very good illustration of Borzage's genius with actors. Francis was very good at comedy, but some felt that she was limited as a dramatic actress, and Brent rarely seemed to get past a certain level of emotional remove. Having her respond to his placidity with loving smiles and good humor is a choice only Borzage would have made. But what ultimately moves me the most about *Living on Velvet* is the spectacle of a man loved by a woman, *truly* loved, with all his frailties and weaknesses. He's on the verge of a complete breakdown, but he's the man she loves, and nothing can change that. It's an extremely delicate, heartbreaking picture, and no one else could possibly have made it except Frank Borzage.

MARTIN SCORSESE
Director

Lonely Are the Brave
1962, David Miller

SCREENPLAY: Dalton Trumbo; based on the novel *Brave Cowboy*, by Edward Abbey
CAST: Kirk Douglas, Gena Rowlands, Walter Matthau, Michael Kane, Carroll O'Connor, William Schallert, George Kennedy, Karl Swenson
U.S.; B & W

For those lucky enough to have been spared a traumatic childhood, movies offer a vicarious initiation into grief and loss. Having survived the blows of *Bambi* and *Old Yeller* by age thirteen, I was ready for the more adult desolation of *Lonely Are the Brave*.

Loss is a foregone conclusion from the opening shot of the face of Jack Burns (Kirk Douglas), a modern-day cowboy imprisoned by the barbed wire and jet contrails that fence in the land and sky. He's back in New Mexico to check in on his old anarchist pal Paul Bondi (Michael Kane), who's serving time for helping illegal Mexican immigrants. He's also checking in on Paul's wife, Jerry (a luminous Gena Rowlands). The way they look at each other (and pretend they aren't) tells the story of a true love lost to an irresolvable conflict: Jack won't sacrifice his freedom and independence to give her a home and a family.

Freedom versus conformity is the fundamental theme of most Hollywood genres, especially the Western. Because Jack must be free, his story is a series of leave-takings: from Paul, who won't join Jack in his jailbreak (Jack "breaks in" by getting arrested for assaulting a cop); from Jerry, who knows he won't ever return; even from one of his molars, punched out by a sadistic prison guard (Arthur Kennedy, getting in some licks before pounding Paul Newman in *Cool Hand Luke*).

What Jack won't sacrifice is Whisky, his skittish, spirited palomino mare, and the two ride off together to cross a mountain ridge and a highway to escape to Mexico. Though the horse becomes more of a burden than a help, Jack won't cut loose from this last bond. That's one reason why Morey (Walter Matthau), the sour local sheriff pursuing the fugitive, nurtures a grudging admiration for his quarry. But Jack's real nemesis, a semitrailer driver (Carroll O'Connor, in his first film) hauling a load of "privies" westward, doesn't even know he exists.

Based on the novel *Brave Cowboy*, by Edward Abbey, flawlessly written by the blacklisted Dalton Trumbo, unobtrusively directed by the journeyman

David Miller, and passionately produced by Douglas himself, this 1962 miniature masterpiece remains as lean, graceful, and heartbreaking as its hero. According to *The Ragman's Son*, Douglas's autobiography, *Lonely Are the Brave* was his favorite of his movies. The same goes for the thirteen-year-old who saw it by chance years ago on TV and felt the romanticized, adolescent virtues of loneliness and bravery embodied in that cowpoke and his horse, all lost on that awful highway in the rain.

PETER KEOUGH
Film editor, Boston Phoenix

The Long Good Friday

1980, John Mackenzie

SCREENPLAY: Barrie Keeffe
CAST: Bob Hoskins, Helen Mirren, Dave King, Bryan Marshall, Derek Thompson, Eddie Constantine, Stephen Davies
U.K.

I am not a Londoner by birth, so my first impressions of London were from movies and television. The film that really captured my imagination was *The Long Good Friday*. I think it still has a particular relevance today. Harold Shand is a tough East End gangster who rose to the top by killing, recruiting, or frightening his rivals away. Now he would like to become a legitimate businessman and help build a new London. But he fails and loses everything. Bob Hoskins plays Harold like a bulldog in a suit. He's a brilliantly versatile actor, and for me this is his finest performance.

DAVID MORRISSEY
Actor

Lord Love a Duck

1966, George Axelrod

SCREENPLAY: Larry H. Johnson and George Axelrod; based on the
novel by Al Hine
CAST: Roddy McDowall, Tuesday Weld, Lola Albright,
Martin West, Ruth Gordon, Harvey Korman, Sarah Marshall,
Lynn Carey, Max Showalter, Martin Gabel
U.S.; B & W

One of the best things about being a film archivist is
the opportunity to work on obscure movies that were
childhood favorites of mine, like *Lord Love a Duck*. For
many years, my best friend and I were the only people
we knew who had even seen this zany satire. The term
"black comedy" could have been invented to describe
this nasty view of greed and sex in sunny Southern
California in the '60s. How could you go wrong with
a movie that features Tuesday Weld as a spoiled L.A.
high school beauty, Lola Albright as her stripper mom,
and Ruth Gordon as the manipulative mother-in-law?
Roddy McDowall, thirty-seven at the time, plays Weld's
too-brilliant classmate who helps her get whatever she
wants. The priceless cast also includes future Mama
Lion band member Lynn Carey, future *Carol Burnett
Show* comedian Harvey Korman, and former Playmate
of the Year Jo Collins. But Albright is the standout;
many actresses have won Oscars for performances inferior to her inspired portrayal of the pretty but alcoholic
loser who constantly embarrasses her daughter.

Two years ago I made a new print of *Lord Love
a Duck* that screened at the American Cinematheque
in Hollywood as part of a retrospective of uniquely
'60s films. The film was so well received that the
Cinematheque screened the film again. See the film in a

theater if you can—comedies are so much funnier with an audience around you.

JOHN KIRK
Film archivist and writer

Los olvidados (The Young and the Damned)
1950, Luis Buñuel

SCREENPLAY: Luis Buñuel and Luis Alcoriza
CAST: Alfonso Mejía, Roberto Cobo, Estela Inda, Miguel Inclán, Alma Delia Fuentes, Francisco Jambrina, Jesús García Navarro
MEXICO; B & W; IN SPANISH

The title in English is *The Young and the Damned*, but most people know this 1950 Luis Buñuel film by its original Spanish title, *Los olvidados* (*The Forgotten Ones*), which is a more accurate description. This is no ordinary tale of youthful rebellion. Buñuel's story of juvenile delinquents roaming the streets of Mexico City looks more like a social documentary: stark, poignant, never condescending. At the center of the narrative is a murder; one kid seeks revenge for the time he spent in a correctional facility and ends up killing one of his mates. But the killing is hardly what the film is about. Rather than focus on one particular incident, Buñuel is interested in capturing the cruel, poverty-stricken environment that turns children into criminals. There are hardly any sympathetic characters in this film, but there are no real villains, either. They are all victims of a world that is inexorably oblivious to their needs.

Buñuel had been living in Mexico for a few years when he made *Los olvidados*. Chronicling problems common to many large cities, the film might have been inspired by his native Spain, a country that was also plagued by serious social wounds at the time. But it was in Latin America that *Los olvidados* resonated

most powerfully. Buñuel has influenced several generations of Latin American filmmakers, many of whom
continue to make films about juvenile delinquents. It is
both a tribute to Buñuel's talents and a sad reminder
of Latin America's enduring social illnesses that, half a
century after it was made, *Los olvidados* has lost little
of the power it had when it was first released.

VINICIUS NAVARRO
Assistant Professor, Film Studies, Georgia Institute of Technology

Lost in La Mancha

see p. 137

Love Me Tonight

1932, Rouben Mamoulian

SCREENPLAY: Samuel Hoffenstein, Waldemar Young, and
George Marion Jr.; based on the play *Tailor in the Château*,
by Léopold Marchand and Paul Armont
CAST: Maurice Chevalier, Jeanette MacDonald, Charles Ruggles,
Charles Butterworth, Myrna Loy, C. Aubrey Smith,
Elizabeth Patterson, Ethel Griffies, Blanche Frederici,
Robert Greig
U.S.; B & W

As far as movie musicals go, they reached a sort of
perfection and sophistication very early on. René Clair's
sublime *Le million* (1931) paved the way for two
American musicals that have rarely been equaled or bet-
tered. *One Hour with You*, directed by Ernst Lubitsch
and George Cukor, is a sly piece of enchantment.
But *Love Me Tonight*, which came out the same year
and shared the same star, Maurice Chevalier, is the
hands-down winner because of the masterfully witty
work of Rodgers and Hart. Sure, *Top Hat* was to
come along in 1935, and while Fred Astaire and Richard

Rogers and Irving Berlin's work is sensational, the plot of that film never comes close to the imaginative heights of *Love Me Tonight*. It's worth seeing just for its two wonderfully complex opening sequences, "The Song of Paree" and the dazzling "Isn't It Romantic." Both numbers are triumphs of editing. The film sustains its level of wit *almost* to the very end, but so what if the last drops of champagne fall a little flat? By that time you're so high, any flaw seems minor. It's not surprising that a decade later, Rodgers and director Rouben Mamoulian would work together again in the groundbreaking *Oklahoma!* The seeds for musical adventure are planted here.

JOHN GUARE
Playwright

M

Madame DuBarry

see *Passion*, p. 173

Mademoiselle

1966, Tony Richardson

SCREENPLAY: Jean Genet
CAST: Jeanne Moreau, Ettore Manni, Umberto Orsini,
Keith Skinner, Jane Beretta, Rosine Luguet, Mony Reh
FRANCE/U.K.; B & W; SHOT IN FRENCH AND ENGLISH

Mademoiselle is one of those rare films, for the '60s
anyway, that was shot simultaneously in French and
English. The cast for both languages was the same,
and the takes were virtually identical. I was too young
to see the film in its initial English-language theatrical
release, but I remember the scathing reviews it got—to
call it a disaster would be putting it mildly. But because
I work for MGM, which owns the film, I offered to
make a print to be shown as part of a Jeanne Moreau
series put on by the L.A. County Museum of Art's Film
Department. Without giving it much thought, I printed
the English version. Upon seeing it, I had to admit the
film just didn't work. I was intrigued by the story but
the English-speaking French actors (including Moreau)
performed awkwardly. I had to spend so much effort
just trying to understand the heavily accented dialogue
that I couldn't get caught up in the drama.

A couple of years later, when the Berlin Film Festival
planned to give Jeanne Moreau a lifetime-achievement
award, she asked that *Mademoiselle* be shown at
the ceremony. Remembering the disastrous English-
language print I'd made, I assumed that the French

version had to be better. The difference was *astounding*.
What had been so awkward in English became, when
the actors spoke in their native tongue, a masterpiece.
Moreau plays one of the evilest characters in the history of cinema—but then, with a story by Jean Genet,
could we expect anything less? I translated the French
dialogue for the English subtitles and sent it off to the
festival, where it was a great success. Apparently a film
that was too disturbing for a '60s audience was just
right for a more jaded audience forty years later.

   Mademoiselle is now available on DVD, but I recommend you try to see this print on the big screen, as it
features some of the most spectacular black-and-white
cinematography you'll ever see.

   JOHN KIRK
   Film archivist and writer

Man Bites Dog
1992, Rémy Belvaux, André Bonzel, and Benoît Poelvoorde

SCREENPLAY: Rémy Belvaux, André Bonzel, Benoît Poelvoorde,
and Vincent Tavier
CAST: Benoît Poelvoorde, Jacqueline Poelvoorde-Pappaert,
Nelly Pappaert, Hector Pappaert, Jenny Drye, Malou Madou,
Willy Vandenbroeck
BELGIUM; B & W; IN FRENCH

Man Bites Dog is a mockumentary about a serial killer
and proof, once and for all, that there's really no such
thing as a true documentary. Everything starts to go
wrong when the earnest, floppy-haired film crew gets
pulled into assisting with the crimes.

   NELLY REIFLER
   Writer

A Man Escaped (Un condamné à mort s'est échappé, ou Le vent souffle où il veut)
1956, Robert Bresson

SCREENPLAY: Robert Bresson; based on the memoir
by André Devigny
CAST: François Leterrier, Charles Le Clainche, Maurice Beerblock,
Roland Monod, Jacques Ertaud, Jean Paul Delhumeau,
Roger Treherne, Jean Philippe Delamarre, César Gattegno,
Jacques Oerlemans, Klaus Detlef Grevenhorst,
Leonhard Schmidt
FRANCE; B & W; IN FRENCH

Based on an account by André Devigny of his escape
from Fort Montluc in Lyons, which took place just a few
hours before he was to be executed, the film is rooted in
reality. But, at the same time, it is also highly abstract.
The hero, Fontaine, has a universal quality: he represents a larger social type—an Everyman-as-prisoner-
of-war in occupied France, and his anonymity becomes
part of his universality. Fontaine is also something of
an abstraction in a religious sense. Though sentenced
to death, he escapes. The central character's progress is
toward a spiritual rebirth, a kind of resurrection, at the
very least an escape from death to a new life.

The film's secondary title is *Le vent souffle où il veut*,
or *The Spirit [or wind] breathes where it will*, which is
taken from the third chapter of St. John's Gospel. The
film works out, in a secular fashion, a crucial religious
paradox. The will of God works in mysterious ways:
it saves some but not others. Another prisoner, Orsini,
attempts to escape but fails, and he is shot. Fontaine
succeeds. At the very moment that Orsini is shot (heard
offscreen), Fontaine is reading aloud the words of Jesus
to Nicodemus—"the spirit breathes where it will."

Everything that happens to Fontaine is, like Grace, both predetermined and the product of his own will. His escape is predetermined, a given that is stated in the film's own title. Yet it is also the end result of his own will, his determination to escape, which constitutes the bulk of the film's action—that is, the cutting through the oak door, the fashioning of ropes and hooks, and so forth.

Bresson's characters are not defined by traditional means; they don't possess the basic elements of motivation found in Hollywood films—greed, lust, jealousy, guilt—elements that are generally considered to supply psychological depth or roundness to characters. We understand them in terms of their will, energy, obstinacy—traits that apply more to spirit than to anything else. As film theorist Amédée Ayfre says, "There is always something fundamental and mysterious in them which escapes us": they refuse to provide us with the sort of information that can enable us to sympathize or identify with them. "This is why, even in their most extreme confidences, they never fundamentally reveal anything but their mystery—like God himself."

The prison setting isolates the characters by keeping them in separate cells and restricting their contact to a few prescribed moments—the descent into the courtyard and the washroom, moments that are themselves carefully regulated. The counterthrust of the film is toward contact, toward an overcoming of the barriers that separate the characters. The film works against isolation. Moments of contact become "miraculous." Fontaine breaks out of his cell, crosses the corridor to the cell of a comrade, and speaks to him. It is a moment in which he has defeated the barriers that the institution has created. Like his escape with fellow prisoner Jost, it is an act of transcendence over the concrete space in which he is entrapped.

The characters struggle against their enclosure, their isolation; that's why the shot of Fontaine and Jost walking off together at the end is so significant. Not only are they together but they have ascended, as it were, into a transcendent space—the spaces seen earlier in the film cannot hold or contain them. The real has given way to its essence; the essence of confinement is the cell; the essence of freedom and escape is the spatially amorphous night.

JOHN BELTON
Professor of English and Film, Rutgers University

Man of Aran
see p. 93

Marius
see p. 116

Paddy Chayefsky

In an age of high-tech, computer-generated visuals, it's easy to overlook the achievement of Paddy Chayefsky. But the writer's influence endures in many contemporary movies trying to approximate real life. Chayefsky brought the rhythms and confusions of everyday speech first to television and then to the movies. In *Marty*, his defining work, he wanted to capture the distinct dialogue of the Bronx as if it had been wiretapped. Listen to Ernest Borgnine in the 1955 movie or, better yet, to Rod Steiger in the 1953 live television drama, and you hear words that seem to come directly from the street—repetitions and non-sequiturs that reflect the way we actually talk. Instead of the poetic musings of Tennessee Williams or the didactic arguments of Arthur Miller, Chayefsky tapped into the sloppiness of the human mind, trying to articulate longings not always expressible in mere words. His imprecise dialogue was perfect for the emerging graduates of the method school of acting, who delved inward to create character. In the most famous scene in *Marty*, Angie asks: "Well, what do you feel like doing tonight?" Marty answers with the same words he says every Saturday night: "I don't know, Angie. What do you feel like doing?" This metropolitan duet of male camaraderie has been replayed in many a subsequent movie about two guys yearning for action in the big city.

RON SIMON
Curator of Television, The Museum of Television & Radio

Memories of Underdevelopment
1968, Tomás Gutiérrez Alea

SCREENPLAY: Tomás Gutiérrez Alea and Edmundo Desnoes; based on the novel *Memórias inconsolables*, by Edmundo Desnoes
CAST: Sergio Corrieri, Daisy Granados, Eslinda Núñez, Beatriz Ponchova, Omar Valdés, René de la Cruz
CUBA; B & W; IN SPANISH

Memories of Underdevelopment was a must-see film back in the early '70s, after having been banned in 1968 as part of the Cuban quarantine. Years later, I watched it again because I was interested in viewing films that use voice-over throughout.

In *Memories of Underdevelopment*, Cuban director Tomás Gutiérrez Alea interlaces fiction and documentary in an experimental way, giving us an exquisite portrait of a man (Sergio) and his identity crisis during the Cuban Missile Crisis.

The film has many highlights, including the scene in which Sergio says good-bye to his wife and family as they leave for Miami, documentary footage of Russian ships entering the harbor, and Sergio's visit to Hemingway's home. But the voice-over is my favorite part. Alea uses the technique beautifully, keeping it straightforward but also using it to show the complex inner life of a man suspended between two worlds.

Alea went to the Centro Sperimentale di Cinematografia in Rome for two years at the height of the neorealist movement. He returned to Cuba revitalized by the activity of Roman street life and became a founding member of the revolutionary cinema organization ICAIC.

MAUREEN SELWOOD
Animator and video installation artist

Miami Blues

1990, George Armitage

SCREENPLAY: George Armitage; based on the novel by
Charles Willeford
CAST: Alec Baldwin, Jennifer Jason Leigh, Fred Ward, José Pérez,
Obba Babatundé, Charles Napier, Martine Beswicke, Nora Dunn,
Paul Gleason
U.S.

Some reasons why I love the movie *Miami Blues*:

• The opening scene. "Spirit in the Sky" plays over the credits. Fade up on puffy white clouds flaring in the sun. It looks like heaven. Cut to Junior (Alec Baldwin), looking out the window of a plane, enjoying the view. From here on you know in your gut that Junior is happily doomed.
• Junior—while impersonating a police officer—to a noisy suspect: "Remain silent."
• The popping sound Junior makes when he takes a swig of beer, as if his body were a closed circuit.
• Susie (Jennifer Jason Leigh) walking around the side of a bed with the proud posture of a little girl.
• Moseley (Fred Ward) realizing that his new partner thinks he's a joke.

- Sanchez (Nora Dunn) effortlessly projecting a full life for her character.
- The tension generated between Junior and Moseley over dinner and a few beers.
- The water pistol that needs a price check.
- Susie reciting a recipe for pie as her heart breaks.
- Baldwin proving that great film acting is when it doesn't feel as if anyone's watching.
- The perfectly inevitable combined with the perfectly surprising.
- Despite our better judgment, our longing for a happy ending.

DYLAN KIDD
Writer and director

Million Dollar Legs

see p. 160

The Miracle

1991, Neil Jordan

SCREENPLAY: Neil Jordan
CAST: Beverly D'Angelo, Donal McCann, Niall Byrne, Lorraine Pilkington, J. G. Devlin, Cathleen Delaney, Tom Hickey, Shane Connaughton
U.K./IRELAND

Everyone loves *The Crying Game*, but *The Miracle*, made just before it, may be better—even if everyone stays the same gender. Set in an Irish seacoast town, it's the story of two bright, imaginative teenagers who like to make up stories about the people they see. Fantasy turns into obsession when a beautiful blond American actress (Beverly D'Angelo) captures the fancy of young Jimmy, an aspiring jazz musician. There's a big narrative twist in this one, too, but you'll see it coming from afar. The plot is not the point: it's the movie's lyrical, seductive style—shot through with startling dream sequences—that mesmerizes.

DAVID ANSEN
Movie critic, Newsweek

Miracle in Milan (Miracolo a Milano)
1951, Vittorio De Sica

SCREENPLAY: Cesare Zavattini, Vittorio De Sica, Suso Cecchi d'Amico, Mario Chiari, and Adolfo Franci; based on the novel *Toto il buono,* by Cesare Zavattini
CAST: Emma Gramatica, Francesco Golisano, Paolo Stoppa, Guglielmo Barnabò, Brunella Bovo, Anna Carena, Alba Arnova
ITALY; B & W; IN ITALIAN

In the '50s, when I was a film student at the university in Prague, the only Western films the Communist government approved for viewing by the general public were the Italian neorealist films. To be clear, they were welcomed because they were critical of capitalist society and this served the Communist propaganda machines well. One day, in the screening room of my school, I saw a new film: Vittorio De Sica's *Miracolo a Milano*. After that day, whenever the film was shown at school, I was there. More than twenty times.

The film is a tragicomedy, a bittersweet fairy tale for adults about Milan's homeless, portrayed with such gusto and understanding of human nature that it took my breath away. Touching and funny, disturbing and soothing . . . there are so many gripping observations of human peculiarities, and such brilliant characterizations of personalities that today, after almost fifty years, I still remember the faces of the extras in this film more vividly than the faces of many leading performers in the hundreds of films I have seen since.

A little tragicomic history: despite the film's strong socialist sentiments, the Czech government still refused to allow *Miracolo a Milano* to be shown to the general public. Their reason: at the end of the film, the homeless people, defeated, seize the brooms of Milan's street sweepers and fly off, flying higher and higher, toward a place where life is more just. The censors concluded from the position of Milan's Cathedral that they were heading toward the West—reason enough to ban the film.

MILOS FORMAN
Director

Miracle of Morgan's Creek

see p. 72

Miracolo a Milano

see *Miracle in Milan*

Mirage

1965, Edward Dmytryk

SCREENPLAY: Peter Stone; based on the novel *Fallen Angel*, by Howard Fast (as Walter Ericson)
CAST: Gregory Peck, Diane Backer, Walter Matthau, Kevin McCarthy, Jack Weston, Leif Erickson, Walter Abel, George Kennedy, Robert H. Harris
U.S.; B & W

Screenwriter Peter Stone created a simple but effective template with his smash success *Charade*: pair a charming couple, drop them in the middle of intrigue, and watch the witty sparks fly. In the overlooked, Hitchcock-inspired *Mirage*, Stone teams another photogenic duo (Gregory Peck and Diane Baker)—but with darkly off-kilter results. Directed by Edward Dmytryk

(of the Hollywood Ten), the noirish *Mirage* hardens
the banter a touch and jarringly abandons standard
dissolves for straight cuts to delineate the disturbing
flashbacks of amnesia victim David Stillwell (Peck). Shot
on location in New York City in appropriately gritty
black and white, *Mirage* chases David through a maze
of blackouts and nuclear secrets, against the backdrop
of a *Pawnbroker*-esque Quincy Jones score. With Walter
Matthau as a soft-boiled Sam Spade, *Mirage* is an odd
little gem that is worth tracking down.

MARK QUIGLEY
Manager, Research & Study Center,
UCLA Film & Television Archive

RECOMMENDED VIEWING: As a companion piece, also see Stone's
Arabesque (1966, directed by Stanley Donen), which yet again joins
a handsome couple (Gregory Peck and Sophia Loren) in the throes
of intrigue.

Moby Dick
1956, John Huston

SCREENPLAY: Ray Bradbury and John Huston; based on the novel
Moby-Dick, by Herman Melville
CAST: Gregory Peck, Richard Basehart, Leo Genn, Orson Welles,
James Robertson Justice, Harry Andrews, Bernard Miles,
Noel Purcell, Edric Connor, Mervyn Johns, Joseph Tomelty,
Royal Dano, Fredrick Ledebur
U.K.

When Orson Welles was called out to Hollywood to
make his fortune (and a splash) he considered making
a film based on *Moby-Dick*. But John Barrymore had
already put the book on the screen twice in the previous decade. His first version was the silent *Sea Beast*,
an execrable thing in which Ahab loses his leg and then
his girl. Barrymore made the movie again a couple years

later, this time as a talkie with his subsequent main squeeze, Joan Bennett; this one he called *Moby Dick*.

Later in the 1940s, so the story goes, John Huston (son of screen actor Walter Huston) took up Welles's suggestion to make *Moby Dick*, starring his father. Huston's film did not happen right away. He needed a screenwriter, and it was not until the early '50s that he coerced Ray Bradbury into doing the job. Gregory Peck, who fifteen years earlier had made a stir playing the nutcase Dr. Edwardes in Hitchcock's *Spellbound*, had a gift for scene chewing that made him just right for the role of Ahab. By 1956, Welles himself had seasoned into leviathan proportions and played Father Mapple, the preacher who sermonizes about Jonah before the *Pequod* makes its fateful departure. Unsurprisingly, Huston's film version of *Moby-Dick*, even with Bradbury's capable screenplay, captures only a fraction of what goes on in Melville's epic novel. The movie is all Ahab; it forgets about Ishmael.

It is harder to film a sea adventure than to write one. It's not the salt and spray that are hard to depict, but the desolation and the absolute unforgiving nature of the sea. In film, the camera's very presence provides the viewer with a sense of security—the cameraman, director, and crew would save you if you began to sink. And then there is the matter of the whale. In Melville's narrative, skillful description is enough to ignite the reader's imagination into creating his or her own frightening image of a whale. But in film, the image is ready-made, and that unhuntable whale must be a very carefully constructed piece of rubber to capture the imagination.

Huston knew these limitations. He made the best white rubber whale the industry could manage. And it is convincing, sort of. Rather than attempt a film equivalent of Melville's literary alienation of the sea, he shifted his camera to focus on the whaling ship and whaling life. The quiet anticipation of the whalers rocking in their boats, waiting for the whale to breach, the sea birds hovering nearby, waiting for what carnage might emerge—these are memorable images. He even developed the technique of superimposing color onto the black-and-white shots so that the film's texture approaches the feel of nineteenth-century engravings.

Not satisfied with Huston's efforts, Welles staged the memorable *Moby-Dick Rehearsed* in which a troupe of actors, having just done *King Lear*, attempts a version of *Moby-Dick*. But in the end, people want their rubber whales, and Welles's stage production had a limited run. Huston's film has fared somewhat better; Peck's performance seems to have escaped our postmodern disdain for dramaturgy and histrionics. Patrick Stewart's more recent rendering of Ahab (in the 1998 made-for-TV *Moby Dick*) seems far too restrained compared with Peck's benchmark performance: we want more stumping and fire; we want to feel the heat of his obsession coming off the screen. Peck played Father Mapple in this later version, the role Welles played in Huston's version. Peck must have eyed Stewart with the same awareness with which Welles had eyed Huston: I can do this better.

JOHN BRYANT
Professor of English, Hofstra University, and editor for The Melville Society

The Mothering Heart
1913, D. W. Griffith

CAST: Lillian Gish, Walter Miller, Kate Bruce, Viola Barry,
Gertrude Bambrick, Josephine Crowell, Adolphe Lestina,
Joseph McDermott, Charles Murray, Charles West
U.S.; B & W; SHORT; SILENT

The freshest film I have seen in a long time is D. W.
Griffith's *The Mothering Heart*, a two-reeler made
with Lillian Gish in 1913, two years before *The Birth
of a Nation*. The best of the shorts Griffith made at
Biograph Studios (*Musketeers of Pig Alley*, *A Corner
in Wheat*) look more revelatory, in their modesty and
forthrightness, than the famous epics that came later.
Gish considered it "a milestone in my career, primarily
because, with two reels to work with, Mr. Griffith could
concentrate more on the effects he wanted and exercise
more subtlety in the direction." For those who think
silent acting hammy and absurd, watch the many subtle
mood changes and character shadings Gish accom-
plishes in a short period of time—from girlish tenderness to mature conjugal love, joy, uncertainty, jealousy,
suspicion, disillusionment, fury, grief, numbness, and
forgiveness. It's like a six-hour miniseries condensed
to twenty-three minutes. You should enjoy this largely
unknown treasure, which is shot with a good deal of
restraint and tact.

PHILLIP LOPATE
Professor, Hofstra University

RECOMMENDED READING: Richard Schickel, *D. W. Griffith: An
American Life*. Limelight Editions, 2004.
RECOMMENDED VIEWING: *Griffith Masterworks*, a 2002 seven-DVD
boxed set by Kino International that includes the Biograph Shorts
1909–1913 (twenty-two short films including *The Mothering Heart*,

Musketeers of Pig Alley, and *A Corner in Wheat*), *The Birth of a Nation*, *Intolerance*, *Broken Blossoms*, and *Orphans of a Storm*.

Lyda Roberti

Million Dollar Legs
1932, Edward F. Cline
SCREENPLAY: Henry Myers, Nicholas T. Barrows, Joseph L. Mankiewicz, and Ben Hecht (uncredited)
CAST: Jack Oakie, W. C. Fields, Andy Clyde, Lyda Roberti, Susan Fleming, Ben Turpin, Hugh Herbert, George Barbier, Dickie Moore, Billy Gilbert
U.S.; B & W

Three Cornered Moon
1933, Elliott Nugent
SCREENPLAY: S. K. Lauren and Ray Harris; based on the play by Gertrude Tonkonogy
CAST: Claudette Colbert, Richard Arlen, Mary Boland, Wallace Ford, Lyda Roberti, Tom Brown, Hardie Albright
U.S.; B & W

Although she's known today only to film aficionados, the delectable Lyda Roberti appeared in two of the funniest screwball comedies of the early '30s and all but stole them both. *Million Dollar Legs* is often described as "Dada-esque," and that's not far off base. The writers included Ben Hecht and Joseph Mankiewicz, and it was directed by the fairly unknown Edward Cline (this was by far his best film). It stars Jack Oakie as a traveling brush salesman, and W. C. Fields, atypically, as the bombastic dictator of the mythical kingdom of Klopstakia (where all the women are named Angela and all the men are named George). It's all fast and furious (just a touch over an hour) and makes no sense whatsoever: Oakie winds up recruiting Klopstokians for the 1932 Olympics; Fields's ministers try to overthrow him by use of arm wrestling; Oakie's love interest (the future Mrs. Harpo Marx, incidentally) keeps the national anthem written on her grandfather's tanned hide. The supporting cast is a movie buff's rose garden: Hugh Herbert, Ben Turpin, Andy Clyde. But it's Roberti who sticks in my mind: doing an evil parody of Garbo's *Mata Hari* (released in '31), she plays Mata Machree, the Woman No Man Can Resist. A bizarre combination of Jean Harlow and Fanny

Brice, the Polish-born Roberti slinks and "oys" and rolls her eyes and sings ("Eet's terrific vhen I get hot"). As wonderful and hilarious as *Million Dollar Legs* is, the film seems to fade when she goes offscreen.

Roberti can also be seen in a slightly less absurdist screwballer, the 1933 *Three Cornered Moon* (based on the play by the delightfully named Gertrude Tonkonogy). It's the story of the large, empty-headed Rimplegar family of Brooklyn, forced to face the Depression when their stock (the above-mentioned *Three Cornered Moon*) goes bust. Roberti plays Jenny, the Swedish maid, and her few moments onscreen are pure gold. But there's not an off moment in this sharp but heartwarming tale; at seventy-seven minutes, it flies by. Again, the cast is a dream: dithery Mary Boland as the clan's matriarch; Claudette Colbert as the daughter; the hunky Richard Arlen as her beau; and Wallace Ford as one of her brothers. The movie skitters lightly around Communism, art versus labor, sexual harassment, and suicidal despair—but somehow it never becomes preachy. *Three Cornered Moon* never was as big a cult hit as some other screwball comedies of its day, but it is well worth ferreting out. Sadly, Lyda Roberti's career was cut short when she died of heart disease at the age of thirty-one.

EVE GOLDEN
Writer

My Man Godfrey
1936, Gregory La Cava

SCREENPLAY: Morrie Ryskind, Eric Hatch, and Gregory La Cava (uncredited); based on the novel *1101 Park Avenue*, by Eric Hatch
CAST: William Powell, Carole Lombard, Alice Brady, Gail Patrick, Eugene Pallette, Alan Mowbray, Jean Dixon, Mischa Auer
U.S.; B & W

There are lots of great William Powell movies, but the one I have the most fun with is *My Man Godfrey*. It has a great cast starring Powell, Carole Lombard, and Eugene Pallette. It also has a fantastic screenplay, and Gregory La Cava's direction seems effortless. The Depression-era plot involves a skid-row bum, Godfrey (Powell), who is snatched up by a spoiled rich girl, Irene (Lombard), as part of a scavenger hunt. Irene decides Godfrey would make a good protégé so she takes him home and he becomes the family's butler. Mix in a few horrified, snobbish family members and the superb Pallette as the father at his wit's end, and you have *My Man Godfrey*.

ADAM DURITZ
Songwriter

My Voyage to Italy (Il mio viaggio in Italia)
1999, Martin Scorsese

Written by Suso Cecchi d'Amico and Raffaele Donato
Narrated by Martin Scorsese
U.S./ITALY; B & W AND COLOR; DOCUMENTARY; IN ENGLISH, ITALIAN, FRENCH, AND GERMAN

Nothing I have ever seen better explains the nexus between documentaries and fictional features in film history than Martin Scorsese's marvelous four-hour documentary, *Il mio viaggio in Italia* (*My Voyage to Italy*), a two-part history of Italian cinema. Scorsese narrates the film himself, and his setup for the film explains the overall concept better than I ever could: "This is not a film for cinephiles; it is a recruiting film for cinephiles." And recruit he does, by leading the viewer through a fascinating tour of Italian cinema during the years from 1914 (Pastrone's *Cabiria*) to 1963 (Fellini's *8 1/2*). Along the way, he points directly to the documentary as the root of neorealism, which changed filmmaking everywhere, forever.

The first film he examines is Rossellini's *Paisan* (1946), which documents the liberation of Italy. It is here that Scorsese introduces the concept of neorealism, which tries to come as close as possible to reality— in essence, the look and feel of the documentary. He traces neorealism's roots back to Rossellini's early short films about animals and discusses how much of the movement's motivation was a function of funding, which was not easy to come by during and just after World War II. There's a straight line from Rossellini to De Sica's groundbreaking *Bicycle Thief* and his more controversial *Umberto D.* (see p. 250), which was so powerful that the minister of culture publicly criticized the film for "washing dirty linen in public." It felt so real that its fictional nature was lost on the viewers.

Scorsese does not rush you through any of the films, and his entire approach to the subject matter is intensely personal. He opens by showing us an old black-and-white sixteen-inch RCA television, on which he first saw movies as a kid with his Sicilian-American family. "If I had never seen these films . . . I would be a very different person." It was through film that Scorsese learned about his own roots, and *Il mio viaggio in Italia* is his heartfelt gift to all of us.

MICHAEL C. DONALDSON
Former President, International Documentary Association, author, and lawyer

RECOMMENDED VIEWING: After you watch *My Voyage to Italy*, you may want to check out *A Personal Journey with Martin Scorsese Through American Movies* (2000). This is, among other things, six master classes in directing, and must-viewing for anyone who wants to direct a film. It will add enormously to anyone's understanding of film.

N

Nanook of the North
see p. 93

Nausicaä of the Valley of the Wind
1984, Hayao Miyazaki

SCREENPLAY: Hayao Miyazaki; based on the comic book series
"kaze no tani no Naushika" by Hayao Miyazaki
VOICES: Sumi Shimamoto, Mahito Tsujimura, Hisako Kyôda,
Gorô Naya, Ichirô Nagai, Kôhei Miyauchi, Jôji Yanami
JAPAN; ANIMATION; IN JAPANESE

Hayao Miyazaki is a renowned comic-book writer and
a master of Japanese animation. Over the course of his
career, his work has attracted a considerable adult audience—in Japan, his films hold their own against popular
Hollywood films—but he has always remained faithful
to his youthful following. The key to understanding his
ability to connect with children *and* adults can be found
in one of his earliest films, *Nausicaä of the Valley of the
Wind*, an adaptation of one of his own epic comics.

Unlike most other science-fiction films, which have
stark or artificial settings, the earth in *Nausicaä*—set
a millennium after a global war—is filled with lush
greenery, water, and wind. Beautiful, but for a toxic
jungle, Fukai, whose rampant growth threatens human-
ity. While other tribes fight one another to burn down
the forest and regain their power, Nausicaä, a princess
of the Valley of the Wind, discovers that Fukai actually
cleanses the world, and so she seeks ways to coexist
with it.

Miyazaki's impressive imaginary world is comple-
mented by the profound subject matter. But while he is

critical of modern society and its handling of environmental issues, he never portrays the world pessimistically or cynically; rather, he illustrates his concerns with grace and warmth. In his stories, even the enemies are lovable—no one deserves to be hurt or to be blamed. This is why his films are so widely accepted by children, while adults watch them over and over again, seeking a return to their childhood purity in Miyazaki's world.

REINA HIGASHITANI
Filmmaker and film critic

New York Stories

1989, Martin Scorsese: Life Lessons; *Francis Ford Coppola*: Life Without Zoë; *Woody Allen*: Oedipus Wrecks

SCREENPLAYS: Richard Price; Francis Ford Coppola and Sofia Coppola; Woody Allen
CAST: *Life Lessons*: Nick Nolte, Rosanna Arquette, Steve Buscemi, Patrick O'Neal, (with paintings by Chuck Connelly); *Life Without Zoë*: Heather McComb, Talia Shire, Giancarlo Giannini, Carole Bouquet; *Oedipus Wrecks*: Woody Allen, Mia Farrow, Mae Questel, Julie Kavner
U.S.

Though the three films that make up *New York Stories* are each in their own way interestingly odd, they are especially odd as a threesome; there is little to link them save the fact that they take place in New York City. There is one scene in the first film, *Life Lessons*, directed by Martin Scorsese, that still sends shivers down my spine. Lionel (Nick Nolte), a living legend of a painter in his prime, lives and works in a huge loft. Paulette (Rosanna Arquette), his desperate girlfriend and a wannabe painter, is jealous of Lionel's prodigious talent but only dimly understands the forces that drive him to create art. In a late-night scene with no dialogue, just blaring rock music, Lionel finishes a gigantic painting while Paulette looks on. Painting has been depicted countless times on film, but the cinematography of this segment captures the intense reality of the experience better than any I have ever seen. You can almost smell the oil paint as the camera zooms in on the palette and lingers over the swirling action of the brush moving vigorously, almost violently, on the canvas. We see the surface of the canvas "give" as the brush is thrust and dragged across it, back and forth from palette to canvas. The thick viscosity of the paint, the mixing of the colors, the pushing of the paint onto and into the surface of the canvas, all in extreme close-up, is one of the most sensual scenes I have ever witnessed on film.

INA SALTZ
Design director

Night and the City
1950, Jules Dassin

SCREENPLAY: Jo Eisinger; based on the novel by Gerald Kersh
CAST: Richard Widmark, Gene Tierney, Googie Withers, Hugh Marlowe, Francis L. Sullivan, Herbert Lom, Mike Mazurki, Kay Kendall
U.K.; B & W

Despite keen and renewed interest in film noir, one outstanding film of the period continues to be overlooked—Jules Dassin's *Night and the City*. Filmed in 1950 against the grim and gloomy background of postwar London, it features Richard Widmark in one of his earliest but most riveting roles as the small-time hustler and fight promoter Harry Fabian. A distinct type of noir protagonist, Fabian is neither a hero nor an antihero; he is a nonhero, a pathetic character who only recognizes his wasted life and misspent energies at the very end. As Fabian, Widmark is at his manic best, racing from place to place to steal, swindle, or impress a variety of thwarted lowlifes who make up his world.

The plot, which revolves around Fabian's desperate attempt to set up a wrestling match, provides a lurid backdrop for a cast of splendid character actors. Googie Withers is both seductive and ruthless as Helen Nosseross, a woman caught up in a miserable marriage to nightclub owner Francis L. Sullivan. Sullivan, his immense bulk huddled in the corner of his glass-walled office overlooking the nightclub, is at his menacing best. Herbert Lom plays a rival fight promoter, a murderous thug who nonetheless shows true tenderness toward his dying father. And Gene Tierney is perfect as the good-hearted beauty who can't save Fabian from himself or from others. Dassin's *Night and the City* is suspenseful and fast paced. Don't confuse it with the dull 1992 remake; there is no substitute for the original.

RICHARD LAVENSTEIN
Architect

The Night of the Hunter
1955, Charles Laughton

SCREENPLAY: Charles Laughton (uncredited) and James Agee; based on the novel by Davis Grubb
CAST: Robert Mitchum, Shelley Winters, Lillian Gish, James Gleason, Evelyn Varden, Peter Graves, Don Beddoe, Billy Chapin, Sally Jane Bruce
U.S.; B & W

I first saw *The Night of the Hunter* on TV in the summer of 1959, just after I graduated from high school. I fell in love with it immediately, both because of the fine work by the entire cast and the audacious storytelling techniques. And what a surprise it was that the great

actor Charles Laughton, of all people, had directed this
bizarre, frightening, and amazing film.

Fifteen years later, in the summer of 1974, it was
a great thrill for me to visit Laughton's widow, Elsa
Lanchester, at their home in Hollywood. I was working
for the American Film Institute in Washington DC, and
my fellow archivist Anthony Slide and I were sent there
to retrieve boxes of photographs, sketches, and letters
relating to *The Night of the Hunter*. When I expressed
my admiration for the film to Ms. Lanchester, she
recalled her husband's desperation following its poor
critical and box-office reception: "Oh, it just broke
his heart!"

Ms. Lanchester, tired of storing the film's original
rushes, and thinking they could be used for schol-
arly research, sent them to the AFI film school in
Beverly Hills. A few months later, we found out that
Laughton's rushes were indeed being used by the film
students—but not to study. They were using the picture
and magnetic sound trims as "fill leader" to assemble
work prints for their own projects. Appalled, curator
Larry Karr had them shipped to the AFI in Washington
DC immediately. When we opened the boxes, we found
over eighty thousand feet of picture and sound trims
of varying lengths, all wound together on dozens of
interleaved rolls.

I had time to assemble only the first twenty minutes
or so before I left the AFI in 1975 for a new job at
the UCLA Film and Television Archive. The rushes
were stored at the Kennedy Center until 1981, when
Karr arranged to have them sent to me. Over the
next twenty years, all of the material was gradually
unwound, identified, and reassembled. Finally, in the
summer of 2002, preservationist Nancy Mysel and
I screened two and a half hours of the most interesting

rushes at UCLA's Festival of Preservation. No one had seen the rushes since Laughton and film editor Robert Golden discarded them more than forty-five years before.

The rushes are very revealing. Because Laughton didn't want to break the mood, he often left the camera running between takes as he coached the actors. We can hear him direct and motivate each performer. The rushes also help dispel the myth that Laughton disliked the children and that Mitchum had to take over for him. He lavishes considerable attention on the children, Billy Chapin and Sally Jane Bruce, and he works prodigiously to mold the performance of Shelley Winters. He is less apt to interact with the experienced actors—Robert Mitchum, James Gleason, and Lillian Gish. Even so, in the rushes, Laughton does play every single character in the film; as an actor turned director, he was a consummate performer who could portray any role with ease. One almost gets the impression Laughton would have been happiest if he could have dispensed with the cast and played all the parts himself!

The Night of the Hunter is the only classic motion picture of its era for which the original rushes survive, and I am pleased that modern audiences can experience the creation of a uniquely memorable film. I have also been fortunate to meet many members of the cast and crew, including Lillian Gish. And so it is that my love for The Night of the Hunter has found a most unique fruition.

ROBERT GITT
Preservation Officer, UCLA Film & Television Archive

NOTE: In 1999, UCLA Film and Television Archive, in cooperation with MGM Studios, preserved The Night of the Hunter with funding provided by The Film Foundation and Robert Sturm.

Nights of Cabiria (Le notti di Cabiria)
1957, Federico Fellini

SCREENPLAY: Federico Fellini, Ennio Flaiano, and Tullio Pinelli
CAST: Giulietta Masina, François Périer, Amedeo Nazzari,
Franca Marzi, Dorian Gray, Aldo Silvani, Mario Passante,
Pina Gualandari
ITALY/FRANCE; B & W; IN ITALIAN

I don't have a favorite book or song or poem, but
Fellini's *Nights of Cabiria* is my favorite movie. There
will never be another Giulietta Masina. There is a
scene that stays with me that is like a film unto itself: a
famous movie star (charismatically played by Amedeo
Nazzari) takes Cabiria (Masina) out for a night on the
town. Later that night, Cabiria spies on the movie star
and his beautiful girlfriend, observing a life of glamour
and wealth that she will never lead. Another actress
might have evoked jealousy or anger, but without
rancor Masina's Cabiria watches the lovers with melancholic wonder, sad because she will never be one of
these shining people but still happy to know they exist.
I've watched this sequence at least twenty times.

DAVID BENIOFF
Screenwriter and author

1900 (Novecento)
1976, Bernardo Bertolucci

SCREENPLAY: Bernardo Bertolucci, Franco Arcalli, and
Giuseppe Bertolucci
CAST: Robert De Niro, Gérard Depardieu, Donald Sutherland,
Burt Lancaster, Dominique Sanda, Francesca Bertini,
Laura Betti, Werner Bruhns, Sterling Hayden, Anna Henkel,
Alida Valli, Romolo Valli, Stefania Sandrelli
ITALY/FRANCE/WEST GERMANY; IN ITALIAN

The first time I saw Bertolucci's *1900*, I was living in
Emilia Romagna, where I was surrounded by the
cinematographic beauty of this seldom-seen classic. One
night, the Italian television station broadcast the five-hour
film, without interruption or commercials. I watched
it with a family whose ancestors have lived in the region
(the very locale of the film) for twelve generations.

What impressed me most was how perfectly
Bertolucci portrayed the eclipse of feudalism, the death
of fascism, and the radical transformation of agrarian
society (which still existed in the Emilian countryside).
The Italians I lived with were not impressed. They
didn't consider the film epic at all; for them it was
just another snapshot of their history. Whenever I eat
sardines or polenta, or drink a glass of Lambrusco, I am
transported to the "set" of this unforgettable movie.

MARIO BATALI
Chef

No Down Payment
1957, Martin Ritt

SCREENPLAY: Ben Maddow (front for Philip Yordan);
based on the novel by John McPartland
CAST: Joanne Woodward, Sheree North, Tony Randall,
Jeffrey Hunter, Cameron Mitchell, Patricia Owens,
Barbara Rush, Pat Hingle
U.S.; B & W

Martin Ritt's *No Down Payment* is a dark film about
post–World War II suburbia, chock-full of barbecues,
excessive cocktails, and backyard trysts. It takes Hawaiian
shirts, racial slurs, Bermuda shorts, booze, sex,
Southern California optimism, and the mind-numbing
architectural sameness of a suburban ranch-house
development, pops it all into a blender, and then pours

the frothy mix right down the back of your shirt. Life was not fun for these people.

Ross Anderson
Architect

recommended reading: Reyner Banham, *Los Angeles: The Architecture of Four Ecologies*. University of California Press, 2001.

None Shall Escape
1944, André De Toth

screenplay: Lester Cole; story by Alfred Neumann and Joseph Than
cast: Marsha Hunt, Alexander Knox, Henry Travers, Richard Crane, Dorothy Morris, Trevor Bardette, Richard Hale, Ruth Nelson, Kurt Kreuger
u.s.

Before the end of World War II, director André De Toth and screenwriter Lester Cole predicted the International War Crimes Tribunal. *None Shall Escape* is the fictionalized story of Wilhelm Grimm, a Nazi officer (played with great dignity and restraint by the underrated British actor Alexander Knox) who is tried for his actions during the war. He tells the judges his life story and we discover how a seemingly normal, kind, intelligent schoolteacher can become a monster.

None Shall Escape is startling in the way it deals with a subject few other American films took on in the 1940s. Jews are herded into cattle cars to be transported to a concentration camp, and massacred when they rebel. The last survivor, seen as a shadow on a train car, intones the Kol Nidre before being gunned down. This scene, so matter-of-fact, achieves a kind of heroic poetry.

Ric Menello
Screenwriter, film historian, and music video director

NOTE: De Toth and Alexander Knox worked together again in *Man in the Saddle* and *Hidden Fear*. Knox's portrayal of Wilhelm Grimm was one of his few leading roles; it is reported that he was "gray-listed" in the 1950s, meaning he could find work only in B-movies or overseas. Screenwriter Lester Cole was blacklisted for being a Communist sympathizer, one of the Hollywood Ten.

Nora inu
see *Stray Dog*

Novecento
see *1900*

Pandora's Box

Passion (Madame DuBarry)
1919, Ernst Lubitsch
SCREENPLAY: Norbert Falk and Hanns Kräly
CAST: Pola Negri, Emil Jannings, Harry Liedtke, Reinhold Schünzel
GERMANY; B & W; SILENT

Broken Blossoms
1919, D. W. Griffith
SCREENPLAY: D. W. Griffith; based on a story by Thomas Burcast
CAST: Lillian Gish, Richard Barthelmess, Donald Crisp, Arthur Howard, Edward Peil
U.S.; B & W; SILENT

The Last Flight
1931, William Dieterle
SCREENPLAY: John Monk Saunders; based on the novel *Single Lady*, by John Monk Saunders
CAST: Richard Barthelmess, David Manners, John Mack Brown, Helen Chandler, Elliot Nugent, Walter Byron
U.S.; B & W

Love Me Tonight
1932, Rouben Mamoulian
SCREENPLAY: Samuel Hoffenstein, Waldemar Young, and George Marion Jr.; based on the play *Tailor in the Château*, by Léopold Marchand and Paul Armont

CAST: Maurice Chevalier, Jeanette MacDonald, Charles Ruggles, Charles Butterworth, Myrna Loy, C. Aubrey Smith, Elizabeth Patterson, Ethel Griffies, Blanche Frederici, Robert Greig
U.S.; B & W

Applause

1929, Rouben Mamoulian
SCREENPLAY: Garrett Fort; based on the novel by Beth Brown
CAST: Dorothy Cumming, Fuller Mellish Jr., Helen Morgan, Joan Peers, Jack Singer, Henry Wadsworth
U.S.; B & W

The Clock

1945, Vincente Minnelli and Fred Zinnemann
SCREENPLAY: Robert Nathan, Joseph Schrank; story by Paul Gallico
CAST: Judy Garland, Robert Walker, James Gleason, Keenan Wynn, Marshall Thompson, Lucile Gleason
U.S.; B & W

The Night of the Hunter

1955, Charles Laughton
SCREENPLAY: Charles Laughton (uncredited) and James Agee; based on the novel by Davis Grubb
CAST: Robert Mitchum, Shelley Winters, Lillian Gish, James Gleason, Evelyn Varden, Peter Graves, Don Beddoe, Billy Chapin, Sally Jane Bruce
U.S.; B & W

The Good Fairy

1935, William Wyler
SCREENPLAY: Preston Sturges; based on the play by Ferenc Molnár
CAST: Margaret Sullavan, Herbert Marshall, Frank Morgan, Reginald Owen, Eric Blore, Beulah Bondi, Alan Hale, Cesar Romero
U.S.; B & W

A Tree Grows in Brooklyn

1945, Elia Kazan
SCREENPLAY: Tess Slesinger, Frank Davis, and Anita Loos (uncredited); based on the novel by Betty Smith
CAST: Dorothy McGuire, Joan Blondell, James Dunn, Lloyd Nolan, James Gleason, Ted Donaldson, Peggy Ann Garner, Ruth Nelson, John Alexander
U.S.; B & W

My love affair with movies began early—too early, as it turned out, because my first experience occurred when

I was six years old, and it was a disaster. My poor, unsuspecting mother took me to see a silent movie called *Passion*. Pola Negri played Madame du Barry. When they dragged her to the guillotine she pleaded with the French revolutionaries for her life. "Don't kill me!" the title card screamed. "Life is so sweet!"

Now it was my turn to scream: convinced that I was right there, in the middle of the Place de la Révolution, I was carried out of the theater shrieking at the top of my lungs. Mother rushed me home, put me to bed, and phoned for the doctor, but all to no avail; I hollered for several hours.

Through the years I continued to over-respond. (In fact, I do so to this day.) But I learned to control myself sufficiently so that I didn't have to be removed—that was the last thing I wanted. In spite of my terror attack during *Passion*, a 1919 German film by director Ernst Lubitsch, I have never found a place more desirable than a movie theater.

Another silent film that made a lasting impression on me was D. W. Griffith's *Broken Blossoms* (1919). This was—and is—a film of great richness. It is rich in beauty, as visually lovely as a lotus blossom. It is rich in emotion, too; the performances Griffith brought forth from Lillian Gish and Richard Barthelmess are more powerful than anything the screen offers today.

In terms of movies with sound, William Dieterle's first American film was *The Last Flight* (produced by First National in 1931). In an interview in the *New York Times*, Dieterle stated that regardless of all the awards lavished on him later, *The Last Flight* was the movie he believed to be his best. I agree wholeheartedly. We find Mr. Barthelmess again in this one, and his leading lady—the ethereally beautiful Helen Chandler—is every bit as sensitive as Ms. Gish. John Monk Saunders, a popular novelist of the 1920s, wrote the screenplay. His style is reminiscent of Hemingway, but I like him better. Hemingway goes for the jugular; Saunders goes for the heart.

The best musical of all time came from Paramount in 1932: *Love Me Tonight* (see p. 144). Director Rouben Mamoulian gave Maurice Chevalier and Jeanette MacDonald a luster that sparkles as brightly today as it did then (if you can find a good print). Don't bother searching for better songs than those Richard Rodgers and Lorenz Hart wrote for Maurice and Jeanette, because there are none. "Lover," "Isn't It Romantic?" and "The Son of a Gun Is Nothing but a Tailor"—all of the songs are unsurpassable.

Another fine Mamoulian film is *Applause* (Paramount, 1929). I became addicted to Helen Morgan when she sang "Bill" in *Show Boat*, so Mamoulian's hunch that she had the making of a great dramatic actress thrilled and fascinated me. Her performance, under Mamoulian's loving direction, is shattering.

Only Judy Garland came closest to the place in my heart occupied by Helen Morgan. There's nothing esoteric about Judy's movies. Most of them were commercial as well as artistic blockbusters and need no help from me in attracting attention. However, *The Clock* (MGM, 1945) did become slightly lost in the shuffle. Too bad, because her acting had never been stronger. It was the second time she teamed with Vincente Minnelli, and he found depths of feeling in his wife (they married shortly after making *The Clock*) that none of her other work has quite matched. And Robert Walker's performance is equally good.

Charles Laughton directed only one movie, *The Night of the Hunter* (1955; see p. 167). It was received without excitement by critics, and this wounded Mr. Laughton so deeply that he never put on the director's hat again. Our loss, more than his. I find it a breathtakingly original film, with ingenious directorial touches and wonderful performances by Robert Mitchum, two splendid child actors, Shelley Winters, and the inimitable Lillian Gish. Good actresses don't die; they just get better.

Did you happen to see *The Good Fairy*? If you did, I don't have to tell you what a charmer it is. Preston Sturges wrote the screenplay in 1935 for Universal. He adapted it from a play by Ferenc Molnár, turning it into a vehicle for Margaret Sullavan. Although Sturges wasn't the director, it has many of the earmarks of a Sturges comedy masterpiece: the hilarious dialogue, the sweetness, and the stable of great character actors he loved to assemble (Frank Morgan, Reginald Owen, Alan Hale, Beulah Bondi, and Eric Blore). This is Morgan's best and funniest performance, and Herbert Marshall scores beautifully as the *inamorato* of Luisa Gingelbusher (Sullavan). William Wyler directed it with his usual skill and taste; Sturges himself couldn't have done it better.

Elia Kazan directed his share of blockbusters, but the film of his that I cherish the most is *A Tree Grows in Brooklyn* (1945). James Dunn, Dorothy McGuire, and Joan Blondell are superb; but it's the portrayal of young Francie by Peggy Ann Garner that knocks me out every time I watch it, year after year. With due respect to Judy Garland, Jackie Cooper, Margaret O'Brien, and Shirley Temple, I believe it to be the best performance by a juvenile ever.

HUGH MARTIN
Songwriter

O

Of Mice and Men
see p. 237

Open City (Roma, città aperta)
1945, Roberto Rosselliero

SCREENPLAY: Roberto Rossellini (uncredited), Federico Fellini, and Sergio Amidei
CAST: Aldo Fabrizi, Anna Magnani, Vito Annichiarico, Nando Bruno, Harry Feist, Maria Michi, Marcello Pagliero
ITALY; B & W; IN ITALIAN

Open City had a far more profound effect on me and on many other filmmakers, as well as viewers, than is commonly realized. It was a major part of a new way of cinematic storytelling: neorealism. You're *there*. You're a part of it. This film rips your heart out as you see and feel the desperation of ordinary people who have had their families and friends torn away from them, their freedoms denied, and their lives shattered by the takeover of their Italian city during World War II. Brace yourself for the emotionally wrenching scene in which Pina (Anna Magnani) runs down the street, weeping and begging, as her priest faces her from the back of a fast-moving truck full of men being taken to their deaths. I still get tears when I think about that scene. *Open City*, along with other Italian films of the same period, made filmmakers around the world think about film in a totally different way, inspiring so many of the neorealist films that we cherish today.

ARTHUR HILLER
Director

Capturing History

O Thiassos (The Travelling Players)
1975, Theo Angelopoulos
SCREENPLAY: Theo Angelopoulos
CAST: Eva Kotamanidou, Aliki Georgouli, Stratos Pahis, Maria Vassiliou, Petros Zarkadis
GREECE; IN GREEK

El santo oficio (The Holy Office)
1974, Arturo Ripstein
SCREENPLAY: José Emilio Pacheco and Arturo Ripstein
CAST: Jorge Luke, Diana Bracho, Claudio Brook, Ana Mérida, Rafael Banquells, Nathanael León, Zonia Rangel
MEXICO; IN SPANISH, HEBREW, AND LATIN

The movies that have the most resonance for me are those in which writers and directors capture a small part or a great sweep of their own history, thereby documenting a story that might otherwise be overlooked by the rest of the world. These people are often unknown in Hollywood, and work thousands of miles away from the mainstream filmmaking world, both literally and philosophically. One celebrated example of this is *Z*, Costa-Gavras's drama about the overthrow of democracy in Greece by the right-wing military junta of the '60s and '70s.

Some of my favorite films are lesser-known works in the same genre. One, coincidentally, can be thought of as somewhat of a prologue to the story told in *Z*: Theo Angelopoulos's *O Thiassos* (*The Travelling Players*). The film follows a family troupe of provincial actors through some of the most traumatic events in twentieth-century Greek history, from World War II to the Greek Civil War and its aftermath. Another film that haunts me is *El santo oficio* (*The Holy Office*), by the great Mexican director Arturo Ripstein. It's set in the sixteenth century during the Inquisition in Mexico.

LES GUTHMAN
Writer, producer, and director

Orpheus (Orphée)

1949, Jean Cocteau

SCREENPLAY: Jean Cocteau
CAST: Jean Marais, François Périer, María Casares, Marie Déa,
Henri Crémieux, Juliette Gréco, Roger Blin, Edouard Dermithe
FRANCE; B & W; IN FRENCH

Orphée, written and directed by Jean Cocteau, is
the truest film about poets and poetry I have yet to
see. When Orpheus enters a bar he used to frequent
and nobody pays any attention to him, he asks the
bartender why. The bartender answers, "You must
astonish them." Any poet who has been around awhile
will feel the aptness of the bartender's words. And
when Orpheus is asked by a tribunal in the underworld,
"What is a poet?" he gives the best answer I know: "A
poet is someone who writes but is not a writer." Like
most poets, Orpheus negotiates two worlds at once:
the everyday world of the living and the underworld of
souls. But the way he does it—by receiving poems via
car radio, by gliding through mirrors—is more thrilling,
and more magical.

MARK STRAND
Poet

O Thiassos (The Travelling Players)

see p. 179

P

The Panic in Needle Park

1971, Jerry Schatzberg

SCREENPLAY: Joan Didion and John Gregory Dunne;
based on the novel by James Mills
CAST: Al Pacino, Kitty Winn, Alan Vint, Richard Bright,
Kiel Martin, Michael McClanathan, Warren Finnerty,
Marcia Jean Kurtz, Raul Julia, Joe Santos, Paul Sorvino
U.S.

A brutal and occasionally brilliant portrait of junkies
on the streets of Manhattan, *The Panic in Needle Park*
features Al Pacino's first lead role in a film, and he
dominates every frame with a passion and force that is
astonishing. Kitty Winn matches him move for move
as his lover, and a young Raul Julia has a small role as
well. Jerry Schatzberg brought a wonderful, if bleak,
documentary feel to this film, and it is the father to just
about every drug-themed film made since, good and
bad. This film is so grimy you'll want to take a bath
after watching it. A true original.

ERIC STOLTZ
Actor

Paracelsus

1943, Georg Wilhelm Pabst

SCREENPLAY: Kurt Heuser
CAST: Werner Krauss, Annelies Reinhold, Harry Langewisch,
Mathias Wieman, Fritz Rasp, Martin Urtel, Herbert Hübner,
Josef Sieber, Harald Kreutzberg
GERMANY; B & W; IN GERMAN

G. W. Pabst—perhaps best known for having unleashed
the stupefyingly beautiful Louise Brooks in movies like

Pandora's Box and *Diary of a Lost Girl*—returned to
Austria after Hitler's ascension to power, having been
living and working abroad. He later claimed that he did
so in order to sell some family property and collect his
mother for a planned emigration to America, but when
Germany invaded Poland, he found himself stuck inside
the Reich. Eventually he made two films there, thereby
earning the enmity of those who would never forgive
him for making any kind of movie within Hitler's
Germany. The second movie, 1943's *Paracelsus*—about
the sixteenth-century physician-alchemist—was widely
considered pro-Nazi. Whether it was or not, it includes
one of the most harrowing dance scenes on record.
As Paracelsus dances, the crowd's reaction begins to
match his movements, and eventually all the people in
the crowd seem hypnotically induced to dance against
their wills. It's a vision of dance as contagion. Imagine
a mass epileptic fit, perfectly synchronized, or a school
of fish tossed onto a dock and gasping and flopping
around together in a horrifying choreography. Most
of the rest of this hard-to-find movie is mundane. But
that scene, once viewed, is an unforgettable portrait
of compulsion and exhilarated abandon, which seems
emblematic of totalitarianism.

JIM SHEPARD
Writer

Paris Is Burning

see p. 102

The Passenger

1975, Michelangelo Antonioni

SCREENPLAY: Mark Peploe and Peter Wollen

CAST: Jack Nicholson, Maria Schneider, Jenny Runacre,
Ian Hendry, Steven Berkoff, Ambroise Bia
ITALY/FRANCE/SPAIN; ENGLISH, SPANISH, GERMAN, AND FRENCH

Displacement and alienation in the modern world
is the theme of Michelangelo Antonioni's 1975 film
The Passenger. Interested in behavior more than plot,
Antonioni allows situations to grow out of the personalities and surroundings of his characters. The final shot
in the film is a technical tour de force: it starts inside
the hotel room of David (Jack Nicholson) and then
slowly moves toward the barred window and through
the bars to the square outside, where the camera pans
around the square before returning to view the room
through the window from the outside. This beautifully
choreographed sequence lasts about fifteen minutes,
without a single cut.

BETTE GORDON
Professor of Film, Columbia University, and director

Passion (Madame DuBarry)

see p. 173

Patterns

1956, Fielder Cook

SCREENPLAY: Rod Serling
CAST: Van Heflin, Everett Sloane, Ed Begley, Beatrice Straight,
Elizabeth Wilson, Joanna Roos, Valerie Cossart, Ronnie Welsh
U.S.; B & W

Rod Serling's 1956 corporate drama explores the
hard logic of capitalism in a sepia-toned universe of
secretarial pools, flannel suits, and mimeographs.
Without being overly sensational, *Patterns* captures the
political tensions, professional anxieties, and personal

costs inherent in the inexorable drive for corporate profit. Perhaps most striking is how the film hints at the dangers of balance-sheet manipulation, laying out a foundation for the increasingly baroque financial constructs that would ultimately bring down the likes of WorldCom and Enron.

Everett Sloane sinks his teeth into the role of Walter Ramsey—the ruthless and efficient CEO anticipating (by decades) the high-octane bluster of Donald Trump and technical savvy of Gordon Gekko. The atmosphere might be dated, but Ramsey's browbeating and manipulation are right out of an episode of *The Apprentice*. Serling suggests that men such as these are "simple, almost childlike," and Ramsey holds sway over his boardroom the way a childhood bully dominates the sandbox.

Fielder Cook's spare direction serves to highlight the rising tension; the personal and professional conflicts are distilled to their essence. Serling doesn't go after any obvious targets in his script, clearly understanding the inevitability of market capitalism, as well as the role it will play in shaping the growing success story of America. Ultimately, what he asks is if there is room for a humanist impulse in the moral calculus of capitalist logic. His open-ended answer: it remains to be seen.

ROB TYMCHYSHYN
Writer

The Peddler (Dastforoush)
1987, Mohsen Makhmalbaaf

SCREENPLAY: Mohsen Makhmalbaaf; story by Alberto Moravia
CAST: Behzad Behzadpour, Zohreh Sarmadi, Esmail Soltanian, Morteza Zarrabi, Moharram Zaynalzadeh
IRAN; IN PERSIAN

Although Mohsen Makhmalbaaf's *Dastforoush* (*The Peddler*) received considerable praise in the late 1980s, it has since been all but forgotten. It remains the perfect example of the direction Iranian cinema would take following the nation's Islamic Revolution, and almost two decades after its release, it's still both a visual pleasure and music to the ears. Shot in Tehran, its hauntingly melancholic atmosphere and dirty yet beautifully decorated sets further a deep, scrutinizing look at the life of the human being.

FARROKH SOLTANI
Film critic, TehranAvenue.com

Pickpocket

1959, Robert Bresson

SCREENPLAY: Robert Bresson
CAST: Martin LaSalle, Marika Green, Pierre Leymarie, Jean Pélégri, Doly Scal, Pierre Etaix
FRANCE; B & W; IN FRENCH

Loosely based on Dostoevsky's *Crime and Punishment*, *Pickpocket* is the portrait of an amoral, lonely man whose erotic obsession with stealing is miraculously transferred to the love of a woman. Bresson, who likened the role of a film director to that of a sleight-of-hand artist, was concerned with the anatomy of theft—the pickpocket's eyes fixed in concentration, his hands moving with graceful assurance—and giving the act the value of a ritual. Indeed, the "ballets of thievery," as Jean Cocteau called them, are among the most beautifully choreographed and edited sequences in cinema.

JOSHUA SIEGEL
Assistant Curator, Department of Film, Museum of Modern Art

Pure Melodrama

A Place in the Sun

1951, George Stevens
SCREENPLAY: Michael Wilson and Harry Brown; based on the
novel *An American Tragedy*, by Theodore Dreiser, and the play
An American Tragedy, by Patrick Kearney
CAST: Montgomery Clift, Elizabeth Taylor, Shelley Winters,
Raymond Burr, Keefe Braselle, Anne Revere
U.S.; B & W

Room at the Top

1959, Jack Clayton
SCREENPLAY: Neil Patterson; based on the novel by John Braine
CAST: Laurence Harvey, Simone Signoret, Heather Sears,
Donald Houston, Donald Wolfit, Allan Cuthberston,
Hermione Baddeley, Raymond Huntley
U.K.; B & W

They're the same story, really. An impoverished, morally
deficient young man longs for a glamorous life, falls for
two women, can't figure out which one he really loves, kills
one of them, and it all turns out pretty badly for everybody.
Pure, unadulterated melodrama . . . but oh, these are terrific films.

George Stevens's *A Place in the Sun* is based on
Theodore Dreiser's novel *An American Tragedy*. The film
is clear and pungent—no small feat when you consider
the length of the novel. Elizabeth Taylor has never been
better, Montgomery Clift makes a bold claim for the title
of America's best actor, and Shelley Winters almost steals
the film as the girl Clift deserts for Taylor. The whole
thing is damn near perfect, which is why it won Oscars for
screenplay, direction, cinematography, editing, costume
design, and music.

In *Room at the Top*, Jack Clayton's seedy 1959 English
version of the morality tale, there's money in the air
all right, but not in people's pockets, and Laurence Harvey
is determined to get his hands on some by marrying the
pretty, virginal, not-a-thought-in-her-head factory owner's
daughter. But he falls hard for a worldly older woman
(Simone Signoret), only to leave her when the pretty daughter
beckons. Clayton's film hasn't the style of Stevens's, but
there's genuine grit, rage, and despair in both his work and

that of cinematographer Freddie Francis. It's representative of that great movement of angry young men who burned up the British screen in the '50s, before the Beatles turned the whole artistic class warfare game upside down a few years later.

GREGORY MOSHER
Director, Initiative at Columbia University, director, and producer

RECOMMENDED VIEWING: It's hard to go wrong with any of Stevens's work. Of special note are the documentary films he shot during the final months of World War II: *That Justice Be Done* (1945); *Nazi Concentration Camp* (1945); and *The Nazi Plan* (1945).

Pinocchio

1940, Hamilton Luske and Ben Sharpsteen

SCREENPLAY: Ted Sears, Webb Smith, Joseph Sabo, Otto Englander, William Cottrell, Aurelius Battaglia, and Erdman Penner; based on the novel *The Adventures of Pinocchio*, by Carlo Collodi

VOICES: Dickie Jones, Walter Catlett, Frankie Darro, Cliff Edwards, Christian Rub, Evelyn Venable

U.S.; ANIMATION

My first realization that something more was happening in Disney films occurred while watching the famous scene in *Pinocchio* in which the wooden boy's nose grows as he lies. Anyone familiar with Collodi's children's story knows this episode; and parents attending the first showing of Disney's version in 1940 (like parents today) were no doubt primed to nudge their children and say, "See what happens when you lie?" But the unexpected artistry is that his nose grows, sprouts branches, leaves, blossoms, and a nest with hatching eggs, then—as Pinocchio denies lying—the leaves wither and fall. Those falling leaves of denial are brilliant.

What I tell my children is this: when you watch a
film, look at the edges of the frame. That's where the
illusion gets ragged. Oops, the boom dips into view.
Oops, that dead Indian just moved to avoid a falling
horse. Oops, that Munchkin skipped left, not right. But
in animation, there are no erring or errant actors, no
continuity problems. Look at the edges of a cartoon:
if they are blank or if you see the same picture on
the wall repeatedly racing to the left as a figure in the
foreground is running to the right, you are watching
The Huckleberry Hound Show. But if those background
edges are as engaging as what is in the center of the
frame, you are watching Disney.

Pinocchio is considered Disney's masterpiece (which
may surprise those who exalt *Snow White*) because
of its controlled integration of cartoon fantasy and
emotional realism. Collodi's modern fairy tale is rooted
in the stuff of everyday life—well, life plus one or two
fantasy elements, plus a talking cricket. Adding to the
film's realism is the use of modern film techniques in
the animation: the long tracking shot down into the village and onto Geppetto's porch and, at the bottom of
the screen, the shadows of children heading for school
while Pinocchio bounces in anticipation. This moment
not only evokes the first day of school excitement, but
also gives older viewers a sense of the town. In another
scene shot from Jiminy Cricket's POV (yes, insects do
have their own perspective), the camera seems to hop as
it approaches the devious Fox and then leap perilously
to an unsteady perch on top of his stovepipe hat. In
fact, the only way to talk about this animated film shot
with an utterly fixed camera is as if it were a live-action
film with a movable camera capable of tracking and
panning, shooting from below or above, inside a whale
or outside. Filming a talking cricket on a hat while

in motion is something no camera could actually do, even if crickets could talk. Through animation, film can become more like live-action than live-action film itself.

JOHN BRYANT
Professor of English, Hofstra University, and editor for The Melville Society

A Place in the Sun

see p. 186

Platform (Zhantai)
2000, Jia Zhang-ke

SCREENPLAY: Jia Zhang-ke

CAST: Wang Hong-Wei, Zhao Tao, Liang Jing-Dong, Yang Tian-Yi, Wang Bo

HONG KONG/CHINA/JAPAN/FRANCE; IN MANDARIN AND SHANXI

The most well-known of the sixth-generation Chinese filmmakers (creators of "urban cinema") is Jia Zhang-ke, who frequently depicts disillusioned youths in a fast-changing China (see 1997's *Xiao Wu* and 2004's *The World*). Jia's film, *Platform*, is set during a period often neglected in Chinese films: the decade between 1979 and 1989, a time that began with China's struggle to recover from the devastation of the Cultural Revolution to the years of fast economic and cultural transformation brought on by Deng Xiaoping's reform policy.

The film follows a group of young people from a provincial town who are part of a state-run performance troupe; the dance and music performances' central themes revolve around socialist ideology. Over the course of the film, privatization takes hold, not only of the country but also of the band, which takes on the Westernized name of the All-Star Rock and Breakdance Band. One by one, the characters shed their Mao jackets and peasant-pants and start exploring Western trends and fashion. The men don bell-bottoms, the women buy high heels, and they all listen to pop songs from Hong Kong and Taiwan. Old clashes with new and, most of the time, capitalist desires win over old Communist credos.

The band, however, fails to attract much of an audience. Discouraged, some members leave the troupe to pursue other careers. The band performs on the back of a truck, moving from one town to another, from one trend to the next, presenting its embarrassing and painfully cheesy acts to a handful of spectators. Sometimes the Western overlay looks hilarious, and sometimes it just looks sad. In trying to catch up with the world, these young people fall into a state of alienation, ultimately giving up their dreams. In one particularly devastating scene, one of the former dancers (who is now a tax collector) performs her last triumphant dance alone in a dull government office to music coming from a radio. It is at once glorious and bleak.

LA FRANCES HUI
Senior Program Officer, Cultural Programs and Performing Arts, Asia Society

Playtime
1967, Jacques Tati

SCREENPLAY: Jacques Lagrange and Jacques Tati; English dialogue by Art Buchwald
CAST: Jacques Tati, Barbara Denneck, Jacqueline Lecomte, Valérie Camille, France Rumilly, Rita Maiden
FRANCE/ITALY; IN FRENCH, ENGLISH, AND GERMAN

The first and only French film shot in 70 mm, *Playtime* is Jacques Tati's triumphant concert of wide-screen space, color, and stereophonic sound—a film much maligned on its initial release, but now for the first time painstakingly restored to the director's full-length original version. Set against the stunning backdrop of "Tativille," an imaginary Paris of the future, Tati's gentle satire about the joys and absurdities of everyday life seems more prescient than ever.

JOSHUA SIEGEL
Assistant curator, Department of Film, Museum of Modern Art

An Act of Kindness

The Producers

1968, Mel Brooks
SCREENPLAY: Mel Brooks
CAST: Zero Mostel, Gene Wilder, Kenneth Mars, Estelle Winwood, Renée Taylor, Dick Shawn, Lee Meredith
U.S.

My father, Sidney Glazier, produced *The Producers* (the movie, not the musical). He loved being approached by fans of the movie who could quote favorite lines and lyrics, and he never tired of telling me that he had run into yet another person yelling, "That's our Hitler!" across First Avenue. Several years ago, my father was having lunch in Los Angeles with his nephew, a screenwriter. Harvey Keitel came over to say hello to my cousin. My cousin introduced my father. "Sidney Glazier?" Keitel said. "You won't remember me, but you saved me from eviction thirty years ago."

Apparently Keitel, a struggling actor in New York at the time, had answered a *Producers* casting call for the *Springtime for Hitler* opening-night scene. Every extra would get one hundred dollars. But Keitel wasn't wearing a tuxedo, as the extras had been instructed to do, and the casting director was about to turn him away. My father happened to be standing nearby and waved Keitel through. "He's got a dark suit," he said. "No one'll know the difference."

Sure enough, if you pause your DVD, you can see a non-tuxedoed, very young Harvey Keitel making his way into the theater, one hundred dollars richer.

KAREN SHEPARD
Professor, Williams College, and writer

Przypadek
see *Blind Chance*

The Puppetmaster
1993, Hou Hsiao-hsien

SCREENPLAY: Chu T'ien-wen and Wu Nien-Jen; story by Li Tienlu
CAST: Li Tienlu, Giong Lim, Chung Lin, Ming Hwa Bai,
Fue Choung Cheng, Hung Liou, Tsai Chen-Nan, Yang Liyin
TAIWAN; IN MANDARIN, TAIWANESE, AND JAPANESE

Although he is perhaps the least known of the world's
most talented living filmmakers, Hou Hsiao-hsien has
been widely praised by international critics and film-
festival audiences. In his 1993 film *The Puppetmaster*, the
second installment in a trilogy on the history of Taiwan
(including *City of Sadness*, 1989, and *Good Men, Good
Women*, 1995), Hou looks at the Japanese occupation
through the eyes of puppeteer Li Tienlu. Narrating his
life on- and offscreen, the charismatic Li takes us back
in time: first to his childhood, when men still wore the
braids of the Qing dynasty, then to his early training
in puppet theater, on to performing propaganda puppet
theater for the Japanese, and finally to the day Taiwan
was liberated.

    Li Ping-bien's luxuriant cinematography infuses
the film with golden tones, lending a nostalgic touch.
Employing static deep focus and long takes, the
camera gazes on the characters—Li, his family, and his
peers—as they move in and out of the frame, going
about their everyday lives. Dimly lit interior spaces are
often framed by a door or a screen in the foreground;
characters act in the middle ground while more obscure
activities go on in the background. Often much of the
frame remains in shadow.

There are no close-ups to lay bare the emotions of the characters. As viewers, we need to be comfortable with our role as spectators, as if we were watching puppet theater from a distance. Even Li looks back at his own life as if he were watching a performance. Sitting in front of the camera, he talks directly to us about fortune and fate; what happens in life, he explains, is often beyond our control, and when fortune and fate take over, we can only sit back and watch.

LA FRANCES HUI
Senior Program Officer, Cultural Programs and Performing Arts, Asia Society

Putney Swope

1969, Robert Downey

SCREENPLAY: Robert Downey

CAST: Arnold Johnson, Mel Brooks, Laura Greene, Antonio Fargas, Eric Krupnick, Pepi Hermine, Ruth Hermine, Allen Garfield, Stan Gottlieb

U.S.; B & W AND COLOR

Director Robert Downey Sr.'s *Putney Swope*, an acerbic lampoon of the advertising industry, was one of the first movies to come out of the age of irony. It's the story of Swope (Arnold Johnson), a black man who, surprisingly for the time, becomes the head of a struggling all-white Madison Avenue advertising agency. His first order of business is to replace all Caucasians with an array of '60s-era Black Power stereotypes, until only one white person (played by the great character actor Stan Gottlieb) remains at the agency. Swope then proceeds to bust one advertising taboo after another, and Downey creates a series of biting parodic commercials that are tame by today's standards but were shocking when the film was released. One, for an acne cream,

romantically pairs a black boy and white girl long
before interracial contact on TV was "acceptable." Time
may have dulled some of *Putney Swope*'s hilarity, but it
remains a milestone of alternative filmmaking.

STEVEN HELLER
Columnist, The New York Times Book Review, *art director,
and writer*

NOTE: The director's son, Robert Downey Jr., makes his film debut
here as an infant.

Q

Queen of Outer Space
1958, Edward Bernds

SCREENPLAY: Charles Beaumontand and Ben Hecht (story)
CAST: Zsa Zsa Gabor, Eric Fleming, Dave Willock, Laurie Mitchell,
Lisa Davis, Paul Birch, Patrick Waltz, Barbara Darrow,
Marilyn Buferd, Joi Lansing
U.S.

I love the Gabors. I think of them as a higher life form.
Zsa Zsa has always been my favorite, because she "gets
the joke" and embraces her Gabordom. The pinnacle
of her career was *Queen of Outer Space*, a delightful
example of "I can see the string!" sci-fi. The year is
1958, and four astronauts—all of them dead ringers for
Ward Cleaver—crash-land on Venus. An early highlight
is a bit by Joi Lansing, Marilyn Monroe–ing all over
the place as one of the Ward Cleavers' girlfriends. She
comes to bid her man good-bye wearing a strapless
evening gown, a chiffon wrap, and rhinestone-studded
gauntlets. (She's a welder by day and a drag queen
by night.)

Venus, it develops, is populated solely by Warner
Bros. starlets dressed up like hatcheck girls at the Copa.
Their leader is the evil Yllana (I could get into a rant
about how all non-beautiful women *must* be evil—but
this film is too silly to get one's panties in a bunch
over). Finally we meet Zsa Zsa, who plays Talleah, the
only girl on Venus with a Hungarian accent (throughout, she refers to the Ward Cleavers as "ze Erzmen").
The simple fact that Zsa Zsa Gabor is the planet's
leading scientist gives one pause. The evil queen comes
on to Zsa Zsa's favorite Ward Cleaver, at which Zsa
Zsa turns to the camera and pouts, "I hayd her. I hayd

dot Qvinn!" When I saw this film at a revival house, the audience stood and cheered at that point.

The Copa girls and the Ward Cleavers team up to overthrow Queen Yllana, and much zaniness ensues (including an attack by a hilarious giant rubber spider, which had even an arachnophobe like myself laughing helplessly). Some of the humor, I might add, is intentional (especially from the goofiest of the Ward Cleavers, Dave Willock, whom you'll recognize from about a million 1960s sitcoms). But with lines like "Twenty-six million miles from earth, and the little dolls are just the same!" it's your choice whether to laugh with or at *Queen of Outer Space.*

EVE GOLDEN
Writer

R

Raise the Red Lantern
see p. 199

Rendezvous with Annie
1946, Allan Dwan

SCREENPLAY: Mary Loos and Richard Sale
CAST: Eddie Albert, Faye Marlowe, Gail Patrick, Philip Reed,
C. Aubrey Smith, Raymond Walburn, William Frawley
U.S.; B & W

During WWII and right after, Hollywood made quite a few low-budget, unadorned movies about struggling couples. These films looked at the strains brought on by war and various attempts to adjust to its aftermath with the greatest care—you feel as though there's an unstated fear shared by everyone behind the camera that the characters and their emotions will come undone if they're not treated with the utmost respect. The late, great John Berry's wonderful 1946 movie *From This Day Forward*, about a young vet and his new bride trying to make a go of it in New York City, is one title that comes immediately to mind. Edward Dmytryk's *Till the End of Time*, which got the jump on *The Best Years of Our Lives* by a few months, features a remarkably delicate romance between psychically scarred vet Guy Madison (looking very much like Brad Pitt) and an ethereal Dorothy McGuire as a young woman who's lost her husband in the war. Delmer Daves's *The Very Thought of You* is an extremely modest film with little of the awesome power of his *Pride of the Marines* (the movie William Wyler screened for his crew before he made *Best Years*), but its portrait of a hasty marriage between a young woman and a young man in uniform has a marvelous, heartfelt simplicity.

I think my favorite is Allan Dwan's lilting, lyrical *Rendezvous with Annie*. Dwan started working in movies right at the beginning—in 1909 to be exact, at Essanay Studios. He made his last movie in 1961. Along the way he directed everything from two-reelers to costume epics, Shirley Temple vehicles to films noirs. By 1946, his technique was remarkably fluid and self-assured. Like all of Dwan's best movies, *Rendezvous with Annie* has a good, simple premise. Jeffrey Dolan, a G.I. stationed in wartime London, pines for his wife back home. Two of his friends spirit him onto their plane for a transatlantic run and promise to have him back before his three-day pass is up. He goes to New Jersey for eighteen blissful hours with his beloved Annie, makes her swear that she will never tell anyone he's gone AWOL and never refer to it in her letters, and gets back to London just in time. After the war has ended, he goes home to find all his friends and neighbors looking at him with a mixture of sympathy, pity, and comic disdain. Annie has had a baby, but since his visit was supposed to be a secret she hasn't been able to tell anyone who the father is. Thus Jeffrey's comic predicament.

The film stars Eddie Albert as Jeffrey, and he gives an extremely soulful performance. Albert has an interesting trait that he and Dwan exploit to great effect: he works at a slightly slower pace than the one set by his director and his fellow actors, creating the effect of a genial audience member who's accidentally wandered into a vaudeville skit and become the unwitting straight man. Fittingly for a movie about life during wartime, *Rendezvous with Annie* is the story of a man whose wife means so much to him that he's willing to go through almost anything to see her and then to clear her name.

That sense of devotion is felt at any given instant, and it gives the movie an uncommon warmth and a well-earned uplift. It also informs the beautiful moment when Jeffrey and Annie first see each other.

Jeffrey arrives by train at night, and he's told Annie that they have to be secretive, because no one must know he's there. Dwan shoots their reunion across the expanse of a dark, empty street and puts the couple at opposite diagonal ends of the frame. They walk tentatively toward each other, and when they realize they're once again in the same town, on the same street, after so much time apart, they run into each other's arms. Dwan puts all his hard-won knowledge of pacing, build-up, and composition to work to create an exceptionally fine image here, which comes off like a Norman Rockwell *Saturday Evening Post* cover without the all-American mawkishness. It's one of the few moments of perfect happiness in movies.

KENT JONES
Film critic, writer, and director

Zhang Yimou

Raise the Red Lantern
1991, Zhang Yimou
SCREENPLAY: Ni Zhen; based on the novella *Wives and Concubines,* by Su Tong
CAST: Gong Li, He Caifei, Ma Jingwu, Cao Cuifen, Jin Shuyuan, Kong Lin
CHINA/HONG KONG/TAIWAN; IN MANDARIN

Ju Dou
1990, Zhang Yimou and Yang Fengliang
SCREENPLAY: Lui Heng, based on the novella *Fuxi Fuxi,* by Liu Heng
CAST: Gong Li, Li Bao-tian, Li Wei, Zhang Yi, Zheng Jian
JAPAN/CHINA; IN MANDARIN

One of my favorite movies is *Raise the Red Lantern*, an intensely quiet and beautiful film by Chinese director Zhang Yimou. Zhang's films teach us about life in earlier times (through closely portraying the details of antiquated houses, settings, and everyday objects) while at the same time, they deliver political messages, through metaphor, about life in contemporary China. *Raise the Red Lantern* is set in the dynastic past, with the entire story—of a young girl entering the household of a wealthy man and his other wives and concubines—unfolding within a traditional Chinese house with a courtyard. The sense of confinement is intense (the characters never leave their home) and it enhances the film's emotional depth.

Ju Dou also takes place in the past—in this case, the pre-Communist '20s. Zhang chose this period in an attempt to avoid censorship, but the film was still banned in China. Like *Raise the Red Lantern*, *Ju Dou* is intensely quiet. One scene in particular contains one of the most beautiful and powerful images I've seen on film: red-dyed cloth, yards and yards of it, spilling over a wooden railing. It's simple, direct, and frightfully evocative. The camera work is so amazing you feel as if you are inside the picture.

HEATHER STELIGA
Associate Director of Communication, Miami Art Museum

Repulsion

1965, Roman Polanski

SCREENPLAY: Roman Polanski and Gérard Brach
CAST: Catherine Deneuve, Ian Hendry, John Fraser,
Yvonne Furneaux, Patrick Wymark, James Villiers
U.K.; B & W

Roman Polanski's *Repulsion* is a brilliantly depicted study of a descent into madness. Polanski uses long, elegant sequences of visual storytelling without dialogue. He vividly captures the psychological state of a young woman (Catherine Deneuve) by physicalizing her apartment, which becomes the inside of her mind. Fascinating and disturbing.

BETTE GORDON
Professor of Film, Columbia University, and director

Return from the Ashes
1965, J. Lee Thompson

SCREENPLAY: Julius J. Epstein; based on the novel by
Hubert Monteilhet
CAST: Maximilian Schell, Samantha Eggar, Ingrid Thulin,
Herbert Lom, Talitha Pol
U.K.; B & W

"No one may enter the theater after Fabi enters her bath!"

This was the poster tagline for *Return from the Ashes*,
a smart, eerie thriller that has all but disappeared into
obscurity. As a teenager in Houston, I saw it during
its brief 1965 theatrical run. I was drawn to the film
by my desire to see Samantha Eggar again, as she had
recently caused a sensation in William Wyler's *The
Collector*. I hadn't seen Ingrid Thulin in anything (give
me a break—it was Texas in the '60s!), but I had heard
of Ingmar Bergman's films, so at least I recognized her
name. I was blown away by Thulin's performance and
haunted by John Dankworth's musical score. *Return
from the Ashes* is about a doctor who survives a World
War II concentration camp and returns home (after
being presumed dead) to discover that her scheming
husband is romantically involved with her stepdaughter
from a previous marriage. I won't say more, so you can
experience this gem for yourself.

JOHN KIRK
Film archivist and writer

Roma, città aperta
see *Open City*

Room at the Top
see p. 186

Ruggles of Red Gap
1935, Leo McCarey

SCREENPLAY: Walter DeLeon, Harlan Thompson, and
Humphrey Pearson; based on the novel by Harry Leon Wilson
CAST: Charles Laughton, Mary Boland, Charles Ruggles,
ZaSu Pitts, Roland Young, Leila Hyams, Maude Eburne,
Lucien Littlefield, James Burke
U.S.; B & W

I'm a great fan of forgotten comedies. My favorite comedy (and one of my favorite movies) is an obscure 1935 movie, *Ruggles of Red Gap*, starring Charles Laughton.

Laughton plays Marmaduke Ruggles, an English butler in the service of the Earl of Burnstead. While on a trip to Paris, the Earl loses his man Ruggles in a poker match to Egbert Floud of Red Gap, Washington. Ruggles's sense of responsibility compels him to honor the Earl's bet, and Floud (played, by the way, by actor Charlie Ruggles), a newly rich man from the American West, finds himself with a gentleman's gentleman.

What follows is sublime comedy as Ruggles tries to teach Floud to be proper, and Floud, with a good deal more success, teaches Ruggles how to get drunk. Their Parisian adventures alone would make a fantastic film. Just when you think it can't get any better, the pair sails off to America and heads West—and suddenly the tables are turned. In the end, the English servant discovers the true meaning of liberty, and the desire to be a free man.

A film like *Ruggles of Red Gap* is a welcome reminder that there was a time when major studios made small movies with good directors, good actors, and truly great scripts.

ADAM DURITZ
Songwriter

Running on Empty

1988, Sidney Lumet

SCREENPLAY: Naomi Foner
CAST: Christine Lahti, River Phoenix, Judd Hirsch, Jonas Abry,
Martha Plimpton, Ed Crowley, L. M. Kit Carson, Steven Hill,
Augusta Dabney, David Margulies
U.S.

Running on Empty is one of the most profound films
I've ever seen. The first time I saw it, I was so moved I
was sure I'd been manipulated, so I went back to see it
again. I was wiped out a second time.

Among its many attributes is a unique portrayal of
teenage life. Martha Plimpton and River Phoenix play
young lovers, and their characters and portrayals are
elegant, intelligent, and wise. Judd Hirsch and Christine
Lahti turn in fine performances as Phoenix's parents.
But Steven Hill, who is in the film for about eight minutes, delivers the single best piece of acting I've
ever seen.

Hill plays Annie's (Lahti) father. His scene features
no fancy camera work and no music. And yet, each
time I see it, I am devastated. Watching Hill is like
seeing someone with his skin off. Sitting at a restaurant
table, he barely raises his voice and doesn't gesture
or make faces, but yet I was aware of every fleeting
thought that ran through his mind. Hill presents the
endlessly shifting panorama of feelings Donald has for
his daughter and, in turn, how he covers them up. Hill
does this without showing off, without "performing,"
and without even seeming to care if anyone is watching
at all. I was so inspired by Hill's performance that I
called him up to find out how he did it. He thought I
was joking.

The film has a rich, complex script by Naomi Foner and is brilliantly directed by Sidney Lumet, a director who does everything he can to divert attention from himself. He runs away from the "beautiful shot" and the "actor's moment." All of his films are rooted in reality, almost to the point of naturalism, a style that serves *Running on Empty* perfectly. I can't recommend this film highly enough.

ALAN ARKIN
Actor

S

Safe in Hell

1931, William A. Wellman

SCREENPLAY: Houston Branch; based on the play by
Houston Branch
CAST: Dorothy Mackaill, Donald Cook, Ralf Harolde, John Wray,
Ivan Simpson, Victor Varconi, Nina Mae McKinney,
Charles Middleton, Clarence Muse, Gustav von Seyffertitz
U.S.; B & W

William Wellman's 1931 melodrama, *Safe in Hell*, starts
at whirlwind speed: a call girl accidentally kills her john,
goes on the lam, and finds refuge on a Caribbean island
that has no extradition treaty with the U.S. Once she
has settled into the island's flyblown hotel, inhabited by
a grotesque assortment of fugitives, the film takes on
a mood of languorous corruption worthy of Brecht's
Threepenny Opera. Of the many amazingly unfettered
pre-Code films—*Employees' Entrance*, *Skyscraper Souls*,
Female, and so many more—this is one of the most
extreme and unpredictable.

GEOFFREY O'BRIEN
Editor in Chief, Library of America, and author

Salesman

1969, Albert Maysles, David Maysles, and Charlotte Zwerin

CAST: Jamie Baker, Paul Brennan, Melbourne I. Feltman,
Raymond Martos, Margaret McCarron, Charles McDevitt,
Kennie Turner
U.S.; B & W; DOCUMENTARY

The Maysles brothers' brilliant 1969 documentary,
Salesman, provides a riveting view of the American dream,
a place where commerce, faith, hucksterism, and despair

collide. It is the story of four Bible salesmen trudging through working-class America, preying on its broke (and broken) families. While hardly unheralded, *Salesman* is remembered more as a vital moment in the history of documentary film than as a great film in and of itself.

But look again. It is a prescient, haunting piece of art. The look of it, in black-and-white 16 mm, is unmistakably 1968. Yet, with the Christian Right ascendant in American politics, *Salesman* seems weirdly revelatory.

Ironically, the audience that attended the sensational New York opening in 1969 considered the film nostalgic, thinking that the era of church-bound Americana was on the wane. But boy, were they wrong.

Salesman is more than a portrait of class and capitalist culture. It's a strong film, with drama at its center. It revolves around Paul Brennan, a weary salesman whose touch is fading as he battles despair and loneliness. Paul's dwindling sales spark his increasingly anxious, darkly funny reveries. At the same time, his fellow salesmen treat him with the growing silence and cramped discomfort worthy of a distinctly modern leper: the failure.

Throughout this film, the Maysles brothers let the camera roll and the audience watch, leaving the moral ambiguity of the salesmen intact. The final impact, then, is all the more powerful, stark, and universal.

BRIAN ACKERMAN
Programming Director, Jacob Burns Film Center

The Saragossa Manuscript
see p. 216

The Savage Eye
1960, Ben Maddow, Sidney Meyers, and Joseph Strick

SCREENPLAY: Ben Maddow, Sidney Meyers, and Joseph Strick

CAST: Barbara Baxley, Gary Merrill, Herschel Bernardi, Jean Hidey
U.S.; B & W

A unique blend of documentary and dramatic feature, *The Savage Eye* is one of the strangest films I've ever seen. And the bleakest. And the best. You'll not find the dark side of the American Dream more beautifully and sadly expressed than in this sixty-seven-minute masterpiece.

Judith is young, pretty, newly divorced, newly fallen. She leads us through her days in 1950s Los Angeles: faith-healing ceremonies, pet cemeteries, strip joints, roller-derby arenas, transvestite parties. This is real footage of real people, with Judith and her story somehow seamlessly inserted into each scene. Throughout the film, in a beat voice-over that is sometimes poignant, sometimes silly for trying too hard, she argues with an unseen male voice that claims to be "your angel. Your double. That vile dreamer. Your conscience. Your God. Your ghost."

Directed by Ben Maddow, Sidney Meyers, and Academy Award–winning Joseph Strick, *The Savage Eye* was shot by two-time Academy Award winner Haskell Wexler, renowned photographer Helen Levitt, and Jack Couffer over a period of several years. The film is completely ambitious, torrid, and compelling.

STEVEN HOFFMAN
Creative Director, Sports Illustrated Magazine

NOTE: The DVD edition of *The Savage Eye* features a seemingly incongruous bonus: Joseph Stricks's Academy Award–winning *Interviews with My Lai Veterans.* A totally different style of documentary, by an obviously great documentarian, this straightforward film focuses on five veterans of the My Lai massacre. It explores how such an atrocity could occur, and what it means to those who carried it out.

The Savage Is Loose
1974, George C. Scott

SCREENPLAY: Frank De Felitta and Max Ehrlich
CAST: John David Carson, Lee Montgomery, George C. Scott,
Trish Van Devere
U.S./MEXICO

I have long been fascinated by films directed by successful actors. With that in mind, I recommend George C. Scott's *The Savage Is Loose*, costarring Scott's then wife, Trish Van Devere, and John David Carson. This 1974 film explores the bizarre evolution of a family shipwrecked on an island. A father, mother, and their young son manage to survive in total isolation until the boy grows up and begins to compete with his father for the mother's affection. What can only be described as a biblical conflict ensues, building to an unsettling and fascinating end. From the opening sequence, the film draws us into the minds of these beleaguered characters. Scott did a marvelous job all around.

ALEC BALDWIN
Actor

Scrooge
see *A Christmas Carol*

Series 7: The Contenders
2001, Daniel Minahan

SCREENPLAY: Daniel Minahan
CAST: Brooke Smith, Marylouise Burke, Glenn Fitzgerald,
Michael Kaycheck, Richard Venture, Merritt Wever,
Donna Hanover, Angelina Phillips
U.S.

I saw this film on opening night, and I was sure it was going to be a huge sensation. Instead, after staying in theaters for only a short while, it disappeared. The acting is superb, the script nearly perfect, and the shooting gritty and gorgeous. What happened?

Even those who love violent films like *Reservoir Dogs* are disturbed, repelled, and nauseated by *Series 7*. It's not because it's more violent or cynical than what they're used to seeing. It's because they—we—see ourselves in the film. *Series 7* is Daniel Minahan's vision of the reality-TV show, *The Contenders*, in which contestants are chosen by lottery to kill or be killed. But instead of the stylized hoods who typically blow one another's heads off in most cool indie films, *Series 7* features a pregnant woman and a sensitive artist. The more we see ourselves in these characters, the more uncomfortable we become. I love a good squirm.

NELLY REIFLER
Writer

The Servant

1963, Joseph Losey

SCREENPLAY: Harold Pinter; based on the novel by Robin Maugham
CAST: Dirk Bogarde, Sarah Miles, Wendy Craig, James Fox, Catherine Lacey, Richard Vernon, Anne Firbank, Doris Knox, Patrick Magee, Harold Pinter
U.K.; B & W

If the mark of a great film is that it sticks in your mind forevermore, that you can watch it countless times without being bored by it, and that even the minor characters give memorable performances, then this 1963 Joseph Losey drama fits the bill. Set in a townhouse in Chelsea, just off the mecca of the decade, the King's

Road, *The Servant* brilliantly depicts a master/servant relationship. The servant, Hugo (Dirk Bogarde), is manipulative and mysterious. His master, Tony (James Fox), is upper-class, weak, and naive. The film charts Tony's descent from a model of social acceptability into decadence. He is engaged to Susan (Wendy Craig), a nice girl from the country, but by the film's end, she has left to go back home and Tony's house is full of prostitutes—a decline into debauchery wholly engineered by his scheming servant, Hugo.

The film includes one of the most erotic moments ever filmed. Hugo convinces Tony that he needs more help in the house and finds a young girl, Vera (Sarah Miles), to be a maid. The first time Tony sets eyes on her, she is in the kitchen. He gets no farther than the door. Vera is a '60s cutie: big hair, huge eyes, striped jumper accentuating her ample curves. Their eyes meet. Nothing is said for a while. It's summer. She's not wearing shoes. She shuffles her weight nervously from one hip to the other. "It's hot in here," she says. The erotic tension is palpable—the silence broken only by a faucet dripping in the kitchen sink.

Two days before writing this piece, I was staying with some friends and mentioned that I had chosen to write about this scene. They asked me if I remembered who had played the maid. When I told them Sarah Miles, they exclaimed, "She's our next door neighbor, and she's coming to dinner!" Over dinner we talked about the film and Sarah remembered her parents visiting London shortly after the film's release. They said only two things: "You have sullied the family name" and "The servants will leave." Hugo would have enjoyed that.

CHARLES MARSDEN-SMEDLEY
Museum and exhibition designer

Shadows
see p. 80

The Sin of Nora Moran
1933, Phil Goldstone

SCREENPLAY: Frances Hyland
CAST: Zita Johann, Paul Cavanagh, Alan Dinehart, Claire Du Brey,
John Miljan, Henry B. Walthall, Sarah Padden, Ann Brody,
Aggie Herring, Syd Saylor, Harvey Clark, Otis Harlan
U.S.; B & W

The Sin of Nora Moran is one of only a handful of movies that can be considered "one of a kind"—films that have no precedent and inspire no imitations.

When UCLA Film and Television Archive preservation officer Robert Gitt invited some friends (me included) to a screening of *Nora Moran* a few years ago, all I knew about the film was that it had a minor reputation as an independent feature from the '30s and that its one-sheet poster was the most salacious I'd ever seen for a pre-Code film.

Film historian David Pierce had suggested *Nora Moran* as a candidate for preservation, but before taking it on, Gitt was interested in getting a film-buff reaction. The 16 mm print shown that evening wasn't of the highest quality, but I doubt that even a bum VHS copy could dim *Nora Moran*'s brilliance. The film is neither classic nor camp but a unique melange of both. Although there was one dissenter, the rest of Gitt's audience encouraged him to go ahead with the project. He was able to secure the original nitrate negatives, and the restored *Nora Moran* was exhibited that summer at UCLA's Tenth Festival of Preservation.

Now, don't confuse *The Sin of Nora Moran* with great moviemaking. Think of it instead as a hidden treasure that was always a bit tarnished. The film's extremely low budget hurts it at times, the first seven or eight minutes are stiffly acted and static, and the plot is nothing special (victimized woman descends into a life of degradation). But it's the telling of the story that elevates *Nora Moran* into a class of its own, accomplished by a hypnotically moving camera and a series of flashbacks, flash-forwards, and flashbacks-within-flashbacks so complex that the entire narrative structure quickly ceases to make sense, assuming a free-form, dreamlike quality. Haunting, hallucinatory, artistic, exploitive—*The Sin of Nora Moran* may be the best B-movie of the '30s.

JERE GULDIN
Film preservationist, UCLA Film & Television Archive

Smile

1975, Michael Ritchie

SCREENPLAY: Jerry Belson

CAST: Bruce Dern, Barbara Feldon, Michael Kidd, Geoffrey Lewis, Nicholas Pryor, Joan Prather, Melanie Griffith, Annette O'Toole, Maria O'Brien, Colleen Camp

U.S.

"Raised on hamburgers and soda pop, she's got a winning smile that's hard to top. A credit to her family, the ideal teen, she's all America's daughter, she's a beauty queen."

That's the slogan on the poster for *Smile*, one of the most underappreciated films I've seen. Hilarious and insightful, it exposes the void at the core of certain rural, middle-class lives in America. Made in 1974, it was directed by Michael Ritchie, photographed by Conrad Hall, written by Jerry Belson, and starred Bruce Dern, Barbara Feldon, and thirty-three "Young

American Misses." I served as the second assistant director on the film when it was shooting in Santa Rosa.

This sly satire focuses on a California beauty pageant, a "meat show," with eight Hollywood actresses (including Melanie Griffith, Colleen Camp, and Annette O'Toole) and twenty-five local girls. Michael Kidd does an amazing turn as the pageant's choreographer.

The film was shot in sequence and the last few pages of the script were removed so that no one knew who would win. True to the theory that more pageants are won by an unknown contestant than by a high-profile beauty queen, the winner was not one of our Hollywood leading ladies, but a local girl. On that glittering night, we all got so caught up in the event that we believed it was real. When Shawn Christianson, "Miss Fountain Valley," was crowned California's Young Miss, she wept—and so did we. You'll laugh a lot at this film, and you might even cry a little too.

LAURENCE MARK
Producer

Songs from the Second Floor
2000, Roy Andersson

SCREENPLAY: Roy Andersson
CAST: Lars Nordh, Stefan Larsson, Lucio Vucina, Peter Roth, Klas-Gösta Olsson, Hanna Eriksson
SWEDEN/DENMARK/NORWAY; IN SWEDISH

It's Monday morning in a big city. The weather is fine. People are going to work. There are traffic jams in the downtown area. And, by the way, capitalism has collapsed. It's the end of the world! No more Wall Street! No more NASDAQ!

Films on similar themes are often prodigal of havoc and hysteria: street violence, immorality, the rise of totalitarianism. We've seen it before, in *Metropolis*, *Escape from New York*, *Twelve Monkeys*, and *Brazil*. But *Songs from the Second Floor* (inspired by a quote from a poem by Peruvian-born artist César Vallejo) takes an original and compelling view of doomsday with the subdued elegance of a deadpan comedy—a *Monty Python* farce told in the style of a Beckett play.

How will we find out that global society has fallen apart? According to Roy Andersson's award-winning fable (it amply deserved its Special Jury Prize at Cannes), things go awry, but we barely notice it: streets are unusually congested; more people are laid off from their jobs; and desperate for money, corporations create new anxieties just as they did at the dawn of the year 2000. (Remember Y2K?)

The apocalypse in *Songs from the Second Floor* is told through a sequence of beautifully composed vignettes. A gently unfolding catalog of very strange events, this soft-spoken journal of a cataclysm has the aplomb of a fairy tale: executives invite a clairvoyant with a crystal ball to discuss a long-range plan; a failed entrepreneur decides that Christ's birth is an opportunity to make money, but ultimately fails; unable to cope with recession, the government considers human sacrifices to aid economic recovery. With a dreamlike pace, chaos and madness unfold around the most unlikely heroes: those who "sit down" and refuse to participate in the orgy of self-destruction. These people were called poets. In the dictionary of neoconservatism, they are defined as lunatics or, worse, passive-aggressive terrorists. *Songs from the Second Floor* invites us to empathize with their civil disobedience, in the hope that our own refusal to join in will put an end to the race toward cultural suicide. Beloved are the ones who sit down.

PAOLO CHERCHI USAI
Writer and director

Spanish Dracula
see *Drácula*

The Spirit of the Beehive (El espíritu de la colmena)
see p. 216

Spoorloos
see *The Vanishing*

Stardust Memories
1980, Woody Allen

SCREENPLAY: Woody Allen
CAST: Woody Allen, Charlotte Rampling, Jessica Harper, Marie-Christine Barrault, Tony Roberts, Daniel Stern, Amy Wright, Helen Hanft, John Rothman
U.S.; B & W

An overlooked classic, *Stardust Memories* is Woody Allen's homage to European filmmaking, with an affectionate wink at Fellini's *8 1/2*. This episodic journey through childhood memories, adult fantasies, self-analysis, ennui, and enlightenment is as intelligent and funny as any American comedy ever made. It stars the beautiful and talented European actresses Charlotte Rampling and Marie-Christine Barrault, with support from regulars like Tony Roberts, Louise Lasser, and Jessica Harper. It's shot in gorgeous black and white by the great Gordon Willis. Production designer Mel Bourne provides a striking seaside landscape and a brilliant New York apartment interior. It's a Woody Allen film festival of magic tricks, vaudeville bits, musical comedy numbers, philosophical aliens, sophisticated studio executives, hot-air balloons, and a great jazz score featuring "Stardust" by Louis Armstrong.

ROGER PARADISO
Writer, producer, and director

A Film Cure

The Spirit of the Beehive (El espíritu de la colmena)
1973, Víctor Erice
SCREENPLAY: Víctor Erice, Francisco J. Querejeta, and Angel Fernández Santos
CAST: Fernando Fernán Gómez, Teresa Gimpera, Ana Torrent, Isabel Tellería, José Villasante, Laly Soldevila
SPAIN; IN SPANISH

The Saragossa Manuscript
1965, Wojciech Has
SCREENPLAY: Tadeusz Kwiatkowski; based on the novel by Jan Potocki
CAST: Zbigniew Cybulski, Kazimierz Opalinski, Iga Cembrzynska, Joanna Jedryka, Franciszek Pieczka
POLAND; B & W; IN POLISH

In the Realm of the Senses (Ai no corrida)
1976, Nagisa Oshima
SCREENPLAY: Nagisa Oshima
CAST: Tatsuya Fuji, Eiko Matsuda, Aoi Nakajima, Meika Seri
JAPAN/FRANCE; IN JAPANESE

Film today is by definition a public, democratic, and mass-market phenomenon. People attend in person, they vote with their wallets, and every schoolchild knows the latest box-office grosses. In such a world, film is the very antithesis of a secret. But this was not always the case. As recently as the 1970s—before pay-per-view, summer blockbusters, DVDs, *Entertainment Tonight*, and the Internet—a film could easily be overlooked, lost, or suppressed. A film could be a private matter, a personal secret.

In 1976 I read an article in the *New York Times* about a film called *The Spirit of the Beehive*, which had been made in 1973. Directed by Víctor Erice, it had been banned by the ultraconservative Spanish government and still had not been released in the United States. The author of the article, Richard Eder, had seen it at the Telluride Film Festival and called it "the best Spanish film ever made. It is also one of the two or three most haunting films about children ever made. It is perhaps one of the dozen best pictures made anywhere in the past half-dozen years." Eder's article piqued the interest of an East Side art-house exhibitor, and the film opened in Manhattan in October of 1976.

I had taken a month off from work to recover from a broken heart. I told everyone I was going on holiday, but instead stayed in town. I spent most days and nights at the movies (including every film in the New York Film Festival). I saw Erice's film at the 10:30 a.m. showing on the first day of its run. With its seamless blend of the political and the personal and its enormous heart, the film changed the way I look at movies. When I returned from my "vacation," I told everyone I knew about this brilliant film. It had been my secret, it had belonged to me, but I willingly passed it on to others.

The Spirit of the Beehive was not my first secret film experience. In college I spent a lot of my free time at film societies, where on a spring evening in 1970 I saw a 16 mm print of *The Saragossa Manuscript*, the surrealist masterpiece directed by Pole Wojciech Has, based on the 1813 novel by Count Jan Potocki. Like Pasolini's *Decameron* or Buñuel's *Discreet Charm of the Bourgeoisie*, it is a story within a story within a story, and it enthralled me. During the succeeding years I heard no mention of the film until, while living in London in the early '80s, I saw it listed as the midnight show at the legendary Electric Cinema on Portobello Road. I was the only person in the audience, and when I left, I ran into the projectionist. We started talking, and I mentioned that the film seemed shorter than when I last saw it and that I remembered it ending differently. He looked at me in awe. "I've never met anyone who's seen it with the original ending," he said. "The only prints I know are missing the final scenes. You're a lucky guy."

There was also a time (though it is difficult to imagine in the age of Internet pornography) when sex did not dominate mainstream American culture, so it was an event for a film (like *Last Tango in Paris* or *I Am Curious Yellow*) to explore a sexually explicit theme. At the New York Film Festival in 1976 (during my self-imposed exile) I bought a ticket to *In the Realm of the Senses*, written and directed by Nagisa Oshima. But on the night of the screening, a spokesperson for the festival announced that the film had been declared obscene and seized by customs officials in Los Angeles. They showed us another of Oshima's films and promised to screen *In the Realm of the Senses* once it was released. The appointed day finally came, and we assembled at MoMA to witness Oshima's transcendentally still meditation on fellatio. Toward the end of this beautifully constructed and very sexy film, I felt a tap on my shoulder and was handed a small pink card by the woman seated behind me. The card proposed a very personal reenactment of the scene that we were witnessing on the screen. I respectfully declined—I was, after all, with someone—but as I watched the end of the film, I marveled at the power of the cinema, and the boundless urge to share its secrets.

GEORGE SHEANSHANG
Entertainment attorney

A Stolen Life
1946, Curtis Bernhardt

SCREENPLAY: Catherine Turney; based on the novel by Karel J. Benes
CAST: Bette Davis, Glenn Ford, Dane Clark, Walter Brennan, Charles Ruggles, Bruce Bennett, Peggy Knudsen, Esther Dale
U.S.; B & W

A Stolen Life stars Bette Davis in a memorable dual role as twins: one deep and soulful, the other tarty and shallow. This was Davis's first production for herself, and she hired director Curtis Bernhardt, screenwriter Catherine Turney, and her leading man, newcomer Glenn Ford.

Every time I watch it, it holds up for me. I feel it may have informed, for better or worse, many of my ideas about romantic love. Plus, it features one of the most spectacular sea-storm and boat-wreck scenes ever filmed.

ALLISON ANDERS
Director, screenwriter, and professor

Straight Time
1978, Ulu Grosbard

SCREENPLAY: Edward Bunker, Jeffrey Boam, and Alvin Sargent
(story); based on the novel *No Beast So Fierce*, by Edward Bunker
CAST: Dustin Hoffman, Theresa Russell, Gary Busey,
Harry Dean Stanton, M. Emmet Walsh, Rita Taggart, Kathy Bates,
Sandy Baron
U.S.

Never was a Dustin Hoffman movie released with less
fanfare than this one, yet it contains one of his greatest,
toughest, and least affected performances. Hoffman
plays a ruthless, self-destructive ex-con back on the
streets after six years in the joint, a time bomb waiting
to explode. And explode he does, in an escalating series
of robberies masterfully staged by director Ulu Grosbard.
It's a gritty, unsentimental portrait of L.A.'s seedy underbelly, with an extraordinary ensemble cast that includes
Harry Dean Stanton, Gary Busey, M. Emmet Walsh,
and then newcomer Theresa Russell as a scared, empty
California girl along for the ride. Hoffman was originally
going to direct the film himself but changed his mind
and turned the reins over to Grosbard. They clashed during the making of the movie, but the sparks they created
are memorable—though largely unappreciated in 1978,
when Warner Bros. threw it away.

DAVID ANSEN
Movie critic, Newsweek

Stray Dog (Nora inu)
1949, Akira Kurosawa

SCREENPLAY: Akira Kurosawa and Ryuzo Kikushima
CAST: Toshirô Mifune, Takashi Shimura, Keiko Awaji, Isao Kimura
JAPAN; B & W; IN JAPANESE

Mention Akira Kurosawa, and stunning epics come to mind: *Rashômon*, *The Seven Samurai*, *Yojimbo*. But I prefer Kurosawa's smaller, non–period pieces: focused on daily Japanese life, they are haunting, atmospheric postcards that jot down the hopes and fears of life's bit players.

A striking example is *Stray Dog*, one of Kurosawa's earliest films. It opens with a disconcerting shot of a mangy, unloved mongrel, so beaten, bedraggled, and hungry that all it can do is bare its teeth.

Soon we are following Murakami, a novice homicide detective on a hunt, first for his stolen gun and then for the killer who is using it. Played by an intense young Toshirô Mifune (who went on to work with Kurosawa for most of his career), Murakami takes us on an increasingly desperate search through postwar Tokyo: down empty streets, into the spare, dimly lit suburbs, then back into putrid slums and heat-swamped *kyaba-kura*, or hostess bars.

It's clear that *Stray Dog* was inspired by Hollywood's hard-boiled film noirs, and the subtitles do a fine job translating the toughs' period colloquialisms. But there is a deeper, harder level to this film that is chilling. While any signs of U.S. Occupation Forces are absent (a result of rigid Occupation censorship), the ravages of war hang over all the scenes like a ghost. The killer, living on the same mean streets as the stray dog, has no job, no hope, no future. "Ever since he got home from the war, he's like a stranger," his older sister whispers sadly to the detective, as she looks out of the dilapidated shack that is her home. And when the good-natured police chief gives the despondent Murakami a pep talk, claiming that criminals are simply evil beings who ought to be eliminated without thought, the younger detective rebels: "I just can't bring myself to think that way yet. All those years in the war, so many men became beasts at the slightest provocation, over and over."

Suzanne Charlé
Editor and writer

The Stunt Man
1980, Richard Rush

SCREENPLAY: Lawrence B. Marcus; based on the novel by
Paul Brodeur
CAST: Peter O'Toole, Steve Railsback, Barbara Hershey,
Allen Garfield, Alex Rocco, Sharon Farrell, Adam Roarke,
Philip Bruns, Charles Bail
U.S.

The Stunt Man, directed by Richard Rush, is an entertaining, ambitious, and multilayered film. Combining the American tradition of exhilarating action with a European sensibility that questions and qualifies the action through crafty intelligence, *The Stunt Man*, much like François Truffaut's *Day for Night*, is nothing less than a celebration of filmmaking.

The Stunt Man saga began in 1971, when Rush read the best-selling novel by Paul Brodeur. It took six years to get independent financing because Rush's adaptation didn't fit into a clear category. The screenplay was eventually written by Lawrence Marcus (best known for *Petulia*) and the film was completed in 1978. But it would be two more years before the movie was released, as initially no major studio would take a chance on it. Despite rave reviews at film festivals, Hollywood feared it was too "arty" for mainstream audiences. *The Stunt Man* was finally acquired by 20th Century Fox after it won the Grand Prize at the Montreal Film Festival.

Pauline Kael was right to coin the term "slapstick metaphysics" for this movie. *The Stunt Man* playfully keeps us on our cinematic toes. As Rush explained when I interviewed him, "Almost every scene starts from one point of view and shifts; by the time the scene is over, you've either added a piece of information or changed the mood so that you're looking at the event through a different window. Each scene carries two or three of the four or five story elements. So you've got an interesting house of cards that is constantly teetering and building." Indeed. While Rush made a handful of commercially successful films—including *Getting Straight*, *Freebie and the Bean*, and Jack Nicholson biker movies like *Hells Angels on Wheels* and *Psych-Out*—*The Stunt Man* remains his towering achievement.

ANNETTE INSDORF
Director of Undergraduate Film Studies, Columbia University, and Professor, Graduate Film Division of the School of the Arts, Columbia University

Sullivan's Travels

1941, Preston Sturges

SCREENPLAY: Preston Sturges
CAST: Joel McCrea, Veronica Lake, Robert Warwick, William Demarest, Franklin Pangborn, Porter Hall, Byron Foulger, Margaret Hayes, Robert Greig, Eric Blore, Torben Meyer, Alan Bridge, Jimmy Conlin
U.S.; B & W

Sullivan's Travels revolves around the life of John L. Sullivan (Joel McCrea), a director who is experiencing a crisis of faith. Sullivan makes very successful comedies (several years' worth of "Ants in Your Pants" films), but wants to be taken seriously. With America in the throes of the Depression, he'd like to make a picture that portrays the tragic struggle of the common man, and call it *O Brother, Where Art Thou?* (The Coen brothers borrowed the title, as well as a theme or two.)

In what may be the funniest scene in the movie, Sullivan is chastised by two studio execs. They point out that, living as he does in a huge Hollywood mansion, Sullivan has no idea what the common man goes through. So, to their dismay, he hits the road disguised as a hobo. I don't want to reveal too much of the plot, but by the end, the film manages to be hysterical, romantic, and tragic. And not only does Sullivan find what he's looking for, but he also finds Veronica Lake.

ADAM DURITZ
Songwriter

Superman

1941, Max Fleischer and Dave Fleischer

SCREENPLAYS: Seymour Kneitel, Joe Shuster, Jerry Siegel, Izzy Sparber

VOICES: Bud Collyer, Joan Alexander, Jack Mercer

U.S.; ANIMATION; SHORT

In 1940, the animation studio of Max and Dave Fleischer (Max produced, Dave directed) was approached by Paramount to create a series of cartoon shorts to rival Disney's. The property Paramount wanted was *Superman*, which had debuted in the comics two years earlier. The Fleischers, who made their name on *Popeye the Sailor* and the Betty Boop series, were frankly not interested and said they would do it only if they received a budget of ninety thousand dollars per episode. This was unheard of at the time—the average cost of an animated short back then was ten thousand dollars, tops. To their astonishment, Paramount agreed. The Fleischers took the money and created what most animation historians consider to be the best short-form cartoons of the twentieth century.

These incredible seven-minute movies are like little comic-book poems you'll want to see again and again. These are genuine works of American cinematic art, though never shown on television and only rarely in theaters. The colors, the movement, the music, the design, the voices (Bud Collyer will always be Superman to me), the camera angles, the pacing, and the stunning use of silhouette and rotoscope—these guys were obviously big fans of Orson Welles (who is rumored to be the voice of one of the villains).

The Fleischers made seventeen *Superman* shorts in all, each one of them a gem. "The Mechanical Monsters" is probably the best, with a tracking shot of Superman taking off into the sky that will take your breath away. It also has a mad scientist, a secret underground lair, a fleet of giant evil robots, stolen jewels, and Lois Lane being lowered into a vat of boiling magma. Can the Man of Steel free himself from deadly electrical power lines in time to save her? Can he? *Can he?*

Sorry.

You've *got* to see these.

CHIP KIDD
Graphic designer and writer

RECOMMENDED READING: *Superman, The Complete History: The Life and Times of the Man of Steel*, by Les Daniels, illustrated by Chip Kidd. Chronicle Books, 1998.

Sweet Movie
1974, Dusan Makavejev

SCREENPLAY: Dusan Makavejev
CAST: Carole Laure, Pierre Clémenti, Anna Prucnal, Sami Frye,
Jane Mallett, Roy Callender, John Vernon
CANADA/FRANCE/WEST GERMANY; IN ENGLISH, FRENCH, POLISH,
AND SPANISH

No movie has been more provoking than Dusan
Makavejev's brilliant *Sweet Movie*, in which Carole
Laure plays the winner of the Miss Monde "most vir-
gin" contest and finds herself shuttled through a series
of sexual escapades involving, in no particular order, a
golden penis, a love cramp, and posing nude in melted
chocolate. In another strand of the film, Anna Planeta
(Anna Prucnal) sails a barge, filled to the brim with
sugar, luring children and sailors aboard.

I studied with Makavejev when I was seventeen,
and upon seeing the movie with him, I told him that I
was engaged by the political story lines, and beginning
to understand what he was trying to achieve with his
collage of documentary and fiction. He responded in
his deep gruff voice, "You Americans, you just need it
to be in color!" (Most all his earlier works are in black
and white.)

Despite the movie's experimental structure, there
are enormously moving moments, such as when sugar-
teased children's dead bodies come to life, as well as
the best documentary-to-fiction transition in cinema,
between Laure posing for an advertisement in melted
chocolate and documentary footage of a Yugoslavian
mass grave exhumation.

DAN ALGRANT
Filmmaker

Sweet Sweetback's Baadasssss Song
1971, Melvin Van Peebles

SCREENPLAY: Melvin Van Peebles
CAST: Simon Chuckster, Melvin Van Peebles, Hubert Scales,
John Dullaghan, West Gale, Niva Rochelle, Rhetta Hughes,
Nick Ferrari, John Amos, Mario Van Peebles
U.S.

As a child, whenever I told my father that I liked a
movie, whether it be *The Breakfast Club* or *Gandhi*, he
would always have the same response: "The best movie
I have ever seen is a movie called *Sweet Sweetback's
Baadasssss Song*." My parents saw the film when they
were living in Newark in the early '70s. It was a time of
racial strife in America, and the city was just recovering
from the infamous Newark riots of 1969. Years later,
when I was in college, I was assigned to read an article
on *Sweet Sweetback* for one of my classes, so I decided
to rent the movie.

The film opens in a brothel, where a young boy is
taken in, fed, and coerced into having sex with one of
the prostitutes. With this act he gets his name, Sweet
Sweetback. The credits roll and the cast is listed simply
as "The people of the black community."

I first watched this film twenty years after it was
made, but many of the issues brought up in the movie—
racist and abusive cops and the need for black people to
stick together—are still valid today. In the VHS copy I
rented, writer/director Melvin Van Peebles introduced
the film himself, explaining that his goal was to make
an entertaining movie with an important message. He
stressed that it was a movie made specifically for black
people, because there really weren't any films like it at
the time. But the success of *Sweet Sweetback* would
soon change that, as Hollywood took notice and began

making blaxploitation films. To anyone who is mildly interested in this genre or in Quentin Tarantino films, I quote my father, "The best movie I have ever seen is a movie called *Sweet Sweetback's Baadasssss Song.*"

INGRID BROMBERG KENNEDY
Graphic designer and gallerist

Symphony of Six Million

1932, Gregory La Cava

SCREENPLAY: Bernard Schubert and J. Walter Ruben
CAST: Ricardo Cortez, Irene Dunne, Anna Appel, Gregory Ratoff, Noel Madison, Lita Chevret, John St. Polis, Julie Haydon
U.S.; B & W

Symphony of Six Million is almost unknown today, but despite being made in 1932, its moral point is still valid. Much of its charm is also what is wrong with it. It's the story of a young boy named Felix who grows up in an immigrant Jewish neighborhood in New York's Lower East Side. After years of study and determination, Felix (Ricardo Cortez) becomes a doctor and leaves his local clinic to become a physician to high society matrons. Meanwhile, back in the Lower East Side, a girl named Jessica (a wonderfully miscast Irene Dunne) needs surgery, and Felix's father has a brain tumor. When he operates on his father, the musical score (by Max Steiner) plays the Kol Nidre, which doesn't seem quite right. His father dies, but Felix returns to his roots, opens a clinic, and, one assumes, cures Jessica. Corny? Yes. But it's also engaging, fast moving, and a fine example of why motion pictures are an invaluable document of the past.

RICHARD P. MAY
Former Vice President of Film Preservation, Warner Brothers

RECOMMENDED READING: Peter E. Dans, M.D., *Doctors in the Movies: Boil the Water and Just Say Aah.* Medi-Ed Press, 2000.

T

Tabu: A Story of the South Seas
1931, F. W. Murnau and Robert J. Flaherty

SCREENPLAY: F. W. Murnau and Robert J. Flaherty
CAST: Anne Chevalier, Matahi, Hitu, Jean, Jules, Kong Ah
U.S.; B & W; SILENT

A collaboration between the famous documentarian
Robert Flaherty and the legendary German director
F. W. Murnau, *Tabu: Story of the South Seas* is a
strange tale, beautifully shot (cinematographer Floyd
Crosby won an Oscar) and largely improvised with
nonactors. Although the visuals far overpower the story
itself, it's still a treat.

Murnau was known mainly for studio pictures (such as
Nosferatu, *Faust*, and *Sunrise*) but *Tabu* was shot on location using largely available light, which was fairly uncommon in filmmaking in 1931. Murnau died soon after the
film's release, leaving too short a film legacy. Had he lived,
he probably would have ascended to the popularity and
fame of his countrymen Fritz Lang and Ernst Lubitsch.

ERIC STOLTZ
Actor

Tales of Manhattan
1942, Julien Duvivier

SCREENPLAYS: Ben Hecht, Ferenc Molnár, Donald Ogden Stewart,
Samuel Hoffenstein, Alan Campbell
CAST: Charles Boyer, Rita Hayworth, Ginger Rogers, Henry Fonda,
Charles Laughton, Edward G. Robinson, Paul Robeson,
Ethel Waters, Eddie "Rochester" Anderson, Thomas Mitchell,
Cesar Romero, Gail Patrick, Roland Young, George Sanders
U.S.; B & W

Built around a unique five-part structure and featuring a string of unforgettable performances by a veritable laundry list of screen legends including Rita Hayworth, Henry Fonda, Ginger Rogers, and Charles Boyer, *Tales of Manhattan* offers an extraordinary array of delights.

A tailcoat is sent to the home of Paul Orman (Charles Boyer), a famous theater actor. As he tries on the exquisitely made garment, Orman learns that it comes with a disclaimer: it had been cursed by the man who made it. At the home of his lover (Rita Hayworth), Orman incurs the wrath of her husband, who shoots him. But Orman gets up and brushes himself off, then walks to his car and driver waiting outside, only to collapse into the backseat, having given the performance of his life.

The next segment, a frothy screwball comedy, reveals the secrets men hide in their coat pockets. Henry Fonda and Ginger Rogers play a delicious cat-and-mouse game around a sofa, a chair, and a cheating fiancé who ends up losing his bride to his best man. The following segments contain perhaps the most memorable performances of all—Charles Laughton as a struggling composer who is finally given the opportunity to conduct his life's work, and Edward G. Robinson as a man fallen on hard times who gets an invitation to his college reunion. Of course, both men get to wear the tailcoat, but to go into any more detail would rob the viewer of the film's greatest pleasures.

Watch this film and really understand the magic of cinema. The coat, without uttering one word, tells the whole story.

ANNE LANDSMAN
Screenwriter

The Tall Target

1951, Anthony Mann

SCREENPLAY: Art Cohn, George Worthing Yates, and
Daniel Mainwaring (as Geoffrey Homes)
CAST: Dick Powell, Paula Raymond, Adolphe Menjou,
Marshall Thompson, Ruby Dee, Richard Rober, Will Geer,
Florence Bates
U.S.; B & W

Anthony Mann was one of Hollywood's finest directors
in the '50s, and yet he is still not sufficiently appreciated. His outstanding pictures, such as *Border Incident*,
The Furies, *Devil's Doorway*, *The Naked Spur*, *The Far
Country*, *The Tin Star*, and *Man of the West*, deserve
greater recognition. Though most of Mann's best work
was in Westerns, one of his best films is *The Tall Target*,
a most unusual thriller starring Dick Powell. By 1951,
Powell's years as a crooning juvenile in Busby Berkeley
extravaganzas were long behind him, and he was well
into his film noir period (begun with 1944's *Murder, My
Sweet*), having completely reinvented himself as a solid
dramatic actor.

The Tall Target begins in 1861 New York. Powell
plays a police sergeant convinced that an assassination
attempt will be made on president-elect Abraham
Lincoln (to whom the title refers). The sergeant boards
a Washington-bound train determined to prevent
Lincoln's murder. Plenty of volatile, suspicious characters are onboard. What a setup: a film about an assassination attempt on Lincoln set four years before
the actual event and not long before the outbreak of
the Civil War. Our knowledge of what's to come
infuses the film with tingling overtones that the filmmakers wisely chose not to overexploit.

From the expansiveness of smoky train stations to the narrow alleys of train corridors, the film is a beauty. The motion-picture camera has always loved trains, and this movie quickly becomes one of those irresistible locomotive-driven suspense yarns in which all the plot elements fall seamlessly into place. *The Tall Target* is a lesson in economy; it lasts a mere seventy-eight minutes, yet nothing about it feels stinted. Strikingly photographed in black and white by Paul C. Vogel, the imagery alternates between scenes of ravishing visual depth and close-ups of startling impact. It's also dramatically satisfying, thanks to an intelligent screenplay that is both tautly drawn and emotionally resonant.

The Tall Target is a little film, but it outclasses most of the biggies that overshadowed its 1951 release. It has urgency, style, and smarts, and we should expect nothing less with Anthony Mann at the controls. One more thing: in this film from the '50s about an assassination attempt on a president, Powell's character's name is, coincidentally, John Kennedy.

JOHN DiLEO
Writer

Tampopo
1985, Juzo Itami

SCREENPLAY: Juzo Itami

CAST: Ken Watanabe, Tsutomu Yamazaki, Nobuko Miyamoto, Koji Yakusho, Rikiya Yasuoka, Kinzo Saura, Shoji Otake

JAPAN; IN JAPANESE

A send-up of John Ford Westerns, *Tampopo* is a wacky, pun-filled "Udon Eastern." Strong silent type Goro (Tsutomu Yamazaki) rides into town in a shiny Mack truck, à la Clint Eastwood, and, tipping his hat, criticizes the noodles made by a despondent widow,

Tampopo (Nobuko Miyamoto). Tampopo begs for
Goro's guidance, and soon the search is on to find the
perfect noodle—a search that goes on no matter how
long or how inane. A cornucopia of food lovers follows,
creating a hilarious tableau of food passion. Staying true
to the genre, the good guys win in the end, and the
hero rides off into the sunset. A film that is as loopy
and pliant as the freshest udon.

SUZANNE CHARLÉ
Editor and writer

Taxi!

1932, Roy Del Ruth

SCREENPLAY: Kubec Glasmon and John Bright; based on the play
The Blind Spot, by Kenyon Nicholson
CAST: James Cagney, Loretta Young, George E. Stone,
Guy Kibbee, Leila Bennett, Dorothy Burgess, David Landau
U.S.; B & W

Film historians call them simply "pre-Code." They're
the unexpected movies made in Hollywood in the
too-brief period between 1930 and 1934, between the
birth of sound and the introduction of the suffocatingly
moral Production Code. "More unbridled, salacious,
subversive, and just plain bizarre than what came after-
wards," writes Thomas Doherty in his book *Pre-Code
Hollywood*. "They look like Hollywood cinema but the
moral terrain is so off-kilter they seem imported from
a parallel universe." It's an upside-down world where,
as shown in 1932's *Taxi!*, tough Irish street kid James
Cagney speaks excellent Yiddish.

Cagney knew the language because it was the lingua
franca of the streets he grew up on in the Yorkville
neighborhood of Manhattan. Cagney told biographer
John McCabe that he especially liked Yiddish because

"it's the one great language of vituperation . . . We Irish and German and other ethnic kids always envied our Jewish buddies their ability to insult." Cagney, playing cabdriver Matt Nolan, used Yiddish in conversations with Jack Warner and, according to McCabe, enjoyed referring to the studio head, in a particularly choice epithet, as a *schvontz.*

Knowing of the actor's gift for Yiddish, screenwriter John Bright crafted a scene in which Nolan, ordinarily feisty enough to start a fight, takes a few minutes off to help a desperate Jewish man who needs directions to Ellis Island so that he can meet his arriving wife. Cagney asks him, in Yiddish, where he wants to go. When the astonished man asks if he is in fact Jewish, Cagney responds with a playful affirmative, *"Vu den, a shay-getz?"* ("What else, a Gentile?") all done in the kind of fluent Yiddish even Jewish actors of today would have trouble matching.

KENNETH TURAN
Film critic, Los Angeles Times

RECOMMENDED READING: Thomas Doherty, *Pre-Code Hollywood: Sex, Immorality, and Insurrection in American Cinema 1930–1934,* Columbia University Press, 1999.

They Caught the Ferry
1948, Carl Theodor Dreyer

SCREENPLAY: Carl Theodor Dreyer; story by Johannes V. Jensen
CAST: Joseph Koch
DENMARK; B & W; SHORT; IN DANISH

It's true that the cinematic language spoken by Danish director Carl Dreyer (1889–1968) is one of the purest and most evocative of the form's history. (He's also one of my all-time hands-down favorite directors—right up there with Ozu, Vigo, Bresson, and Keaton.) But just to get things straight, Dreyer, in fact, does not fit neatly into the "purist aesthete" category where cinema history tries to contain him. Before directing he was a café pianist, a corporate bookkeeper, a tabloid journalist, and a balloon pilot. And let's not forget that his second feature was entitled *Leaves from Satan's Book* and that his third, *The Witch Woman*, was in essence a sex film. His next one, *Chained* (or *The Story of the Third Sex*), was about a man's internal torment over his homosexual urges (shades of *Ed Wood*!). Dreyer was also regarded as an obstinate brat and was a well-known pain in the ass to producers and financiers. This, of course, was due to his fanatical insistence on complete aesthetic control over his work.

In any case, by 1948 Dreyer, by then a true master, was having trouble securing financing for his feature projects (and had yet to deliver two of his greatest films—*Ordet* made in 1955 and *Gertrud* made in 1964). Auspiciously, the Danish government approached him (or maybe vice versa) to direct, of all things, a traffic-safety film for public-service purposes. Dreyer accepted the offer but decided to use a tragic motorcycle ride as his subject—therein unexpectedly creating what is possibly the very first Euro-biker movie.

Entitled *They Caught the Ferry*, it's now a rarely seen eleven-minute black-and-white masterpiece and is only slightly disguised by its original intention. It's both a perfectly miniaturized youth horror film and the likely precursor to a subgenre of motorcycle flicks (including, among many others, *The Wild One*, *Girl on a Motorcycle*, *Blonde in Black Leather*, *The Loners*, and maybe even *Easy Rider*, since the bikers die in the end).

On another level, *They Caught the Ferry* could also be seen as a kind of thumbnail encapsulation of the tragic criminal-youth-on-the-run love-story genre, with

Nicholas Ray's *They Live by Night* being my personal favorite. Just imagine *They Live by Night* transposed to a single motorcycle ride—the whole thing reduced to two wheels and minus the entire plot! Talk about cinematic purity.

Dreyer's jewel-like movie begins with a ferryboat docking, then various cars and motorbikes unload into a small city or town. Among the vehicles disembarking is the film's focus: a young couple on a motorcycle—she in the saddle behind, arms encircling him. And, as in all good biker movies, these two characters are "born to be bad" (even if only in a clean, 1948, Scando-trash kind of way). After all, they're on a motorcycle, they're not wearing helmets, and, if nothing else, they just drive way too fast.

The couple exits the town. She holds on even tighter as the bike flies down rural roads past trees and Scandinavian farmland. Daringly, they overtake cars and other motorcycles, barely avoiding farm animals in the process.

They arrive at a fork in the road and make a quick wrong decision, then have to turn around and accelerate back up to their previous breakneck speed. In the process, Dreyer employs a beautifully balanced variety of camera positions: shots from the bike, blurred POVs of the passing landscape, inserts of the vibrating needle on the speedometer, shots of their ecstatic faces intercut with the bike's spoked wheels spinning above the surface of the road . . . Breathtaking.

Then, eventually, their ecstasy hits a snag. The motorcycle catches up to a slow-moving, black, boxlike hearse—complete with an ominous skeleton painted on its rear doors. The bike makes several attempts to overtake the sinister vehicle, but each time it is blocked. Dreyer carefully picks his moment to reveal the driver of the hearse—an emaciated ghoul clad in black, grinning maniacally from behind the wheel! Dr. D., the Reaper.

Accelerating wildly, they make yet another attempt to pass, but again the hearse swerves, intentionally forcing the motorcycle off the road. The bike catapults across a ditch, then slams head-on into a tree. Fade to black.

Fade up from black: the final shot of the film mimics its opening. This time, though, the ferryboat is preparing to depart. Two coffins have been loaded on. They contain the corpses of our young riders, making the return trip. Dead. They caught the ferry.

JIM JARMUSCH
Director

NOTE: The original version has no accompanying music, instead effectively relying on variations of the motorcycle's engine to provide a "score" for the film. However, Tom Verlaine (guitarist extraordinaire and former leader of the legendary New York rock band Television) created a new score for *They Caught the Ferry* in 2000.

They Won't Believe Me
1947, Irving Pichel

SCREENPLAY: Jonathan Latimer
CAST: Susan Hayward, Robert Young, Jane Greer, Rita Johnson, Tom Powers, George Tyne, Don Beddoe, Frank Ferguson
U.S.; B & W

With a noir screenplay by Jonathan Latimer, this trickily constructed little thriller features a stunningly unexpected performance by Robert Young. In a mode far removed from *Father Knows Best*, he plays a small-town philanderer whose machinations lead him into a labyrinth of unforeseen consequences.

For a double feature on the perils of infidelity, try pairing this with Arthur Lubin's equally devious *Impact*.

GEOFFREY O'BRIEN
Editor in chief, Library of America, and author

Sunday Afternoon

The Thief of Bagdad
1940, Michael Powell, Ludwig Berger, and Tim Whelan
SCREENPLAY: Miles Malleson and Lajos Biró
CAST: Conrad Veidt, Sabu, June Duprez, John Justin, Rex Ingram, Miles Malleson, Morton Selten, Mary Morris
U.K.

Things to Come
1936, William Cameron Menzies
SCREENPLAY: H. G. Wells; based on the novel *The Shape of Things to Come*, by H. G. Wells
CAST: Raymond Massey, Edward Chapman, Ralph Richardson, Margaretta Scott, Cedric Hardwicke, Maurice Braddell, Sophie Stewart, Derrick De Marney, Ann Todd
U.K.; B & W

Of Mice and Men
1939, Lewis Milestone
SCREENPLAY: Eugene Solow; based on the novel by John Steinbeck
CAST: Burgess Meredith, Betty Field, Lon Chaney Jr., Charles Bickford, Roman Bohnen, Bob Steele, Noah Beery Jr.
U.S.; B & W

Before there was home video, there was "home" video on a ten-inch black-and-white RCA TV screen in Detroit, at least as I remember it. There were no videotapes or DVDs, but thanks to Sunday afternoon and late-night television programming, we had plenty of old films to keep us fascinated. I sat for hours glued to the television screen, thrilled by the many wonderful experiences in my own mini-cinema. Three films in particular remain burned into my memory. The first is *The Thief of Bagdad*—not the *really* old one with Douglas Fairbanks, but the one directed by Ludwig Berger in 1940, starring Conrad Veidt and Sabu, and produced by Alexander Korda. It was truly one of the great special-effects spectacles of its time. Second, I loved

William Cameron Menzies's *Things to Come*, starring
Raymond Massey—one of the most original, prescient
science-fiction tales ever, envisioned by the great H. G.
Wells. And, third, one of the most emotional films ever:
Lewis Milestone's screen adaptation of John Steinbeck's *Of
Mice and Men*, starring Burgess Meredith, Lon Chaney Jr.,
Bob Steele, and Betty Field.

Check these out. You might not find them scheduled
as part of a Sunday-afternoon television matinee that often
anymore, but thanks to the "new" home video, they're still
around.

ROBERT K. SHAYE
Cochairman/Co-CEO, New Line Cinema

The Third Man

1949, Carol Reed

SCREENPLAY: Graham Greene; based on the novella by
Graham Greene and Alexander Korda

CAST: Joseph Cotten, Alida Valli, Trevor Howard, Orson Welles,
Pail Hörbiger, Ernst Deutsch, Erich Ponto, Siegfried Breuer,
Hedwig Bleibtreu

U.K.; B & W

Orson Welles delivers the famous speech in Carol
Reed's *The Third Man* as Harry Lime, the friend
whom Holly Martens (Joseph Cotten) thought was
dead. Instead Lime has become a drug lord in
postwar Vienna.

"Oh, don't be so gloomy," says Lime. "In Italy, for
thirty years under the Borgias, they had warfare, terror,
murder, bloodshed—they produced Michelangelo,
Leonardo da Vinci, and the Renaissance. In Switzerland,
they had brotherly love, they had five hundred years of
democracy and peace, and what did that produce? The
cuckoo clock."

Audiences and critics alike heard that line and
thought, "How Graham Greene. Only Greene could

write a line like that!" But the line is not in Greene's original script. As Greene himself enjoyed noting, it was ad-libbed by Welles. Reed thought it was perfect—perfectly Graham Greene.

SCOTT SIMON
Host, National Public Radio's Weekend Edition

¡Three Amigos!
1986, John Landis

SCREENPLAY: Steve Martin, Lorne Michaels, and Randy Newman
CAST: Chevy Chase, Steve Martin, Martin Short, Joe Mantegna, Jon Lovitz, Phil Hartman, Alfonso Arau, Tony Plana, Patrice Martinez
U.S.

Back in 1986, when I was a second-string reviewer for the *Chicago Reader*, I had my funny bone put on hold for a time as I was sent out to every Hungarian film about suicide and confessional documentary about a parent dying of cancer that came down the pike. I'm not complaining, but I was relieved when at last I got a shot at a regular picture: *¡Three Amigos!*

Of course, I wasn't about to slack off just because it was a lowbrow Hollywood comedy directed by mainstream talent John Landis and starring popular funny guys Steve Martin, Chevy Chase, and Martin Short. No, I planned to watch it with the same analytical detachment I would normally bring to East German melodramas about war guilt. And as it turned out, if looked at in the right way, *¡Three Amigos!* presented a lot to think about. First, there was the whole artifice-versus-reality problem. The amigos of the title are a trio of silent-film stars fired by their ruthless studio head. Desperate for work, they accept an invitation from the Mexican village of Santa Poco to come and "put on a show" for the "infamous El Guapo." Once there, they discover that, as Martin's character whispers, "it's real" ("and *I've already been shot*," he adds, near tears).

Reality, or another movie, or several of them? The obvious allusions include *The Seven Samurai* via *The Magnificent Seven*, as well as *The Wild Bunch* (wasn't that Alfonso Arau, who played a bandito in Peckinpah's groundbreaking Western, in the role of El Guapo?). On the surface a dumb-ass, adolescent comedy, *¡Three Amigos!* concealed a dazzling, subversive masterpiece of postmodern pastiche deconstructing several film genres, including the silent comedy, the Western, and the musical, and, indeed, even the notion of the postmodernist pastiche itself. As I was jotting these thoughts down I was interrupted by the sound of someone laughing continuously, tonelessly, mirthlessly. People were annoyed and complaining. The culprit, of course, was me. Perhaps the laughing started as early as the first mention of the amigos' names: Lucky Day (Martin), Dusty Bottoms (Chase), Ned Nederlander (Short). I smile, witlessly, even now as I write them down. Or maybe it started with Ned's explanation of what "infamous" means ("more than famous"). But definitely it began long before the scene, set in a bar, in which the amigos cow Mexican gunslingers into singing the chorus of "My Little Buttercup" (songs by Randy Newman, who also played the Singing Bush and co-wrote the film with Martin and Lorne Michaels) or the scene where Ned regals non-comprehending peasant children with the story of his meeting Lillian Gish. By the time Ned utters the immortal line, "Sew, very old one, sew like the wind!" I was beyond restraint or shame.

Dumb, very dumb. But necessary, too: how long can one watch movies merely as a disconnected intellect? As Lucky Day explains near the end, "We all have our

own El Guapo. Ours just happens to be a big dangerous guy named El Guapo." My El Guapo? Perhaps
taking movies too seriously, or not seriously enough.

PETER KEOUGH
Film editor, Boston Phoenix

Three Cornered Moon
see p. 160

A Time to Love and a Time to Die
1958, Douglas Sirk

SCREENPLAY: Orin Jannings; based on the novel by
Erich Maria Remarque
CAST: John Gavin, Lilo Pulver, Jock Mahoney, Done DeFore,
Keenan Wynn, Erich Maria Remarque, Thayer David,
Agnes Windeck, Klaus Kinski, Jim Hutton
U.S.

Taken from the novel by the highly regarded German
author Erich Maria Remarque (best known for penning
All Quiet on the Western Front), *A Time to Love and
a Time to Die*'s dramatic and bittersweet antiwar love
story and message had widespread appeal. In 1937, after
years of trying to avoid the political machinations of the
Nazi regime, Douglas Sirk fled Germany with his Jewish
wife and eventually immigrated to the United States.
The Remarque story had incredible relevance to the
director's personal experiences regarding the demise of
powerless individuals in Germany during World War II.

A fairly recent newcomer to the Universal lot,
actor John Gavin was cast as the story's protagonist,
a German soldier named Ernst Graeber. Even though
Gavin was of Spanish descent, he was perfectly capable
of passing as "Aryan" and is quite dashing in the role.
Returning home from the Russian front, Graeber is

confronted with the devastation of his town, the disintegration of spirit, and the sincerity of his friends. In a very touching, simplistic manner that counterbalances the horrors surrounding his short respite, Graeber falls in love with Elizabeth Kruse (played by lovely German actress Lilo Pulver), who happens to be the daughter of a political prisoner. The two form a strong bond as they search for loved ones and find moments of comfort among the devastation.

The unsophisticated performances by the two leads are believable and sincere, but hardly groundbreaking. In fact, the casting of American actors (Gavin, Jock Mahoney, Keenan Wynn, and Jim Hutton) as the film's main German characters tends to weaken its credibility at times, a fact that becomes even more apparent with the casting of German performers in the minor roles (including Remarque himself in an effective cameo as a teacher opposed to Hitler's regime).

Although filmed on location in Germany among the still-standing ruins of World War II, the picture has a definite Universal back-lot feel. From the opening credits of the cherry blossoms in the rain to the haunting closing images of the fatalistic finale, cinematographer Russell Metty attaches an eerie gloss and glamour to a rather grim subject. The outcome is as beautiful as it is unsettling.

The film retains many of the qualities of classic melodramas of the time, qualities that, when all is said and done, probably hurt the film's integrity. But the subtle yet powerful film techniques used celebrate what Sirk would define as the "brevity of happiness." The universality of such classic Sirkian themes seems to have overcome his films' "fluff" status, long held against them by critical and academic communities. Thanks to the current revitalization of interest in melodrama, this straightforward and poignant love story, surrounded by the ominously relevant ramifications of war, will hopefully touch a chord for those who revisit this "lost" film.

TODD WIENER
Motion picture archivist, UCLA Film & Television Archive

T-Men
1948, Anthony Mann

SCREENPLAY: John C. Higgins; based on the short story by Virginia Kellogg
CAST: Dennis O'Keefe, Mary Meade, Alfred Ryder, Wallace Ford, June Lockhart, Charles McGraw, Jane Randolph, Art Smith
U.S.; B & W

Among the several superb collaborations between director Anthony Mann and cinematographer John Alton (including *Raw Deal* and *Border Incident*), *T-Men* is perhaps the greatest, and its critical and financial success catapulted the two erstwhile poverty-row filmmakers to the A-list at MGM studios. This scorching crime procedural, filmed on location in the popular semi-documentary style of its era (replete with a stern-voiced narrator), follows a painstaking investigation by two treasury agents (played by Dennis O'Keefe and Alfred Ryder) as they go undercover to infiltrate a vicious gang of counterfeiters. Utilizing stark brutality (particularly in a famous steam-bath murder scene) and brilliant black-and-white chiaroscuro lighting, Mann and Alton turn familiar material into a noirish nightmare depicting the seamy underbelly of postwar urban America.

MICHAEL SCHEINFELD
Writer

RECOMMENDED VIEWING: Other films directed by Anthony Mann: *Desperate* (1947); *He Walked by Night* (a.k.a. *The L.A. Investigator,*

1948); *Raw Deal* (1948); *Border Incident* (1949); *Reign of Terror* (a.k.a. *The Black Book*, 1949).

Tokyo Story
1953, Yasujiro Ozu

SCREENPLAY: Kôgo Noda and Yasujiro Ozu
CAST: Chishu Ryu, Chieko Higashiyama, Setsuko Hara, Haruko Sugimura, Sô Yamamura, Kyôko Kagawa
JAPAN; B & W; IN JAPANESE

My friends say that I think every movie is too long. It's true. I'm a film editor, and even I think some of the movies I've cut myself are too long. But there is not a single frame that I would excise from Yasujiro Ozu's *Tokyo Story*.

The pacing of this film reflects the sensibility of an aging couple with whom we journey to visit their children in Tokyo. Through this couple's eyes, we see the rapidly accelerating pace of everyday life that is overtaking their world, a world their children willingly inhabit. I doubt that many would sympathize with their harried, self-involved offspring.

Ozu provides a timeless metaphor for us to witness and evaluate the changes post—World War II Japan underwent. Although the film has a bias, it is a beautiful snapshot of a time that is gone forever.

GERALDINE PERONI
Film editor

A Touch of Zen
1969, King Hu

SCREENPLAY: King Hu; story by Pu Song-ling
CAST: Chang Ping-yu, Hsu Feng, Pai Ying, Tien Feng, Roy Chiao, Tien Peng
TAIWAN; IN MANDARIN

Not underrated by those who have seen it, but still far too little known. King Hu's three-hour masterpiece, *A Touch of Zen*, is a leisurely told, stunningly photographed story that sublimely mixes rebels, monks, princesses, martial artists, painters, and nagging mothers in an adventure that keeps emerging onto new levels of comedy, intrigue, and combat, culminating in a mood of spiritual exaltation.

GEOFFREY O'BRIEN
Editor in chief, Library of America, and author

The Travelling Players
see *O Thiassos*, p. 179

A Tree Grows in Brooklyn
see p. 174

Trouble in Paradise
1932, Ernst Lubitsch

SCREENPLAY: Samson Raphaelson and Grover Jones; based on the play *The Honest Finder*, by Aladar Laszlo
CAST: Miriam Hopkins, Kay Francis, Herbert Marshall, Charles Ruggles, Edward Everett Horton, C. Aubrey Smith, Robert Greig, Leonid Kinskey
U.S.; B & W

If you've ever heard of the phrase "the Lubitsch touch," you know it refers to the most elegant and raucous amoral comedy, all done by indirection and suggestion. Ernst Lubitsch's *Trouble in Paradise* is the tale of two thieves who fall for each other. The moonlit dinner where they meet and pick each other's pockets is one of the greatest love scenes in any medium. "I hope you don't mind if I keep your garter," he says at the end of the scene . . . and she hadn't even missed it. Then they team up, and he falls for their intended victim.

Screenwriter Samson Raphaelson was a Broadway playwright whose tearjerker *The Jazz Singer* was made into the first talkie, with Al Jolson. But Raphaelson had nothing to do with that film and everything to do with this one and with his next collaboration with Lubitsch, 1940's charming *Shop Around the Corner* with Margaret Sullavan and James Stewart. That one takes place in a more or less recognizable world filled with earnest working people. But *Trouble in Paradise* floats in a parallel universe of romance and style that you feel must exist *somewhere*—if you could only meet the right person. It's the high-water mark of cinematic wit.

JOHN GUARE
Playwright

True Confessions
1981, Ulu Grosbard

SCREENPLAY: John Gregory Dunne and Joan Didion; based on the novel by John Gregory Dunne
CAST: Robert De Niro, Robert Duvall, Charles Durning, Kenneth McMillan, Ed Flanders, Cyril Cusack, Burgess Meredith, Rose Gregorio, Dan Hedaya
U.S.

Rose Gregorio's performance as an utterly spent hooker in *True Confessions* offers subtle shadings on what has to be the most clichéd of all women's roles. Robert Duvall's jaded cop and Robert De Niro's unctuous priest add to the bitter pleasures of this film, but it's Gregorio, featured in only a few scenes, who truly makes *True Confessions* memorable.

MEGAN RATNER
Associate Editor, Bright Lights Film Journal

Turtle Diary
1985, John Irvin

SCREENPLAY: Harold Pinter; based on the novel by Russell Hoban
CAST: Glenda Jackson, Ben Kingsley, Richard Johnson,
Michael Gambon, Rosemary Leach, Eleanor Bron, Harriet Walter,
Nigel Hawthorne
U.S.

Films featuring Glenda Jackson have been favorites of ours since we first saw her opposite Peter Finch in *Sunday Bloody Sunday*, a classic 1971 film that won the young actor her second Academy Award nomination. In Jackson's roles, her no-nonsense British pragmatism, sharp wit, and intelligent approach consistently come together with an unanticipated measure of vulnerability. The result, invariably, is an undertow of eroticism, mischief, and mysteriousness that gives every one of her films a richly nuanced core.

One of her lesser-known films is *Turtle Diary*. Harold Pinter's quirky screenplay doesn't waste a word of dialogue or include one unnecessary scene as it tells the story of two lonely people with a common obsession: the desire to liberate three giant turtles from an aquarium. Neaera (Glenda Jackson) is a successful, eccentric writer who lives alone in a world of meticulous order and restraint. Her passion for life percolates at full boil, just below a carefully manicured surface. William (Ben Kingsley) is a clerk in a bookstore, divorced and living alone in a rented room. Both Neaera and William seek solace in their ritual visits to an aquarium, where they watch three giant turtles swim, trapped in their tiny tank. George (Michael Gambon), the aquarium keeper, completes the trio of turtle conspirators.

Authenticity is what Jackson brings to all of her films, whether they are lighthearted romances or tragic dramas. When Jackson was elected MP, British Parliament's gain was the film fan's loss.

MARY SCHMIDT CAMPBELL AND GEORGE CAMPBELL JR.
Dean, Tisch School of the Arts; President, Cooper Union for the Advancement of Science and Art

Carole Lombard

Twentieth Century

1934, Howard Hawks
SCREENPLAY: Ben Hecht, Charles MacArthur; based on the play *Napoleon of Broadway*, by Charles Bruce Millholland, Ben Hecht, and Charles MacArthur
CAST: John Barrymore, Carole Lombard, Walter Connolly, Roscoe Karns, Charles Lane, Etienne Girardot, Dale Fuller, Ralph Forbes, Edgar Kennedy
U.S.; B & W

Twentieth Century, one of the early screwball comedies, is distinguished by a typically outrageous performance by John Barrymore, playing an egotistical producer, and Carole Lombard, in her first substantial film role, playing his protégé. Their free-for-all performances show what can happen when great talent is gathered together and directed well.

Initially, neither Barrymore nor the director, Howard Hawks, was pleased with Lombard's acting. She lacked energy and was apparently intimidated by Barrymore, who made his disapproval of her performance known to Hawks, who then spoke to Lombard. Richard Bann tells this anecdote about that conversation and what followed: Hawks asked her, "What would you do if a man told you to get fucked?" To which Lombard replied, "I'd kick him right in the balls."

Hawks asked her some other provocative questions, and Lombard got angry. He said, "Go back there and kick him and wave your arms and do any damned thing you want to do." Lombard took him seriously and made history. Hawks said proudly, "We made the picture in three

> weeks. I just turned them loose. And she was a star after that picture."
>
> ELLIOT SILVERSTEIN
> Director

Two-Lane Blacktop
1971, Monte Hellman

SCREENPLAY: Will Corry and Rudolph Wurlitzer
CAST: James Taylor, Warren Oates, Laurie Bird, Dennis Wilson, David Drake, Richard Ruth, Harry Dean Stanton, Alan Vint
U.S.

Two-Lane Blacktop, by Monte Hellman, is one of my favorite movies. It stars Warren Oates, Harry Dean Stanton, and two of the cutest boys ever put on screen: rock stars James Taylor and Dennis Wilson. This film never ceases to thrill me.

ALLISON ANDERS
Director, screenwriter, and professor

RECOMMENDED VIEWING: *Monte Hellman: American Auteur* (1997), a documentary directed by George Hickenlooper.

U

Umberto D.
1952, Vittorio De Sica

SCREENPLAY: Cesare Zavattini and Vittorio De Sica
CAST: Carlo Battisti, Maria-Pia Casilio, Lina Gennari
ITALY; B & W; IN ITALIAN

With masterpieces like *Open City*, *Germany Year Zero*, and the remarkable *Viaggio in Italia* to his credit, Roberto Rossellini may well be the best-known director of the Italian neorealism movement. But if I had to pick my favorite example of this form, I'd have to go with Vittorio De Sica's *Umberto D.*, the story of an old, penniless man trying to get rid of his dog. The camera vanishes, and it's just you and the two of them. How it ends up being a profound statement on the human condition is one of the mysteries of art. Imagine if *Lassie Come Home* or *Milo and Otis* had been written by Sophocles. Unbearably moving.

JOHN GUARE
Playwright

Un condamné à mort s'est échappé, ou Le vent souffle où il veut
see *A Man Escaped*

Un flic (Dirty Money)
1972, Jean-Pierre Melville

SCREENPLAY: Jean-Pierre Melville
CAST: Alain Delon, Richard Crenna, Catherine Deneuve, Riccardo Cucciolla, Michael Conrad, Paul Crauchet, Simone Valère, André Pousse
FRANCE/ITALY; IN FRENCH

Jean-Pierre Melville has been justly celebrated for such brilliant, resonant crime films as *Le samourai*, *Le cercle rouge*, and *Bob le flambeur*. *Un flic* (*Dirty Money*) is his most underrated film, dismissed by French and British critics upon its release as a tired rehashing of his previous work.

Melville has never been interested in originality or realism in his stories or characters. The criminal's code of honor, the betrayed hood seeking revenge even if it costs him his life, the relationship between the cop and the criminal—all of these themes are given new life by Melville's cool, meditative style. His technique is to take the conventions of the genre and strip everything else away; the result is a form of urban poetry.

The film has a stark, ritualized quality that signals the end of Melville's journey toward abstraction. Alain Delon plays Commissaire Edouard Coleman, a disillusioned cop who has seen too much of the dirty world he inhabits. Richard Crenna (doing a damn good job of dubbing himself in French) plays his friend Simon, a nightclub owner and master criminal. Catherine Denueve plays Cathy, Simon's mistress and accomplice who is having an affair with Coleman.

Is it any wonder that when these three "friends" get together for a drink (in a beautiful sequence without words) they avoid looking into each other's eyes? They steal furtive glances, stare off into space, and gaze at their drinks. Melville can do more with a glance or a shot of Coleman playing jazz on the piano, smiling at Cathy, than most directors can do with a whole page of dialogue.

Even those who don't find *Un flic* among Melville's best films are willing to admit that the opening scene is one of his greatest wordless sequences. The aftermath of the final shootout at dawn, as the characters leave the scene, is filled with the curious mixture of romantic fatalism and world-weary cynicism that was Melville's gift to crime film.

Ric Menello
Screenwriter, film historian, and music video director

V

Valley of the Dolls
1967, Mark Robson

SCREENPLAY: Helen Deutsch and Dorothy Kingsley; based on
the novel by Jacqueline Susann
CAST: Barbara Parkins, Patty Duke, Susan Hayward, Paul Burke,
Sharon Tate, Tony Scotti, Martin Milner, Charles Drake,
Alexander Davion, Lee Grant, Robert H. Harris, Joey Bishop,
George Jessel, Jacqueline Susann
U.S.

Valley of the Dolls is often described as a tasteless piece
of outrageous, trashy camp—to which I say, "Duh.
That's why I love it!" In fact, though many "serious"
critics feel *Valley* is the worst film ever made, I can't
find anything wrong with it. This camp classic, based
on Jacqueline Susann's smash novel about three show-
biz lovelies and their battles with pills, works on every
conceivable level. It's an eye-opening fashion show, a
giddy musical, and a behind-the-scenes cautionary tale.
It's also brimming with real-life gossip, like how Susan
Hayward replaced Judy Garland as the over-the-hill
barracuda Helen Lawson. It's probably a good thing
Judy dropped out, because Helen's nemesis—Neely,
a spunky upstart on pills played by Patty Duke—was
based on the young her! Beyond the gossip, the big
hair, the nutty dialogue ("That little whore makes me
feel nine feet tall!"), and the outlandish situations (a
love duet sung in a rehab center), *Valley of the Dolls*
is as engrossing and fun to watch today as when it
came out.

MICHAEL MUSTO
Columnist, The Village Voice

The Vanishing (Spoorloos)
1988, George Sluizer

SCREENPLAY: Tim Krabbé; based on the novel *The Golden Egg*, by Tim Krabbé
CAST: Bernard-Pierre Donnadieu, Gene Bervoets, Johanna Ter Steege, Gwen Eckhaus, Bernadette Le Saché, Tania Latarjet, Lucille Glenn, Roger Souza
NETHERLANDS/FRANCE; IN FRENCH AND DUTCH

Mention *The Vanishing* at a party. You'll instantly know who's seen it. "The Dutch one," they'll say emphatically (to distinguish it from the inferior American remake). They'll nod, and their eyes will say "whoa" or "ho-ly shit." But as much as they may want to talk about this haunting little masterpiece of terror, they know that those who haven't seen it should remain in the dark. This is a thriller that defies the genre; it has no special effects, no supernatural forces, no red herrings, and not one drop of blood, and yet, with the help of one of film's best-rendered sociopaths, it truly terrifies.

TAD HILLS
Author and illustrator

Vérités et mensonges
see *F for Fake*

W

The Wannsee Conference
1984, Heinz Schirk

SCREENPLAY: Paul Mommertz; script derived from the minutes of the 1942 Wannsee Conference
CAST: Robert Atzorn, Friedrich G. Beckhaus, Gerd Böckmann, Jochen Busse, Hans-Werner Bussinger, Harald Dietl, Peter Fitz, Reinhard Glemnitz, Dieter Groest, Martin Lüttge
WEST GERMANY/AUSTRIA; DOCUMENTARY; IN GERMAN

The Wannsee Conference is a dramatization of the transcribed notes from the meeting that sealed the fate of millions of Jews during World War II. You sit there for eighty-two minutes, the exact length of time that it took to plan the extermination of Jews, homosexuals, and political undesirables. You listen to the exact conversation—word for word. Nothing is embellished; nothing is added. Everything—the location of the shoot (a home in a Berlin suburb), the offstage barking of dogs, the officer's casual banter—is exactly as it was.

The Wannsee Conference was later made into a BBC/HBO movie called *Conspiracy* with fictionalized dialogue and big-name actors (Stanley Tucci, Kenneth Branagh, and Colin Firth). It's good, but not as good as this chilling re-creation shot in real time.

MICHAEL C. DONALDSON
Former President, International Documentary Association, author, and lawyer

A Wedding
1978, Robert Altman

SCREENPLAY: Robert Altman, John Considine, Patricia Resnick, and Allan F. Nicholls

CAST: Desi Arnaz Jr., Carol Burnett, Mia Farrow, Geraldine Chaplin, Amy Stryker, Nina Van Pallandt, Dina Merrill, Lauren Hutton, Lillian Gish, Vittorio Gassman, Paul Dooley, Dennis Christopher, John Considine, John Cromwell, Pam Dawber, Howard Duff, Dennis Franz, Peggy Ann Garner, Viveca Lindfors, Pat McCormick U.S.

Only three guests show up for Dino Sloan Corelli and Margaret "Muffin" Brenner's wedding, and two of them arrive late: one on a motorbike, the other on a horse. Over a hundred people have sent their regrets and it's clear that neither the self-sufficient Dino (Desi Arnaz Jr.) nor the born-again Muffin (Amy Stryker) have any real friends. But between the two families, there's more than enough to go around of joy, hope, deception, jealousy, and bigotry. Robert Altman captures it all in his powerful comic masterpiece, *A Wedding*.

There's so much going on here: snobbery, idealism, compromise, romance, disappointment, racial and sexual intolerance. The editing is to die for and there are no weak performances: Carol Burnett, Geraldine Chaplin, Vittorio Gassman, and Mia Farrow have never been better. Nina Van Pallandt, a singer who rarely acted, is extraordinarily convincing, and Pat McCormick purrs like a plump marmalade cat. Enough. Just see the movie.

MICHAEL RATCLIFFE
Film critic and writer

The World of Geisha
1973, Kumashiro Tatsumi

SCREENPLAY: Kumashiro Tatsumi; based on the short story "The Inside Lining of the Four-and-a-Half Mat Room," by Nagai Kafu
CAST: Junko Miyashita, Hideaki Esumi, Moeko Ezawa, Gô Awazu, Nahomi Oka, Meika Seri, Hatsuo Yamatani
JAPAN; IN JAPANESE

Soft porn can be quite serious cinema in Japan. When the studio system fell apart after the golden age of Ozu and Mizoguchi, soft porn movies (called "pink films" in Japan) were still mass produced, offering opportunities for young filmmakers. Many of today's best Japanese commercial directors, such as Suo Masayuki (*Shall We Dance?*) and Kurosawa Kiyoshi (*Cure*), got their training in pink films—especially when the major studio Nikkatsu, which nearly went bankrupt in 1971, decided to save itself by turning to porn (imagine Warner Bros. making nothing but skin flicks!). But pink films have also earned critical respect, in part because they were sometimes political. Kumashiro Tatsumi was the most critically successful director in Nikkatsu's brand of pink cinema—called "Nikkatsu Roman Porno"—and he used his film *The World of Geisha* to take a hard jab at censorship authorities.

Sexual censorship of movies in Japan, enforced by the independent agency Eirin under the watchful eyes of the police, has always been rather strict—pubic hair was long forbidden and even today showing genitals is strictly verboten (thus the soft, not hard, porn). Several Nikkatsu directors and Eirin inspectors were actually arrested for approving and releasing several films in 1972. Making a pink film at Nikkatsu studio in 1973 must have been a very tense experience, indeed. What made matters worse was Kumashiro's audacious decision to adapt a banned story to film. Publication of the story, attributed to the famed novelist Nagai Kafu, had long been forbidden, and when a publisher tried to print it once more, in 1972 of all years, the police prosecuted again.

The World of Geisha ostensibly depicts a "day in the life" of a brothel, commenting on all this by making visible what usually tries to remain invisible: censorship.

Not only does the film cite famous censorship incidents in Japanese history, such as the massive expunging of references to rice riots in 1919—which resulted in blank newspaper pages—it also "censors" itself in an extreme way that can only make the viewer conscious of the abuse of power involved. Large black rectangles invade the screen to cover up the naughty bits, and even some of the dialogue displayed on intertitles suffers censorship. For instance, a woman in ecstasy moans "I'm coming," but using the exact same techniques of fascist-era Japan it's rendered, "I'm XXing" (unfortunately the subtitler for the U.S. DVD version missed the entire point and filled in the XXs). This battle over censorship corresponds to a story that is in some ways a war of the sexes set in a militarist era.

In *World of Geisha*, Kumashiro is not just critiquing the suppression of free expression, he is calling for resistance by moviegoers. Just as the prewar Japanese tried to subvert censorship by mentally filling in what had been XX'd out, Kumashiro challenges his viewers to fill in what has been blocked out in his film. The imagination, he seems to say, will struggle to be free, no matter how oppressive authorities can be.

AARON GEROW
Assistant Professor in Film Studies, Yale University

RECOMMENDED VIEWING: *A Woman with Red Hair* (1979), directed by Kumashiro Tatsumi; *A Woman Called Sada Abe* (1975), directed by Tanaka Noboru.

The Wrong Box
1966, Bryan Forbes

SCREENPLAY: Larry Gelbart, Lloyd Osbourne, and Burt Shevelove; based on the novel by Robert Louis Stevenson

CAST: Jeremy Lloyd, John Mills, Michael Caine, James Villiers, Wilfrid Lawson, Graham Stark, Dick Gregory, Ralph Richardson, Peter Cook, Dudley Moore, Peter Sellers
U.K.

Made during one of Britain's many golden ages of humor (this one circa '66), *The Wrong Box* assembles a who's who of British comic actors: John Mills, Ralph Richardson, Michael Caine, Peter Sellers, and—in their film debuts—Dudley Moore and Peter Cook.

Based on a story by Robert Louis Stevenson, the action is set in motion when members of a Victorian gentleman's club agree to contribute a tidy sum to a tontine (or lottery, for viewers on this side of the pond), the full sum of which will fall, with considerable interest, to the last surviving son.

The list of potential winners is quickly cut down, as lads meet vainglorious deaths available only to the Empire's ruling class. An overeager twit of a lieutenant commands his men to fire (twice)—in front of the cannon. A foppish dandy, intent on impressing a bevy of beauties by showing off his prize falcon, lifts off its hood and, looking into the bird's eyes, commands it to attack. Another kneels to be knighted and Her Royal Highness makes a fatal slip of the sword—frightfully sorry.

Soon, only two doddering brothers remain, a pompous pedant and a rickety blackguard. Ancient enemies, they live side by side in twin townhouses and, according to an even more ancient butler, haven't spoken to each other for forty years. These would-be heirs and their loving (Caine and Nanette Newman) and not-so-loving (Cook and Moore) kin reel through a maze of murderous plots and cracked confusions that includes, but is not limited to, a train wreck, a serial killer, a less-than-ethical physician played to distracting perfection by Sellers, a covey of kittens, and a confusion of corpses, caskets, and hearses drawn by racing horses. You might want to cry uncle, but no one will hear you.

SUZANNE CHARLÉ
Editor and writer

X–Z

The Young and the Damned
see *Los olvidados*

Youth Runs Wild
1944, Mark Robson

SCREENPLAY: John Fante
CAST: Bonita Granville, Kent Smith, Jean Brooks, Glen Vernon,
Vanessa Brown (as Tessa Brind), Arthur Shields,
Lawrence Tierney, Dickie Moore
U.S.; B & W

The producer Val Lewton and his team of young directors turned out one simple, poetic, inventive low-budget
horror film after another between 1942 and 1946, at
RKO. Each film was a model of craft and ingenuity,
remarkably alive to the expressive potential of objects,
shadows, corridors, rooms just offscreen, and the
sounds emanating from within. Each was shot through
with allusions and references, both literary and historical. The Lewton hallmark was a fine eye for detail and
a quietly understated performance style. The action in
each film had an air of overall calm, deftly punctuated
with screams, footsteps, and the shocking after-effects
of violent encounters: in *The Leopard Man*, one of the
best Lewtons, a little girl's murder is represented by a
pool of her blood running under her mother's locked
front door and filling a seam in the tiled floor.

Lewton also made two non-horror films at RKO,
an adaptation of Maupassant's "Boule de suif," called
Mademoiselle Fifi, and a contemporary portrait of
"problem" teenagers called *Youth Runs Wild*. As usual
with Lewton, the quiet delicacy of the action and the

rip-roaring title make for a sweetly comical mismatch. *Youth Runs Wild* is, as they say, a compromised film, starring Bonita Granville as a troubled teenaged girl with too much time on her hands, finally saved by the generosity of the kid next door and his caring family. Lewton's original cut was much tougher, less sentimental (the script was written by the novelist John Fante), and quite a few scenes were re-shot. Lewton wanted a drama, the bosses wanted a civics lesson—he asked to have his name removed and they refused. Nonetheless, this film has always stayed in my mind. The picture of small town life, from Granville's uncaring parents cracking open a beer after a hard day at the defense plant to the smalltime menace of the local playboy (played by the great Lawrence Tierney), feels movingly accurate. Leonard Maltin may be right—*Youth Runs Wild* probably has more value as a time capsule than anything else. But it's a lovely time capsule, a sweet portrait of American life as seen through the eyes of some remarkably sensitive and intelligent craftsmen.

KENT JONES
Film critic, writer, and director

Yukinojo henge
see *An Actor's Revenge*

Yurisai
see *Lily Festival*

Zhantai
see *Platform*

INDEXES

INDEX OF CONTRIBUTORS

Over the last twenty years, BRIAN ACKERMAN has programmed several art theaters in Manhattan, including the 68th Street Playhouse, the 57th Street Playhouse, and the Eastside Playhouse as well as the premier suburban art house in the country, the Fine Arts Cinema in Scarsdale, New York. He is now founding programming director of the Jacob Burns Film Center in Pleasantville, New York, a unique suburban collaboration with the Film Society of Lincoln Center. (*Salesman*, p. 205)

DOUG AITKEN is a multimedia artist known for his innovative installations. He has had many screenings and exhibitions, both in the U.S. and abroad. His 2007 installation *Sleepwalkers* at the Museum of Modern Art in New York reimagined the museum's facade as a giant screen onto which a film was projected. (Film as a Subversive Art, p. 83)

DAN ALGRANT is a New York filmmaker whose credits include *Naked in New York*; *People I Know*, starring Al Pacino; and the HBO series *Sex and the City*. (*Sweet Movie*, p. 225)

WOODY ALLEN is one of the most respected and prolific American filmmakers. He has written and directed more than forty films, appearing in many of them. His films have received innumerable honors, including three Academy Awards. Some of the most memorable are *Bananas* (1971), *Sleeper* (1973), *Annie Hall* (1977), *Zelig* (1983), *Broadway Danny Rose* (1984), *Purple Rose of Cairo* (1985), *Crimes and Misdemeanors* (1989), *Husbands and Wives* (1992), *Bullets over Broadway* (1994), and *Match Point* (2005). Allen is a devoted amateur jazz clarinetist and has a standing weekly engagement performing in New York City. (*The Hill*, p. 105)

ALLISON ANDERS describes herself as a "filmmaker against all odds," adding, "If I can do it, *anyone* can." She has eight feature films to her credit: *Border Radio*, *Gas Food Lodging*, *Mi Vida Loca*, *Grace of My Heart*, *Four Rooms*, *Sugartown*, *Things Behind the Sun*, and *The Circle Game* (documentary). She has received a Peabody Award (2002), a MacArthur Fellowship (1995), a Shine Award (2002), and a New York Film Critics Circle Award (1992). She's also the single mother of three children: Tiffany, Devon, and Ruben. (*Alice in the Cities*, p. 16; *A Stolen Life*, p. 218; *Two-Lane Blacktop*, p. 249)

KURT ANDERSEN is a novelist (*Heyday*, *Turn of the Century*), essayist, columnist (*New York, The New Yorker, New York Times Magazine*), public radio host (*Studio 360*), and former editor (*Spy, New York*). (*Berlin: Symphony of a Great City*, p. 28)

ROSS ANDERSON is the founder of Anderson Architects, an award-winning design firm with the expertise to program, plan, design, and manage projects requiring the integration of architecture, planning, and urban design. Previously, he was a founding partner (with Frederic Schwartz) of Anderson/Schwartz Architects. A recipient of the Rome Prize in architecture from the American Academy in Rome, Anderson has won many awards from Architectural Record and the New York chapter of the American Institute of Architects (AIA), where he is a member of the college of fellows. He has taught at Yale, Columbia, and Carnegie Mellon universities and the Parsons School of Design. (*No Down Payment*, p. 171)

WES ANDERSON is the director, co-writer, and producer of *Bottle Rocket* (1996), *Rushmore* (1998), *The Life Aquatic with Steve Zissou* (2004), and *The Darjeeling Limited* (2007). Anderson was nominated for an Academy Award for his 2001 film *The Royal Tenenbaums*. He has also held the role of producer for Noah

Baumbach's film *The Squid and the Whale.* (Peter Hyams Double Bill: *Busting*; *Capricorn One*, p. 42)

DAVID ANSEN was *Newsweek*'s movie critic from 1977 through 2008, and he continues to review movies there as a contributing editor. He has written television documentaries on Groucho Marx, Bette Davis, Greta Garbo, and Elizabeth Taylor and is a member of the New York Film Critics Circle, the National Society of Film Critics, and the Los Angeles Film Critic Association. (*Baxter*, p. 25; *Deep End*, p. 64; *Dreamchild*, p. 69; *Funny Bones*, p. 87; *The Hours and Times*, p. 104; *The Miracle*, p. 153; *Straight Time*, p. 219)

ALAN ARKIN is a founding member of Chicago's Second City Theater. He received a Tony for *Enter Laughing*; an Obie for *Little Murders*; a Golden Globe for *The Russians Are Coming, The Russians Are Coming*; and two New York Film Critics Circle awards. He has written seven books, one of which, *The Lemming Condition*, was chosen to be placed in the White House Library. (*Running on Empty*, p. 203)

KEN AULETTA has written for *The New Yorker* magazine since 1977, contributing the "Annals of Communications" column and profiles since

1992. He is the author of ten books, including *Three Blind Mice: How the TV Networks Lost Their Way*; *Greed and Glory on Wall Street: The Fall of the House of Lehman*; *The Highwaymen: Warriors of the Information Super Highway*; and *World War 3.0: Microsoft and Its Enemies*. Four have been national best sellers. His eleventh book will explore the future of media. (*The Americanization of Emily*, p. 19)

DR. NEAL BAER has been nominated for seven Emmys, three Golden Globes, and two Writers Guild Awards. Now the executive producer of the TV series *Law & Order: Special Victims Unit* and former executive producer of *ER*, Dr. Baer graduated from Harvard Medical School in 1996 and completed his internship in pediatrics at Children's Hospital Los Angeles in 2001. (*The Big Heat*, p. 32)

ALEC BALDWIN is an actor who has appeared in many films, television shows, and theatrical productions. His favorite restaurant is Shun Lee. His favorite color is red. He is right-handed. His middle name is Rae. (*The Savage Is Loose*, p. 208)

JEANINE BASINGER is Corwin-Fuller Professor of Film Studies at Wesleyan University in Middletown, Connecticut, where she founded the Wesleyan

Cinema Archives and serves as its curator as well as chair of the Film Studies Department; she is also the 1996 winner of Wesleyan's Binswanger Prize for Excellence in Teaching. She has written ten books on film, among them *American Cinema: 100 Years of Filmmaking*, the companion book for a PBS television series; *Silent Stars*, which won the National Board of Review's William K. Everson Award for Film History; and her latest, *The Star Machine*. Basinger has contributed articles to the *New York Times Magazine*, *American Film*, and *Film Comment*. She is a trustee emeritus of the American Film Institute (which awarded her a doctorate of humane letters in 2006), a trustee of the National Board of Review, and adviser to The Film Foundation's *Story of Movies* program. (*Bunny Lake Is Missing*, p. 43)

In 2002, MARIO BATALI was honored as the James Beard Foundation's "Best Chef: New York." He is chef and owner of New York restaurants Babbo, Lupa, Esca, and Otto and has written three cookbooks: *Simple Italian Food*; *Holiday Food*; and *The Babbo Cookbook*. (*1900 [Novecento]*, p. 170)

NOAH BAUMBACH was born and raised in Park Slope, Brooklyn. He is the writer and director of such films as *Kicking and Screaming*, *The Squid*

his film *Killer of Sheep* was inducted into the Library of Congress National Registry. Born in Vicksburg, Mississippi, Burnett received his B.A. and M.F.A. from the University of California, Los Angeles. (*Ganja and Hess*, p. 90)

STEPHEN H. BURUM has been a cinematographer for more than thirty-five years, working on such films as *The Outsiders, Rumble Fish, The War of the Roses, Hoffa, The Untouchables,* and *Mission: Impossible.* (American Society of Cinematographers, p. 18)

GEORGE CAMPBELL JR. is president of the Cooper Union for the Advancement of Science and Art. He earned a Ph.D. in theoretical physics from Syracuse University and is a graduate of the Executive Management Program at Yale University. A recipient of the 1993 George Arents Pioneer Medal in Physics, he is a fellow of the American Association for the Advancement of Science and the New York Academy of Sciences. He has published several papers and is coeditor of *Access Denied: Race, Ethnicity, and the Scientific Enterprise.* (*Turtle Diary*, p. 247)

MARY SCHMIDT CAMPBELL, B.A., M.A., PH.D.; HON.: D.F.A., PH.D., was appointed dean of the Tisch School of the Arts in 1991 and associ-ate provost for the arts in December 2004, a post she held until 2007, when she was appointed chair of the New York State Council of the Arts. Previously, she was New York City commissioner of cultural affairs from 1987 to 1991, in the Edward I. Koch and David Dinkins administrations. She came to city government after serving as executive director of the Studio Museum in Harlem from 1977 to 1987. Campbell is a fellow of the American Academy of Arts and Sciences and serves on the boards of the American Academy in Rome, the New York Shakespeare Festival, and the United Nations International School. She holds honorary degrees from the College of New Rochelle, Colgate University, City University of New York, and Pace University. She is the coauthor of *Harlem Renaissance: Art of Black America* and *Memory and Metaphor: The Art of Romare Bearden, 1940–1987.* (*Turtle Diary*, p. 247)

SUZANNE CHARLÉ is a writer and editor who divides her time between New York and Indonesia. Her work appears in the *New York Times, The Nation, Ford Foundation Report, American Prospect,* and other publications. She was editor of *Indonesia in the Soeharto Years: Issues, Incidents, and Images,* published in 2007 by the Lontar Foundation.

(*Legong: Dance of the Virgins*, p. 127; *Stray Dog*, p. 219; *Tampopo*, p. 231; *The Wrong Box*, p. 258)

CHEN SHI-ZHENG is a director, choreographer, singer, and actor. Born in China, he became a leading traditional opera actor before immigrating to the United States in 1987. In 2000 he received the title of Chevalier in the Order of Arts and Letters from the French government. His staging of Tang Xianzu's complete *The Peony Pavilion* premiered as part of the Lincoln Center Festival and was subsequently presented in Paris, Milan, Perth, Denmark, Vienna, Berlin, and Singapore. Recent directing projects include *The Orphan of Zhao* for Lincoln Center Theater and Verdi's *Vespers of 1610* with the Handel and Haydn Society. Chen's directorial film debut, *Dark Matter*, starring Liu Ye and Meryl Streep, was released in 2007 and won the Alfred P. Sloan Prize at the 2007 Sundance Film Festival. In addition, he directed *Rise and Fall of Madame Mao's Hero* for France 3 TV. (*The East Is Red*, p. 71)

CASSANDRA CLEGHORN teaches English and American studies at Williams College. Her poems have been published in such journals as *Paris Review*, *Yale Review*, *Southwest Review*, and *Seneca Review*. (*Ball of Fire*, p. 21)

KAREN COOPER became director of the Film Forum in 1972, building it from a tiny screening room with fifty folding chairs to its current incarnation: a three-screen cinema that is New York's most prestigious exhibitor of independent-film premieres and repertory programming. She is head programmer for the selection of premieres. Cooper has received an award from the New York Film Critics Circle for her programming as well as an honorary doctorate from the American Film Institute. (*Cinéma Vérité: Harlan County U.S.A.*; *Paris Is Burning*; *Crumb*, p. 102)

JOHN DiLEO is the author of *100 Great Film Performances You Should Remember—But Probably Don't* (2002) and *And You Thought You Knew Classic Movies!* (1999). (*The Tall Target*, p. 230)

MICHAEL C. DONALDSON is the former president of the International Documentary Association and an attorney with Donaldson & Callif, specializing in independent film and theater. He is the author of the authoritative *Clearance and Copyright: Everything You Need to Know for Film and Television*, 3rd ed.; *Negotiating for Dummies*, 2nd ed.; and *Fearless Negotiating*. (*American Dream*, p. 18; *Burden of Dreams*, p. 46; *My Voyage to Italy*, p. 162; *The*

Wannsee Conference, p. 255; A Meager Existence: *Nanook of the North*; *Man of Aran*; *The Gleaners and I*, p. 93)

ADAM DURITZ is lead singer of the band Counting Crows. The group's most recent album, *Saturday Nights & Sunday Mornings*, was released in 2008. (*The Adventures of Buckaroo Banzai across the 8th Dimension*, p. 10; *Gettysburg*, p. 94; *My Man Godfrey*, p. 161; *Ruggles of Red Gap*, p. 202; *Sullivan's Travels*, p. 222)

RICK ELLIS is a food stylist, writer, and culinary historian based in New York City. With a library of more than five thousand volumes on American cookery, he is still searching for a first edition of *Fannie Farmer*. (Turtle Soup: *The Age of Innocence*, p. 14)

LOUISA ERMELINO is the author of three novels celebrating New York City, her Italian heritage, and the power of women: *Joey Dee Gets Wise*, *The Black Madonna*, and *The Sisters Mallone*. She works at *InStyle* magazine, where she is chief of reporters. (*Big Deal on Madonna Street*, p. 30)

BRUCE FEIRSTEIN is a longtime columnist at the *New York Observer*, a contributing editor at *Vanity Fair*, and best-selling author (*Real Men Don't Eat Quiche*). His best-known screenwriting credits include the James Bond films *GoldenEye*, *Tomorrow Never Dies*, and *The World Is Not Enough*. He is responsible for the female "M" (Dame Judi Dench) calling Bond a "sexist misogynist dinosaur" and for the Robert Maxwell–inspired character Elliot Carver (portrayed by Jonathan Pryce) declaiming: "The distance between insanity and genius is only measured by success." (A Hollywood Primer, p. 107)

Czechoslovakian director MILOS FORMAN directed his first English-language film, *Taking Off* (1971), for which he won several awards including a Special Jury Prize at Cannes. Following this triumph, Forman directed the decathlon sequences of the multinational Olympic documentary *Visions of Eight* (1973) and then moved on to what many consider his masterpiece, *One Flew over the Cuckoo's Nest* (1975), which won Oscars in all five major categories, including best director. He again won the Oscar for his direction of *Amadeus*, a liberal retelling of the life of Mozart (as seen through the eyes of Antonio Salieri). Forman served as director of Columbia University's film division and directed such critically acclaimed films as *Hair* (1979), *The People Vs. Larry Flint* (1996), and *Man on the Moon* (1999). (*Miracle in Milan*, p. 154)

DAVID FRANCIS joined the staff of the British Film Institute's National Film Archive as television acquisitions officer in 1959, the same year he graduated from the London School of Economics. He was instrumental in the design and construction of the J. Paul Getty Jr. Conservation Centre at Berkhamsted for the archive as well as London's Museum of the Moving Image and the National Audio-Visual Conservation Center for the Library of Congress. He was awarded the Order of the British Empire by Her Majesty the Queen for services to film preservation, is an honorary fellow of the British Kinematograph Sound and Television Society, and is a recipient of the Prix Jean Mitry and Mel Novikoff Award. He has served as vice president and executive committee member of the International Federation of Film Archives; in 2001, he retired from his position as chief of the Motion Picture, Broadcasting, and Recorded Sound Division at the Library of Congress. He is the coauthor (with Raoul Sobel) of *Chaplin: Genesis of a Clown.* (*The Exploits of Elaine*, p. 73)

JAMES FREY is originally from Cleveland and now lives in New York. He is the author of *A Million Little Pieces, My Friend Leonard,* and *Bright Shiny Morning.* (*Conan the Barbarian*, p. 54)

AARON GEROW is assistant professor in film studies and East Asian languages and literatures at Yale University. He has published extensively on Japanese film, old and new. (*The World of Geisha*, p. 256)

ROBERT GITT is preservation officer for the UCLA Film and Television Archive. He has restored many historic films, including Frank Capra's *Lost Horizon* (1937); Howard Hawks's *The Big Sleep* (1945 pre-release version); John Ford's *My Darling Clementine* (preview version, 1946); Orson Welles's full-length *Macbeth* (1948); Budd Boetticher's director's cut of *Bullfighter and the Lady* (1951); and *Seven Men from Now* (1956). In collaboration with Richard Dayton, he helped restore the first successful two-color Technicolor feature, *The Toll of the Sea* (1922), and the first three-color Technicolor feature, *Becky Sharp* (1935), directed by Rouben Mamoulian. Gitt and the university received the British Film Institute Archival Achievement Award in 1991, and in 1995 he was awarded the Prix Jean Mitry. He is a member of the Academy of Motion Picture Arts and Sciences. (*The Night of the Hunter*, p. 167)

EVE GOLDEN is the author of five books on film and theater history, most recently biographies of actresses Anna Held and Kay Kendall. (*The Best of Everything*, p. 29; *Queen of Outer Space*, p. 195; Lyda Roberti: *Million Dollar Legs*; *Three Cornered Moon*, p. 160)

BRUCE GOLDSTEIN is repertory director for the Film Forum and a partner at Rialto Pictures. (*The Cameraman*, p. 47)

BETTE GORDON is a director and independent filmmaker whose film *Luminous Motion* opened to rave reviews in 2000 and was selected by the Locarno, Toronto, Munich, and Florida film festivals. Gordon is best known for *Variety* (1984), which premiered at the Cannes Film Festival's prestigious Director's Fortnight. During the fall of 1996, *Variety* and *Empty Suitcases*, one of her early short films, were presented as part of the Whitney Museum of American Art's retrospective *New York/No Wave Cinema*. Gordon's work in television includes segments of *Tales of the Darkside* and *Monsters*; German television's *Seven Women Seven Sins*; Showtime's *Love Streets*; and two films for Playboy's cable TV network, as part of their Director's Showcase series. She has been trailing director for HBO's *Oz* and NBC's *Law and Order: Criminal Intent*. Gordon is the Vice-Chair of the School of the Arts Film Division at Columbia University. She is also a staff writer

for *Bomb*, a journal of theater, film, art, and literature. (*Caged Heat*, p. 47; *Dance, Girl, Dance*, p. 61; *The Passenger*, p. 182; *Repulsion*, p. 200)

HENRY GRIFFIN is a screenwriter and filmmaker in New Orleans. His films include *Mutiny* and *Tortured by Joy*, and the forthcoming feature *Flip Mavens* (working title). He is currently artist-in-residence at the University of New Orleans. (*Drácula*, p. 67; *Hellzapoppin'*, p. 103)

TOM GRUENBERG's "lifetime commitment" to film began at age fourteen, when he took a job tearing movie tickets. Decades later, he is now in the business of selling tickets as a producer, exhibitor, and distributor. (*City Lights*, p. 53)

JOHN GUARE is the award-winning playwright (Tony, Obie, and New York Drama Critics Circle awards) of such plays as *House of Blue Leaves*, *Six Degrees of Separation* (for which he also wrote the screenplay), *Lydie Breeze*, and *A Few Stout Individuals*. He wrote the Oscar-nominated screenplay for Louis Malle's *Atlantic City*. He coedits the *Lincoln Center Theater Review*, is a council member of the Dramatists Guild, was elected to the American Academy of Arts and Letters, and serves on the executive board of PEN American Center. (*An*

Actor's Revenge, p. 9; *Love Me Tonight*, p. 144; *Trouble in Paradise*, p. 245; *Umberto D.*, p. 250)

JERE GULDIN has worked for the UCLA Film and Television Archive since 1984, specializing as a film preservationist (of mainly silent films and animation) since 1998. He has contributed articles on animation preservation to several magazines and journals. (*The Sin of Nora Moran*, p. 211)

LES GUTHMAN has written, produced, and directed nine documentary films, including *Corwin, Three Nights at the Keck, The Hudson Riverkeepers*, and *The Waterkeepers*. He has executive produced more than three dozen hour-long documentaries, including *Into the Tsangpo Gorge, Farther Than the Eye Can See, The Bihac, Bosnia Kayak Club, Into the Thunder Dragon, Liquid off the Throne of Shiva*, and *The Robert F. Kennedy Human Rights Award on PBS*. He is also the creator, writer, and executive producer of a television series based on the magazines *Discover* and *Outside*. (Capturing History: *O Thiassos* [*The Travelling Players*]; *El santo oficio* [*The Holy Office*], p. 179)

CURTIS HANSON wrote screenplays during the 1970s, including 1978's *The Silent Partner*. In the 1980s and 1990s, he directed such thrillers as *The Bedroom Window* (1987), *Bad Influence* (1990), and the box office hit *The Hand That Rocks the Cradle* (1992). His 1997 film *L.A. Confidential* earned nine Academy Award nominations, including the Oscar awarded to Hanson and his writing partner, Brian Helgeland, for best adapted screenplay. Hanson's other films include *The River Wild* (1994), *Wonder Boys* (2000), *8 Mile* (2002), *In Her Shoes* (2005), and *Lucky You* (2007). (*Killer of Sheep*, p. 121)

STEVEN HELLER was art director for the *New York Times* for thirty-three years, originally of the Op-Ed page and, for almost three decades, of the *New York Times Book Review*. Currently, Heller is cochair of the MFA Designer as Author Department, acts as special consultant to the President of SVA for New Programs, and writes the "Visuals" column for the *New York Times Book Review*. He is the author of more than eighty books on design, political art, and popular culture, including *The Graphic Design Reader*; *Cuba Style*; *Merz to Emigré and Beyond: Progressive Magazine Design of the 20th Century*; and *Counter Culture: The Allure of Mini-Mannequins*. (*Fail Safe*, p. 76; *Putney Swope*, p. 193)

Based in New York City, REINA HIGASHITANI is currently a producer for Downtown Community Television Center, a nonprofit media center. Her first independent feature-length documentary, *Shall We Sing?*, has been broadcast nationwide on PBS and won the Excellence Award at the Tokyo Video Festival. She is associate producer of the work-in-progress feature documentary *Kusama, Princess of Polka Dots*, by Heather Lenz. Her recent camerawork credits include director Volker Barth's *The Sperm Whale Mystery*, scheduled to broadcast on ARTE. A scholar of film, Higashitani is a frequently published critic, writing reviews and essays for newspapers and magazines including *Marie Claire Japan*. In addition, she is often involved in programming film festivals and translating Japanese films for U.S. distribution. Higashitani received her master's degree in cinema studies from New York University's Tisch School of the Arts. (*Nausicaä of the Valley of the Wind*, p. 164)

ARTHUR HILLER directed docudramas and dramas for CBC Radio and Television, followed by stints directing several of NBC's Matinee Theatre productions and many prestigious Playhouse 90 dramas, including *Massacre at Sand Creek*, which earned him an Emmy nomination. He became a director of choice for some of the industry's best-known series, including *Naked City*, *Alfred Hitchcock Presents*, *Gunsmoke*, *Ben Casey*, and *Route 66*. Hollywood's film industry beckoned, leading to a string of successful and critically acclaimed films, including *The Americanization of Emily* (1963); *The Out-of-Towners* (1969); *Love Story* (1970), for which he was honored with a Golden Globe as well as an Academy Award nomination; *Plaza Suite* (1971); *Hospital* (1971); *Man of La Mancha* (1972); *The Man in the Glass Booth* (1975); *Silver Streak* (1976); *The In-Laws* (1978); *Making Love* (1981); *Outrageous Fortune* (1986); and *The Babe* (1992). (*Open City*, p. 178)

TAD HILLS has written and illustrated many books for children including the *New York Times* bestselling *Duck & Goose* and *Duck, Duck, Goose*. Hills lives in Brooklyn NY with his wife Lee Wade, their two kids Elinor and Charlie, and their dog—the inspiration for his next book, *When Rocket Learned to Read*. (*The Vanishing* [*Spoorloos*], p. 254)

During a twenty-year career in the New York film industry, SAM HOFFMAN has produced, directed, and assistant directed numerous films, shorts, and commercials including *The Royal Tenenbaums, School of*

Rock, *The Producers*, *Donnie Brasco*, *Dead Man Walking*, and *Groundhog Day*. Currently, he is executive producing the film *Every Day*, for Ambush Entertainment. Hoffman graduated with honors from the University of Pennsylvania. He lives in New York City with his wife, Andrea Crane, and their son, Jack. (*Big Lebowski*, p. 33)

In 1989, STEVE HOFFMAN redesigned *Sports Illustrated* and became its creative director. He is instrumental in maintaining a consistent *Sports Illustrated* brand image in endeavors as diverse as Web design, books, and corporate projects. He has also designed formats and special issues for *Newsweek*, *Harper's Bazaar*, and *Business Week* and served as a design consultant to Bergdorf Goodman, Time Inc., and New York University. (*The Savage Eye*, p. 206)

HIKARI HORI is a visiting professor of the East Asian Languages and Cultures Department at Columbia University. Previously, she was a senior curator of the Film Department of the Japan Society of New York. She has worked as a research associate at the National Film Center in Tokyo and taught at Barnard College. (*Gamera 3: Revenge of Iris*, p. 89; *Lily Festival*, p. 134)

ISRAEL HOROVITZ's plays have been translated and performed in as many as thirty languages worldwide. Among the best known are *The Indian Wants the Bronx*, *Line*, *The Primary English Class*, *Park Your Car in Harvard Yard*, and *My Old Lady*. His films include *The Strawberry Statement*, *Author! Author!*, *James Dean*, and *Sunshine*, for which he won the European Film Academy Award for best screenwriting. His other awards include two Obies, the Prix du Jury of the Cannes Film Festival, and the Prix Italia, among many others. (*Federal Hill*, p. 78)

MATTHEW HOROVITZ is a television producer for the National Basketball Association. He lives in New York City. (Vanilla Ice: *Cool As Ice*, p. 56)

LA FRANCES HUI is senior program officer of cultural programs and performing arts at the Asia Society. For the past few years, she has served on the Features Selection and Screenplay Competition committees for Asian CineVision's annual Asian American International Film Festival. She recently curated a Cultural Revolution film series at the Asia Society, has interviewed filmmakers Ang Lee and Patrick Tam, and has written for the online journal *Cinevue*. (*Days of Being Wild*, p. 62;

Kwaidan, p. 123; *Platform*, p. 189; *The Puppetmaster*, p. 192)

ANJELICA HUSTON has appeared in a boggling variety of films, from *Prizzi's Honor* to *The Grifters* to *The Addams Family*. She has since defined an icy alter ego working with director Wes Anderson in *The Royal Tenenbaums*, *The Life Aquatic with Steve Zissou*, and *The Darjeeling Limited*. (*Dead Man*, p. 63)

ANNETTE INSDORF is director of undergraduate film studies at Columbia University and a professor in the Graduate Film Division of the School of the Arts. She is the author of *Double Lives, Second Chances: The Cinema of Krzysztof Kieslowski*; *François Truffaut*, a study of the French director's work; and *Indelible Shadows: Film and the Holocaust*. She has been a frequent contributor to the *New York Times* Arts and Leisure section, and her articles have appeared in various other publications. Dr. Insdorf is the creator and host of the popular film series Reel Pieces at Manhattan's 92nd Street Y. She served as a jury member at the Berlin Film Festival, among others, and hosts Cannes Film Festival coverage for Bravo/IFC. She is also the executive producer of award-winning short films, including the Oscar-nominated *Shoeshine*, starring Ben Stiller and Jerry Stiller, and *Performance*

Pieces, starring F. Murray Abraham, which was named Best Fiction Short at the 1989 Cannes Film Festival. (*The Stunt Man*, p. 221)

HENRY JAGLOM trained with Lee Strasberg at the Actors Studio and performed in off-Broadway theater and cabaret before moving to Hollywood in the late 1960s. Under contract to Columbia Pictures, he guest-starred on television shows and was featured in several films, including those directed by Jack Nicholson (*Drive, He Said*), Dennis Hopper (*The Last Movie*), and Orson Welles (*The Other Side of the Wind*), each of whom he directed in turn. Although Jaglom's filmmaking career began in the cutting room (when he helped edit the 1969 hit *Easy Rider*), his roots are firmly planted in acting, and he has costarred in four of his own films. He has written, directed, and edited many films, including *Hollywood Dreams*, *Going Shopping*, *A Safe Place*, *Tracks*, *Sitting Ducks*, *Can She Bake a Cherry Pie?*, *Someone to Love*, *New Years Day*, *Eating*, *Venice/Venice*, *Babyfever*, *Last Summer in the Hamptons*, *Déjà vu*, and *Festival in Cannes*. (Mavericks: Welles and Cassavetes: *F for Fake*; *Shadows*, p. 80)

JIM JARMUSCH's feature films include *Permanent Vacation* (1980), *Stranger Than Paradise*

(1984), *Down by Law* (1986), *Mystery Train* (1989), *Night on Earth* (1992), *Dead Man* (1995), *Year of the Horse* (1997), and *Ghost Dog: The Way of the Samurai* (1999) *Broken Flowers* (2005), and *The Limits of Control* (2009). His films have received Independent Spirit Awards as well as prizes from the Cannes Film Festival, the New York Film Critics Circle, and the National Society of Film Critics, among others. His short films include *INT/Trailer/Night* (released as part of a feature-length compilation of films about time, entitled *Ten Minutes Older* [2002]) and a series of short films, all entitled *Coffee & Cigarettes*. Jarmusch has also directed music videos. (*They Caught the Ferry*, p. 233)

MARK JOHNSON produced his first film, *Diner* (directed by Barry Levinson), in 1982. He has since produced *The Natural*; *Good Morning, Vietnam*; and *Rain Man*, for which he won the Oscar for best picture in 1988. More recent films include *A Perfect World*; *Donnie Brasco*; *My Dog Skip*; *Galaxy Quest*; *The Notebook*; *The Chronicles of Narnia: The Lion, the Witch, and the Wardrobe*; *The Hunting Party*; *Shooter*; *The Chronicles of Nardia: Prince Caspian*; and seven episodes of the AMC series *Breaking Bad*. (*The Conformist*, p. 56)

KENT JONES has worn many hats: archivist (for Martin Scorsese's Sikelia Productions), programmer (for New York's Film Society of Lincoln Center), film critic, writer, and director. He began writing for *Film Comment* in 1996, quickly becoming a strong presence at the magazine. Since becoming editor-at-large, he's played a large role in opening the magazine to a more cosmopolitan perspective. As a critic, he's always maintained this perspective himself; he's written extensively in English on French and American cinema for *Cahiers du cinéma*. He recently wrote and directed the documentary *Val Lewton: The Man in the Shadows,* narrated by Martin Scorsese. (*Rendezvous with Annie*, p. 197; *Youth Runs Wild*, p. 261)

LAWRENCE KAHN is professor emeritus of pediatrics at Washington University in St. Louis. Currently one of his major activities is leading a group from the Lifelong Learning Institute in reading and interpreting all of Shakespeare's plays. Beyond that, he takes great pleasure in the practical application of his son's City Secrets series. (Marcel Pagnol Trilogy: *Marius*; *Fanny*; *César*, p. 116)

DAVID BAR KATZ is a writer and director in every medium other than comic books, though he hopes to break into them soon. (*Fiddler on the Roof*, p. 82)

INGRID BROMBERG KENNEDY is co-owner and director of Klaus von Nichtssagend Gallery a contemporary art space in Brooklyn that represents emerging artists from the U.S. and Europe. She is principal of In-Grid Design and designs books, including this one. (*Sweet Sweetback's Baadasssss Song*, p. 226)

PETER KEOUGH has been film editor at the *Boston Phoenix* since 1989. He is a member of the Boston Society of Film Critics and the National Society of Film Critics, for which he edited the collection *Flesh and Blood: The National Society of Film Critics on Sex, Violence, and Censorship.* Among his awards are a fiction grant from the Massachusetts Council of Arts (1990), first prize for film criticism from the Association of Alternative Newspapers (1996), and first prize in arts and entertainment reporting from the New England Press Association (1994, 2001). (*Blind Chance*, p. 37; *The Gold Diggers of 1933*, p. 95; *Lonely Are the Brave*, p. 139; *¡Three Amigos!*, p. 239)

WENDY KEYS was involved in programming for the Film Society of Lincoln Center for more than thirty years, working on such projects as the New York Film Festival and New Directors/New Films for the Museum of Modern Art. She coproduced and directed thirty annual gala tributes at the society, including those for Laurence Olivier, Federico Fellini, Martin Scorsese, Audrey Hepburn, Mike Nichols, and Francis Ford Coppola. Keys also worked on retrospectives and thematic programming at the Walter Reade Theater and served on many panels and juries worldwide. She currently sits on the Film Society's Board of Directors and is on the Executive Committee. (*Light Sleeper*, p. 133)

CHIP KIDD is the author of *The Cheese Monkeys*, a novel about art school. Some people liked it. He has been designing book jackets for Alfred A. Knopf and other publishers since 1986. (*Superman*, p. 233)

DYLAN KIDD is the writer and director of the film *Roger Dodger*, which won the Best Feature Film Award at the first annual Tribeca Film Festival in 2002, and directed *P.S.* in 2004. He lives in Queens with his two cats. (*Miami Blues*, p. 152)

JOHN KIRK started his career as an assistant editor on several television series. Since 1990 he has worked in the technical departments at MGM/United Artists and Sony Pictures. As a former film archivist for both studios, he worked on restoring and preserving such important films as *Some Like It Hot*, *Kiss Me Deadly*, *Persona*, Fellini's *Satyricon*, *The Apartment*, and *Mississippi Mermaid*. (*Lord Love a Duck*, p. 142; *Mademoiselle*, p. 146; *Return from the Ashes*, p. 201)

TIM KITTLESON served as director of the UCLA Film and Television Archive from 1999 through 2006. From 1980 to 1998 he was executive vice president of the Inter national Film and Television Alliance (IFTA) and executive director of its trade event, the American Film Market (AFM). Earlier in his career, he was a documentary film producer under contract to UNESCO and worked as an advertising executive in New York, London, and Paris. (*Alice Doesn't Live Here Anymore*, p. 16; *Bedazzled*, p. 27; *The Innocents*, p. 115; *L'Innocente*, p. 135)

BARBARA KOPPLE, two-time Academy Award–winning producer/director, has made her mark by telling in-depth stories in both nonfiction and fiction films, exploring subjects ranging from the struggles of coal miners to the lives of Woody Allen and Mike Tyson. Her films include *Wild Man Blues*, *Harlan County U.S.A.*, *American Dream*, *Fallen Champ: The Untold Story of Mike Tyson*, *A Conversation with Gregory Peck*, *My Genera-*

tion, and *Shut Up & Sing*. She has also directed commercials and television series, including *Oz*, *Homicide*, and *Addiction*. (*The Battle of Algiers*, p. 23)

ANNE LANDSMAN is a novelist and screenwriter whose first novel, *The Devil's Chimney*, was nominated for the PEN/Hemingway Award, the Janet Heidinger Kafka Prize, QPB's "New Voices" Award, and the M-Net Book Prize. Her work has been featured in *The Believer* magazine, and her latest novel is *The Rowing Lesson*. (*Tales of Manhattan*, p. 228)

SHIRLEY LAURO is a Guggenheim fellow and author of the Tony-nominated *Open Admissions*, *A Piece of My Heart*, *The Contest*, *AKA*, *All Through the Night*, and *Clarence Darrow's Last Trial* as well as many other plays for which she has won numerous awards. She is on the steering committee of the Dramatists Guild. (*Black Narcissus*, p. 36)

RICHARD LAVENSTEIN is a principal at Bond Street Architecture & Design. (*It's a Gift*, p. 117; *Night and the City*, p. 166)

JOHN LINDLEY has been director of photography on such films as *Field of Dreams*, *Father of the Bride*, *You've Got Mail*, *Money Train*, *Pleasantville*, *The Sum of All Fears*, and *Reservation Road*, among others. (*Liquid Sky*, p. 136)

PHILLIP LOPATE is the author of essay collections (*Bachelorhood; Portrait of My Body*), novels (*The Rug Merchant*), and poetry (*The Daily Round*) and editor of *The Art of the Personal Essay* and *Writing New York*. His film criticism is collected in *Totally Tenderly Tragically*. He has served on the New York Film Festival selection committee and as a guest programmer of the Telluride Film Festival. Lopate currently holds the John Cranford Adams Chair at Hofstra University and teaches in the M.F.A. graduate programs at Columbia University, New School University, and Bennington College. (*The Mothering Heart*, p. 159)

SIDNEY LUMET has directed more than forty films, including *12 Angry Men* (1957), *The Pawnbroker* (1964), *Network* (1976), *The Wiz* (1978), *Dog Day Afternoon* (1975), *Prince of the City* (1981), and *The Verdict* (1982). In 2007, he directed the critically acclaimed film *Before the Devil Knows You're Dead* (2007). Lumet has garnered more than fifty award nominations, including an honorary Academy Award in 2005 and the Directors Guild of America Lifetime Achievement Award in 1993. (*Dodsworth*, p. 65)

SUSAN LYALL is a costume designer who has worked with many great directors and actors. Her credits include *Nell* (1994), *The Spanish Prisoner* (1997), *State and Main* (2001), *Flight Plan* (2005), *Invincible* (2006), *Music and Lyrics* (2007), and *Rachel Getting Married* (2008). (*Darling*, p. 61)

LAURENCE MARK has worked in a variety of fields in the movie business, climbing his way up to the executive suite and eventually heading his own production company. As vice president of production at United Artists, he oversaw such features as James L. Brooks's Oscar-winning *Terms of Endearment* and the Eddie Murphy hit *Trading Places* (both 1983). He subsequently joined 20th Century Fox as executive vice president of production; among the features under his watch were David Croenenberg's remake of *The Fly* (1986). In 1986, he formed Laurence Mark Productions, headquartered at Fox, where he was the executive producer of Mike Nichols's comedy *Working Girl* (1988). Mark moved his company to Walt Disney Studios, where he produced *Jerry Maguire* (1996), a film that won the Oscar for best picture. He has continued to produce films, many of which have garnered awards and acclaim, such as the highly anticipated *As Good as It Gets* (1997), *I, Robot* (2004), and *Dreamgirls* (2006). (*Smile*, p. 212)

CHARLES MARSDEN-SMEDLEY is a museum and exhibition designer based in London. (*The Servant*, p. 209)

A native of Birmingham, Alabama, HUGH MARTIN started his career in New York as a vocal arranger. With Ralph Blane, he wrote the score of *Meet Me in St. Louis*, for Judy Garland. Two of its songs, "The Trolley Song" and "Have Yourself a Merry Little Christmas," have become classics. (Pandora's Box: *Passion* [*Madame DuBarry*]; *Broken Blossoms*; *The Last Flight*; *Love Me Tonight*; *Applause*; *The Clock*; *The Night of the Hunter*; *The Good Fairy*; *A Tree Grows in Brooklyn*, p. 173)

ROBERT MARX has served as director of the theater program at the National Endowment for the Arts and the New York State Council on the Arts and was executive director of the New York Public Library for the Performing Arts at Lincoln Center. He is an essayist on theater and opera, has produced off-Broadway plays, and is the voice frequently heard on the intermission features of the Metropolitan Opera's radio broadcasts. (*The Blue Angel*, p. 39)

RICHARD P. MAY has been involved in film distribution and preservation since 1952. He is a member of the Academy of Motion Picture Arts and Sciences, the Association of Moving Image Archivists, and the Society of Motion Picture and Television Engineers, where he is a fellow and chair, Hollywood Section. (*Symphony of Six Million*, p. 227)

ANNETTE MELVILLE has directed the National Film Preservation Foundation since 1997. Created by Congress in 1996, the nonprofit NFPF has provided preservation grants to archives and museums across forty-five states, the District of Columbia, and Puerto Rico and saved more than 1,300 films. (*Cologne: From the Diary of Ray and Esther*, p. 53)

RIC MENELLO is a screenwriter, film historian, and music video director. He co-wrote the feature *Two Lovers* starring Joaquin Phoenix and Gwyneth Paltrow, and was creative consultant on *We Own the Night* both of which were official entries in the Cannes Film Festival. He did the audio commentary for two DVDs of films by Claude Chabrol, *Cry of the Owl* and *Pleasure Party*. The films he has co-written have been entered in the Florence and Bari Film Festivals, Atlanta Fest, Crested Butte (Silver Award for Short Comedy), Slamdance and South by Southwest. He has been nominated for two Billboard Music Video Awards. He also works as a script consultant to actors and directors. (*None*

Shall Escape, p. 172; *Un flic* [*Dirty Money*], p. 250)

DINA MERRILL has starred in twenty-two motion pictures, including *True Colors*. On television, she has guest-starred in innumerable major shows, appearing in series, specials, mini-series, and movies of the week, including *Murder She Wrote, Repeat Performance*, and *The Brass Ring*. Between these appearances, she accomplished two of her major goals: starring on Broadway, in the drama *Angel Street*, and in her first musical, *On Your Toes*. She is vice chair of RKO Pictures. (*Just Tell Me What You Want*, p. 120)

ROGER MICHELL is a film and theater director of, among other projects, *Persuasion, Notting Hill, Changing Lanes*, and *Venus*. (*The Great Escape*, p. 97)

SUSANNA MOORE is a writer whose books include the novel *One Last Look* (Knopf, 2003), the travel book *I Myself Have Seen It* (2003), and *The Big Girls* (Knopf, 2007). (*Fire*, p. 84)

DAVID MORRISSEY has appeared in many films, including *Some Voices, Hilary and Jackie, Robin Hood, Drowning by Numbers, Fanny and Elvis, Call*, and *The Other Boleyn Girl*. His theater credits include *Peer Gynt* (Royal National Theater), *King John* (Royal Shakespeare Ensemble), *Much Ado About Nothing*, and *Three Days of Rain* (West End). He has appeared on television in *Our Mutual Friend, Holding On, Out of Control, One Summer*, and *Pure Wickedness* and is the director (film/TV) of *Bring Me Your Love* and *Sweet Revenge*. (*The Long Good Friday*, p. 141)

GREGORY MOSHER is director of the Arts Initiative at Columbia University. He is a Tony Award–winning director and producer of nearly two hundred stage productions at the Lincoln Center and Goodman Theatres, on Broadway, at the Royal National Theatre, and in the West End. His film *The Prime Gig* was shown at the Venice, London, and Los Angeles film festivals. (*Fat City*, p. 77; *Pure Melodrama: A Place in the Sun; Room at the Top*, p. 186)

MICHAEL MUSTO writes the popular column "La Dolce Musto" in the *Village Voice*. (*Valley of the Dolls*, p. 253)

DIANE NABATOFF has developed and produced a diverse group of films, including *Very Bad Things*, starring Christian Slater and Cameron Diaz; *The Proposition*, starring Kenneth Branagh, William Hurt, and Madeleine Stowe; and *Operation Dumbo Drop*, starring Danny Glover and Ray Liotta. In 1999, she returned to New

York City and, with Liotta and Michelle Grace, founded Tiara Blu Films, where she has produced many projects for both television and film. These include *NARC*, starring Liotta and Jason Patric, and *Take the Lead*, starring Antonio Banderas. While receiving her B.A. degree from Harvard University, Nabatoff was the first female producer of the Hasty Pudding Theatricals and founded the Radcliffe Pitches, the university's first female vocal group. She received an M.B.A. from Harvard Business School. (*Amen.*, p. 17)

VINICIUS NAVARRO is assistant professor of film studies at Georgia Institute of Technology. (*How Tasty Was My Little Frenchman*, p. 106; *Los olvidados* [*The Young and the Damned*], p. 143)

ROB NELSON is a member of the National Society of Film Critics and winner of three editorial awards from the Association of Alternative Newsweeklies. He is an adjunct instructor at the Minneapolis College of Art and Design. Nelson is the former film editor of *City Pages*. He still writes about movies and related topics for such publications as *Film Comment*, *Cinema Scope*, and the *Boston Pheonix*. (*The Heartbreak Kid*, p. 100)

GEOFFREY O'BRIEN is editor in chief of the Library of America and the author of several books, including *Hardboiled America*, *Dream Time: Chapters from the Sixties*, *The Phantom Empire*, *The Browser's Ecstasy*, *Castaways of the Image Planet*, and *Sonata for Jukebox*. He is a contributor to the *New York Review of Books*, *Artforum*, and other publications; he received the Whiting Foundation Writing Award and has been a finalist for the National Book Critic Circle Award in criticism. (*A Christmas Carol*, p. 52; *Safe in Hell*, p. 205; *They Won't Believe Me*, p. 236; *A Touch of Zen*, p. 244)

KATHERINE OLIVER was appointed commissioner of the New York City Mayor's Office of Film, Theatre, and Broadcasting on August 1, 2002. She earlier served as general manager of Bloomberg Radio and Television, where she oversaw ten channels in seven languages. Prior to that, Oliver was a radio and television reporter for CNBC, Financial News Network (FNN), WABC Radio, 1010 WINS, and National Public Radio member station WBGO. She is a board member of the International Academy of Television Arts and Sciences, the Center for Communication, the Museum of the Moving Image, and Early Stages. She is an associate to the board of directors of the International Academy of Television Arts and Sciences, a member of New York Women in Film and Television, and the Junior League. (Location Scout, p. 26)

ROGER PARADISO most recently wrote, produced, and directed *Tony' n' Tina's Wedding.* His other producing credits include Robert De Niro's *City by the Sea*; *The Thomas Crown Affair*, directed by John McTiernan and starring Pierce Brosnan and Rene Russo; and *At First Sight*, directed by Irwin Winkler and starring Val Kilmer and Mira Sorvino. Paradiso was also one of the producers on *Bullet*, for director Julien Temple, and *The Manhattan Project*, for director Marshall Brickman. He wrote and directed the award-winning short films *Looping* and *The Dream Conspiracy*, which played at festivals worldwide and aired on cable television. He has also been unit director on several films as well as a producer/director for commercials, videos, and theater. (*Stardust Memories*, p. 215)

Since founding GreeneStreet Films with Fisher Stevens in 1996, JOHN PENOTTI has produced many of the company's projects, including *A Prairie Home Companion*, *Uptown Girls*, *Swimfan*, *Piñero*, *Illuminata*, and *In the Bedroom*, which was nominated for five Academy Awards. He began his film career working under Sidney Lumet on such features as *Family Business* and *A Stranger Among Us*. (*The Front*, p. 86)

GERALDINE PERONI enjoyed a long collaboration with Robert Altman, editing his films *The Player*, *Short Cuts*, and *The Company*, among others. She also edited *Jesus' Son*, Tim Robbins's *Cradle Will Rock*, Nora Ephron's *Michael*, and Ang Lee's *Brokeback Mountain*. (*Tokyo Story*, p. 244)

ACE G. PILKINGTON is professor of English and humanities at Dixie State College and literary-seminar director for the Utah Shakespearean Festival. He is the author of *Screening Shakespeare from Richard II to Henry V* (University of Delaware Press, 1991) and the play *Our Lady Guenevere*, which was produced by the Utah Shakespearean Festival in 1997. His poetry has appeared in more than sixty publications in five countries. Pilkington is also a member of the Science Fiction Writers of America. (*Galaxy Quest*, p. 88)

DAVID POGUE is a graduate of Yale University and personal-technology columnist for the *New York Times*. He has more than 2.5 million books in print, making him one of the world's best-selling authors of how-to books. He has written or co-written seven books in the For Dummies series and created the Missing Manual series of how-to computer books. (*Gattaca*, p. 92)

SAM POLLARD has worked in the film and television industry for more than thirty years, primarily as an editor of documentaries and feature films. His most notable achievement was serving as editor and coproducer of the Oscar-nominated *4 Little Girls*, directed by Spike Lee. (*Crime Wave*, p. 59)

MARK QUIGLEY manages access services for the UCLA Film and Television Archive and serves as adjunct faculty member for UCLA's Moving Image Archive Studies (MIAS) graduate program. (*Mirage*, p. 155)

TONY RANDALL (1920–2004) is best known for his role as Felix Unger, the fastidious photographer who formed half of TV's "The Odd Couple," from 1970 to 1975. Randall was a comic actor who first stepped on the New York stage in 1941. After serving in the U.S. Army during World War II, he worked on radio and in television, appearing in the series *One Man's Family* (1950–52) and, more famously, costarring with Wally Cox in *Mr. Peepers* (1952–55). He was memorable in the films *Pillow Talk* (1959) and *Lover*

Come Back (1961), romantic comedies starring Rock Hudson and Doris Day, and in the fantasy *The Seven Faces of Dr. Lao* (1964), in which he played multiple roles. His real success, however, came in television, appearing in comedy series and as a guest on talk shows and game shows. (He was a frequent guest of Johnny Carson and David Letterman.) After *The Odd Couple*, he starred in two more comedy series, *The Tony Randall Show* (1976–78) and *Love, Sidney* (1981–83), and appeared in small film roles. In the 1990s, he founded the National Actors Studio and made headlines by becoming a father for the first time at age 77. (*City Lights*, p. 53)

MICHAEL RATCLIFFE is former literary editor and chief book critic of the *Times* in London and former theater critic and literary editor of the *Observer*. Now working freelance, he has written on opera in Britain and on European travel for the *New York Times* and has led specialist cultural tours to Prague, Vienna, Provence, and Berlin. (*A Wedding*, p. 255)

MEGAN RATNER is associate editor for *Bright Lights Film Journal*. She has contributed to *Filmmaker*, *The New York Times*, *BlackBook*, and *Senses of Cinema*. She also writes about art for *Frieze* and

Art on Paper. (*Lamerica*, p. 125; *True Confessions*, p. 246)

NELLY REIFLER is the author of *See Through*, a collection of stories. She has also published stories in such magazines and online journals as *McSweeney's*, *Bomb*, *BlackBook*, *Post Road*, *Failbetter*, and *Exquisite Corpse*. She was assistant editor on the anthology *I Thought My Father Was God*, edited by Paul Auster. Reifler was awarded a Henfield Prize in 1995 and received a grant from the Rotunda Gallery in 2001. She teaches at Sarah Lawrence College. (*Man Bites Dog*, p. 147; *Series 7: The Contenders*, p. 208)

CARRIE RICKEY is a film critic at the *Philadelphia Inquirer*. (*I Know Where I'm Going!*, p. 112)

ROBERT ROSEN is dean of the UCLA School of Theater, Film, and Television, where he oversees programs that include the Department of Film and Television, the Department of Theater, and the Film and Television Archive as well as the school's relationship with the Geffen Playhouse. Rosen is an educator, critic, and preservationist who specializes in issues of media and historical memory. After receiving degrees from Rutgers University in political science and Stanford University in history, he taught in the history departments at Columbia University and the University of Pennsylvania before joining UCLA's Department of Film and Television in 1974. Since 1975 he has served as founding director of The Film and Television Archive, and from 1993 to 1998 he served as chair of the Department of Film and Television. With Martin Scorsese, he organized The Film Foundation, on which he currently serves as founding chair of the Archivists Advisory Council. (*Kiss Me Deadly*, p. 121)

SHAWN ROSENHEIM teaches literature, film, and new media at Williams College. He is married to poet (and fellow Williams professor) Cassandra Cleghorn. (*Creature Comforts*, p. 58; Eddie Bracken: *Hail the Conquering Hero*; *The Miracle of Morgan's Creek*, p. 72)

TOM ROTHMAN is chairman of Fox Filmed Entertainment, the studio responsible for many hit movies including the *X-Men* series, *Ice Age*, *Moulin Rouge*, *Master and Commander*, *Minority Report*, *Napoleon Dynamite*, *Star Wars Episodes 1, 2, and 3*, and *Titanic*. Prior to being named chairman, Rothman held the post of president for the 20th Century Fox Film Group (January–August 2000) and was president of TCF Production (1995–2000). In 1994, he founded and served as first president of Fox Searchlight

Pictures. He is also a member of the board of directors of the Sundance Institute. Rothman was a partner at the New York law firm Frankfurt, Garbus, Klein, and Selz and received the Arthur B. Krim Award from Columbia University. (*The Crucible*, p. 60)

JULIAN RUBENSTEIN is an award-winning writer and journalist based in New York. His work has appeared in such publications as the *New York Times Magazine*, *Rolling Stone*, *Details*, *BlackBook*, *Men's Journal*, and *Salon* and was honored in *The Best American Sports Writing*, *The Best American Crime Writing*, and *The Best American Essays*. He is the author of *Ballad of the Whiskey Robber*. (*F for Fake*, p. 78)

ALBERT S. RUDDY created *Hogan's Heroes* (CBS, 1965–1971), a World War II sitcom, loosely based on the play *Stalag 17*, that depicted the antics of five prisoners of war trying to subvert the Nazi war effort. At the end of the show's five-year run, Ruddy produced several films, including *The Godfather* (1972), for which he won his first of two Oscars for best picture. He returned to television in 1993, creating the successful police drama *Walker, Texas Ranger* (CBS, 1993–2001), starring Chuck Norris as a lawman who believed in handling criminals the old-fashioned way—beating them up. Ruddy continued producing films, eventually striking gold with *Million Dollar Baby* (2004), directed by Clint Eastwood and costarring Hilary Swank and Morgan Freeman. Praised by critics as exquisite and subtle, the film received wide acclaim and won several awards, including his second Oscar for best picture. (*A Big Hand for a Little Lady*, p. 32)

INA SALTZ is principal of Saltz Design, professor of electronic design and multimedia at the City College of New York, and author of *Body Type: Intimate Messages Etched in Flesh*. She was design director of *Golf Magazine*, for which she completed a redesign in 2001. For more than six years, she art-directed the international editions of *Time* and has also been design director of *Worth*, *Golf for Women*, *Worldbusiness*, *PC Tech Journal*, and *High School Sports* magazines. Saltz, who graduated from the Cooper Union for the Advancement of Science and Art, was one of the first art directors to design using a computer; in 1981, she created animated graphics as part of Time Inc.'s Teletext Project, a precursor of the World Wide Web. She has chaired, cochaired, and judged many design competitions, and her honors include awards from major design organizations. Saltz serves as a board member of the Society of Publication Designers and is on the design faculty of the Stanford Professional Publishing Course. (*After Hours*, p. 12; *New York Stories*, p. 165)

NABEEL SARWAR is a corporate lawyer. He studied in the graduate program in television at the Newhouse School of Communications at Syracuse University. (*Dragon's Food*, p. 68; *East Is East*, p. 71; *In Custody*, p. 114)

SIMON SCHAMA is professor of art history and history at Columbia University and art and culture critic for *The New Yorker*. His fifteen-part BBC/History Channel series on the history of Britain drew an estimated 3 to 4 million viewers in the U.K., and his books—*Rough Crossings*; *The Power of Art*; *Citizens: A Chronicle of the French Revolution*; *Landscape and Memory*; and *Rembrandt's Eyes*—have won awards on both sides of the Atlantic. (*Accident*, p. 8; *Le Colonel Chabert*, p. 126; *The Leopard*, p. 131)

MICHAEL SCHEINFELD is senior writer for *TV Guide* and contributes the magazine's "Now Showing on Video and DVD" column. He is also a contributing editor to the annual best-selling reference book *Leonard Maltin's Movie and Video Guide*. Among the publications to which he has written reviews and articles are *The Motion Picture Guide* and *Films in Review*. (*Gun Crazy*, p. 98; *Johnny Guitar*, p. 119; *T-Men*, p. 243)

MARTIN SCORSESE was born in 1942 in New York City and raised in the downtown neighborhood of Little Italy, which later provided the inspiration for several of his films. Scorsese earned a B.S. in film communications in 1964, followed by an M.A. in the same field in 1966, at New York University's School of Film. During this time, he made numerous prize-winning short films, including *The Big Shave*. In 1968, Scorsese directed his first feature film, *Who's That Knocking at My Door?* He served as assistant director and editor of the documentary *Woodstock* in 1970 and won critical and popular acclaim for his 1973 film *Mean Streets*. Scorsese directed his first documentary, *Italianamerican*, in 1974. In 1976, his *Taxi Driver* was awarded the Palme d'Or at the Cannes Film Festival. He followed with *New York, New York* in 1977, *The Last Waltz* in 1978, and *Raging Bull* in 1980, which received eight Academy Award nominations including best picture and best director. Scorsese went on to direct *The Color of Money*, *The Last Temptation of*

Christ, Goodfellas, Cape Fear, Casino, Kundun, and *The Age of Innocence,* among others. In 1996, he completed a four-hour documentary entitled *A Personal Journey with Martin Scorsese through American Movies,* codirected by Michael Henry Wilson; commissioned by the British Film Institute, it celebrated the one hundredth anniversary of the birth of cinema. In 2001, Scorsese released *Il Mio Viaggio in Italia,* an epic documentary that affectionately chronicles his love for Italian cinema. His long-cherished project *Gangs of New York* was released in 2002, earning critical honors including a Golden Globe Award for best director. In 2003, PBS broadcast the seven-film documentary series *Martin Scorsese Presents: The Blues. The Aviator* was released in December 2004, earning five Academy Awards as well as the Golden Globe and BAFTA awards for best picture. In 2005, *No Direction Home: Bob Dylan* was broadcast as part of the American Masters series on PBS and released on DVD worldwide by Paramount Home Entertainment. Scorsese's most recent feature, *The Departed,* was released to critical acclaim in October 2006; it was honored with four Academy Awards, including best picture and best director, as well as the Director's Guild of America, Golden Globe, New York Film Critics, National Board of Review, and Critic's Choice awards for best director. *Shine a Light,* his documentary of the Rolling Stones in concert, was released worldwide on April 4, 2008. He is currently in postproduction on *Shutter Island,* due for release in fall 2009. Additional awards and honors include the Golden Lion from the Venice Film Festival (1995), the AFI Life Achievement Award (1997), the Honoree at the Film Society of Lincoln Center's 25th Gala Tribute (1998), the DGA Lifetime Achievement Award (2003), and the Kennedy Center Honors (2007). Scorsese is founder and chair of The Film Foundation, a nonprofit organization dedicated to the preservation and protection of motion picture history. At the 2007 Cannes Film Festival, he launched the World Cinema Foundation, a not-for-profit dedicated to the preservation and restoration of neglected films from around the world, with special attention to developing countries lacking the financial and technical resources to undertake the work themselves. Scorsese is the founder and chair. (*Living on Velvet,* p. 138; Forgotten Westerns: *Little Big Horn; Canyon Passage,* p. 50)

A leading figure in American independent animation, MAUREEN SELWOOD is the creator of such film projects as *Mistaken Identity, Hail Mary, Flying Circus: An Imagined Memoir, Pearls, This Is Just to Say, The Rug,* and *Odalisque: Three Fantasies of Pursuit.* She has participated in a series of installations and performances, including *As the Veil Lifts* (American Academy in Rome), *As You Desire Me* (American Academy in Rome), and *This Is My House* and *All the Places I Have Ever Lived* (MAK Center for Art and Architecture). She has received grants from the John Solomon Guggenheim Foundation, New York State Council on the Arts, the Jerome Foundation, and the American Film Institute as well as a visiting artist residency at the MacDowell Colony. A recipient of the Rome Prize from the American Academy in Rome, Selwood is currently on the faculty of the Experimental Animation Department at California Institute of the Arts. (*Memories of Underdevelopment,* p. 151)

WILLIAM SERTL has been a travel editor for the past twenty years at *Saveur, Travel & Leisure,* and, most recently, *Gourmet.* (*Dodsworth,* p. 65)

ROBERT K. SHAYE founded New Line Cinema in 1967, guiding the company's growth from a privately held art-film distributor to one of the entertainment industry's leading independent studios and veritable box office force. A University of Michigan graduate with a degree in business administration and a J.D. from Columbia University Law School, Shaye is also a Fulbright Scholar and a member of the New York State Bar and serves on the board of trustees of the Motion Picture Pioneers and the American Film Institute. (Sunday Afternoon: *The Thief of Bagdad; Things to Come; Of Mice and Men,* p. 237)

GEORGE SHEANSHANG is an entertainment attorney in private practice in New York City. He specializes in film, television, publishing, and theater law. His clients include actors, directors, writers, producers, production companies, distributors, financiers, agents, and executives. (A Film Cure: *The Spirit of the Beehive; The Saragossa Manuscript; In the Realm of the Senses* [Ai no corrida], p. 216)

JIM SHEPARD is the author of six novels, including *Project X,* and two story collections, including *Love and Hydrogen.* His most recent book of stories is *Like You'd Understand, Anyway.* Shepard teaches at Williams College. (*Aguirre: The Wrath of God,* p. 15; *Paracelsus,* p. 181)

KAREN SHEPARD is the author of the novels *An Empire of a Woman, The Bad Boy's Wife,* and, most recently, *Don't I*

Know You? She teaches writing and literature at Williams College and lives in Williamstown, Massachusetts, with her husband, novelist Jim Shepard, their three children, and one very strange dog. (*Big Trouble*, p. 34; An Act of Kindness: *The Producers*, p. 191)

JOSH SIEGEL, assistant curator in the department of Film and Media at the Museum of Modern Art, is the organizer or co-organizer of more than fifty exhibitions, including *The Spell of the Picture: Envisioning Henry James*; *The Films of Marguerite Duras*; and *The Lodz Film School of Poland: 50 Years*, as well as tributes to Jeanne Moreau, Don Siegel, Nicholas Ray, Olivier Assayas, and Errol Morris. Siegel also cocurated *Open Ends*, with Kirk Varnedoe and Paola Antonelli, the third cycle of MoMA2000 exhibitions, and coedited the accompanying catalogue, *Modern Contemporary: Art at MoMA Since 1980*. (*An Actor's Revenge*, p. 9; *Duck Soup*, p. 69; *In a Lonely Place*, p. 113; *Pickpocket*, p. 185)

ELLIOT SILVERSTEIN is the director of the films *Cat Ballou*, *The Happening*, *A Man Called Horse*, and *The Car*. He also has two Broadway credits to his name as well as many seasons of summer theater. He served on the National Board of the Directors Guild of America for more than thirty years and was president of the Artists Rights Foundation from 1990 to 2001. Among his honors are the John Huston Award for Artists Rights, the Médaille Beaumarchais from the Société des Auteurs et Compositeurs Dramatiques, and the Robert B. Aldrich Award for Service from the Directors Guild of America. Silverstein managed the theater department of Brandeis University from 1950 to 1952, and he was on the adjunct faculty at the University of Southern California, where he taught directing to graduate students. (Carole Lombard: *Twentieth Century*, p. 248)

RON SIMON has been curator of television at the Museum of Television and Radio since the early 1980s. Among the many exhibitions he has curated featuring screenings and a catalogue are *The Television of Dennis Potter*, *Witness to History*, *Jack Benny: The Television and Radio Work*, and *Worlds without End: The Art and History of the Soap Opera*. Simon is associate professor at Columbia University and Hunter College, where he teaches courses in the history of the media. He has written for many publications, including *The Encyclopedia of Television*, and served as host and creative consultant of the CD-ROM *Total Television*. He is a member of the editorial board of *Television Quarterly* and has lectured at museums and educational institutions throughout the U.S. (Paddy Chayefsky, p. 150)

SCOTT SIMON has been part of National Public Radio's *Weekend Edition*, the top-rated U.S. news and public affairs program, for eighteen years. He is the winner of Peabody, Emmy, and Columbia-Dupont awards for war reporting, personal essays, and political and social reporting. Simon is also the author of three books, including *Pretty Birds*, a novel set in Sarajevo during the Bosnian war. (*The Third Man*, p. 238)

FARROKH SOLTANI is film critic for TehranAvenue.com, an online city magazine based in Tehran, published in Farsi and English. (*The Cow* [*Gaav*], p. 57; *The Peddler* [*Dasforoush*], p. 184)

HEATHER STELIGA is associate director for communications at the Miami Art Museum. Previously, she was president of foggydaycommunications, (which provides marketing and communications services to nonprofit organizations in New York City and New England); director of communications for the School of Visual Arts; and director of public relations for the Asia Society and Museum. (Zhang Yimou:

Raise the Red Lantern; *Ju Dou*, p. 199)

ERIC STOLTZ is an actor and director who has appeared in films, on television, and on Broadway. (*The Panic in Needle Park*, p. 181; *Tabu: A Story of the South Seas*, p. 228; Behind the Scenes: *Hearts of Darkness: A Filmmaker's Apocalypse*; *Living in Oblivion*; *Lost in La Mancha*; *Burden of Dreams*, p. 137)

MARK STRAND is the author of ten books of poetry, and the most recent, *Blizzard of One*, won the 1999 Pulitzer Prize. He has served as Poet Laureate of the United States and is a former chancellor of the Academy of American Poets. (*Dead of Night*, p. 64; *In a Lonely Place*, p. 113; *Orpheus*, p. 180)

KENNETH TURAN is film critic for the *Los Angeles Times*, director of the *Times* Book Prizes, and film critic for National Public Radio's *Morning Edition*. A graduate of Swarthmore College and Columbia University's graduate program in journalism, he is coauthor of *Call Me Anna: The Autobiography of Patty Duke* and sits on the board of directors of the National Yiddish Book Center. His other books include *Sundance to Sarajevo: Film Festivals and the World They Make* and *Never Coming to a Theater Near You: A Celebration of a Certain*

Kind of Movie. (*Léolo*, p. 130; *Taxi!*, p. 232)

ROB TYMCHYSHYN is an aspiring screenwriter, established computer nerd, and former corporate muckety-muck. (*Fireworks*, p. 85; *Patterns*, p. 183)

PAOLO CHERCHI USAI wrote and directed *Passio*, which premiered in North America at the 2007 Tribeca Film Festival. He is cofounder of the Pordenone Silent Film Festival and of the L. Jeffrey Selznick School at George Eastman House. His books include *Burning Passions: An Introduction to the Study of Silent Cinema* (2000), the twelve-volume series *The Griffith Project* (1999–2008), and *The Death of Cinema: History, Cultural Memory, and the Digital Dark Age* (2001). In 2002 he was honored by the French Ministry of Culture with the title of Chevalier de l'Ordre des Arts et des Lettres. (*Songs from the Second Floor*, p. 213)

KEVIN WADE is the author of the plays *Key Exchange, Mr. & Mrs.,* and *Cruise Control* and screenplays for *Working Girl, True Colors, Junior,* and *Maid in Manhattan.* He also co-wrote the screenplays for *Mr. Baseball* and *Meet Joe Black.* Wade lives with his family in Oyster Bay, New York. (*Against All Odds*, p. 12)

WENDY WASSERSTEIN (1950–2006) was a playwright whose credits include *The Heidi Chronicles* (Tony Award, Pulitzer Prize, and Susan Blackburn Prize) and *The Sisters Rosenweig* (Outer Critics Circle Award). She was the recipient of Guggenheim and NEA fellowships. (*The Band Wagon*, p. 23)

TODD WIENER has worked at the UCLA Film and Television Archive for the last nine years and is currently its motion picture archivist. Previously at the archive, he served as assistant motion picture archivist and collection services assistant (where he mastered a "mean" nitrate film cement splice). He is a member and supporter of the Association of Moving Image Archivists (AMIA) and actively participates in its conferences and events. Wiener is particularly proud of his work on the production of the educational and research DVD series *A Century of Sound: The History of Sound in Motion Pictures,* narrated by the archive's preservation officer, Robert Gitt. (*A Time to Love and a Time to Die*, p. 241)

TIM WILLIAMS is head of production at GreeneStreet Films. His production and coproduction credits include the Oscar-nominated *In the Bedroom;* the ALMA Award–winning *Piñero; Swimfan;* and *Just a Kiss.* Prior to joining

GreeneStreet, Williams was a partner with the London-based GriP Theatre, which, over the course of four years, developed into a small but profitable home for a promising company of new writers, directors, and actors on the London fringe. Williams has also worked as set assistant and assistant director for such directors as Sidney Lumet, Mike Nichols, Penny Marshall, and Paul Mazursky and producers Lawrence Mark, Scott Rudin, Larry Gordon, and Burtt Harris. (*Billy Liar*, p. 35)

CHRONOLOGICAL INDEX

1959 *Pickpocket*
1959 *Room at the Top*
1959 *Shadows*
1960 *The Savage Eye*
1961 *The Innocents*
1962 *Lonely Are the Brave*
1963 *An Actor's Revenge*
1963 *Billy Liar*
1963 *The Great Escape*
1963 *The Leopard*
1963 *The Servant*
1964 *The Americanization of Emily*
1964 *The East Is Red*
1964 *Fail Safe*
1964 *Kwaidan*
1965 *The Battle of Algiers*
1965 *Bunny Lake Is Missing*
1965 *Darling*
1965 *The Hill*
1965 *Mirage*
1965 *Repulsion*
1965 *Return from the Ashes*
1965 *The Saragossa Manuscript*
1966 *A Big Hand for a Little Lady*
1966 *Lord Love a Duck*
1966 *Mademoiselle*
1966 *The Wrong Box*
1967 *Accident*
1967 *Bedazzled*
1967 *La collectionneuse*
1967 *Playtime*
1967 *Valley of the Dolls*
1968 *Memories of Underdevelopment*
1968 *The Producers*
1969 *The Cow*
1969 *Putney Swope*
1969 *Salesman*
1969 *A Touch of Zen*
1970 *The Conformist*
1970 *Deep End*
1971 *Fiddler on the Roof*

1971 *How Tasty Was My Little Frenchman*
1971 *The Panic in Needle Park*
1971 *Sweet Sweetback's Baadasssss Song*
1971 *Two-Lane Blacktop*
1972 *Fat City*
1972 *Ganja and Hess*
1972 *The Heartbreak Kid*
1972 *Un flic*
1973 *Aguirre: The Wrath of God*
1973 *The Spirit of the Beehive*
1973 *World of Geisha*
1974 *Alice Doesn't Live Here Anymore*
1974 *Alice in the Cities*
1974 *Busting*
1974 *Caged Heat*
1974 *El santo oficio*
1974 *The Savage Is Loose*
1974 *Sweet Movie*
1975 *F for Fake*
1975 *O Thiassos*
1975 *The Passenger*
1975 *Smile*
1976 *The Front*
1976 *Harlan County U.S.A.*
1976 *In the Realm of the Senses*
1976 *L'Innocente*
1976 *1900*
1977 *Killer of Sheep*
1978 *Capricorn One*
1978 *Straight Time*
1978 *A Wedding*
1980 *Just Tell Me What You Want*
1980 *The Long Good Friday*
1980 *Stardust Memories*
1980 *The Stunt Man*
1981 *Blind Chance*
1981 *True Confessions*
1982 *Burden of Dreams*
1982 *Conan the Barbarian*

INDEX OF DIRECTORS

Taylor Hackford
  Against All Odds
Sachi Hamano
  Lily Festival
Robert Hamer (with Charles
Crichton, Alberto Cavalcanti,
and Basil Dearden)
  Dead of Night
Wojciech Has
  The Saragossa Manuscript
Howard Hawks
  Ball of Fire
  Twentieth Century
Monte Hellman
  Two-Lane Blacktop
Werner Herzog
  Aguirre: The Wrath of God
George Hickenlooper (with
Fax Bahr)
  *Hearts of Darkness: A Film-
  maker's Apocalypse*
Arthur Hiller
  *The Americanization of
  Emily*
Hou Hsiao-hsien
  The Puppetmaster
King Hu
  A Touch of Zen
Brian Desmond Hurst
  A Christmas Carol
John Huston
  Beat the Devil
  Fat City
  Moby Dick
Peter Hyams
  Busting
  Capricorn One
Nicholas Hytner
  The Crucible
Kon Ichikawa
  An Actor's Revenge
John Irvin
  Turtle Diary

Juzo Itami
  Tampopo
Jim Jarmusch
  Dead Man
Norman Jewison
  Fiddler on the Roof
Jia Zhan-ke
  Platform
Neil Jordan
  The Miracle
Shusuke Kaneko
  Gamera 3: Revenge of Iris
Elia Kazan
  A Tree Grows in Brooklyn
Buster Keaton (with Edward
Sedgwick)
  The Cameraman
David Kellogg
  Cool As Ice
Krzysztof Kieslowski
  Blind Chance
Takeshi Kitano
  Fireworks
Kasaki Kobayashi
  Kwaidan
Barbara Kopple
  American Dream
  Harlan County U.S.A.
Alexander Korda (with Marcel
Pagnol)
  Marius
Tatsumi Kumashiro
  World of Geisha
Akira Kurosawa
  Stray Dog
Gregory La Cava
  My Man Godfrey
  Symphony of Six Million
John Landis
  ¡Three Amigos!
Fritz Lang
  The Big Heat
Charles Laughton
  The Night of the Hunter

Christopher Münch
  The Hours and Times
F. W. Murnau (with Robert J. Flaherty)
  *Tabu: A Story of
    the South Seas*
Jean Negulesco
  The Best of Everything
Andrew Niccol
  Gattaca
Elliott Nugent
  Three Cornered Moon
Damien O'Donnell
  East Is East
Nagisa Oshima
  In the Realm of the Senses
Yasujiro Ozu
  Tokyo Story
Georg Wilhelm Pabst
  Paracelsus
Marcel Pagnol
  César
Marcel Pagnol (with Alexander Korda)
  Marius
Dean Parisot
  Galaxy Quest
Nick Park
  Creature Comforts
Louis Pepe (with Keith Fulton)
  Lost in La Mancha
Irving Pichel
  They Won't Believe Me
Benoît Poelvoorde (with Rémy Belvaux and André Bonzel)
  Man Bites Dog
Roman Polanski
  Repulsion
Gillo Pontecorvo
  The Battle of Algiers
H. C. Potter
  Hellzapoppin'

Michael Powell (with Emeric Pressburger)
  Black Narcissus
  I Know Where I'm Going!
  *The Life and Death of
    Colonel Blimp*
Michael Powell (with Ludwig Berger and Tim Whelan)
  The Thief of Bagdad
Otto Preminger
  Bunny Lake Is Missing
Emeric Pressburger (with Michael Powell)
  Black Narcissus
  I Know Where I'm Going!
  *The Life and Death of
    Colonel Blimp*
Nicholas Ray
  In a Lonely Place
  Johnny Guitar
Carol Reed
  The Third Man
Tony Richardson
  Mademoiselle
W. D. Richter
  *The Adventures of Buckaroo
    Banzai Across the 8th
    Dimension*
Arturo Ripstein
  El santo oficio
Michael Ritchie
  Smile
Martin Ritt
  The Front
  No Down Payment
Mark Robson
  Valley of the Dolls
  Youth Runs Wild
Eric Rohmer
  La collectionneuse
Roberto Rossellini
  Open City
Richard Rush
  The Stunt Man

Yang Fengliang (with Zhang
Yimou)
  Ju Dou
Zhang Yimou
  Raise the Red Lantern
Zhang Yimou (with Yang
Fengliang)
  Ju Dou
Fred Zinnemann (with
Vincente Minnelli)
  The Clock
Charlotte Zwerin (with Albert
Maysles and David Maysles)
  Salesman
Terry Zwigoff
  Crumb

BIOGRAPHIES

ROBERT KAHN, creator and editor of the City Secrets series, is an architect in private practice. A recipient of the Prix de Rome from the American Academy in Rome, Kahn has received numerous awards from the New York chapter of the American Institute of Architects (AIA). His work has been featured in many publications, including *Architectural Digest, House & Garden, Metropolitan Home*, the *New York Times Magazine*, and the *New York Times*. A partial list of clients includes Frank Stella; Kevin Kline and Phoebe Cates; Daniel Day-Lewis and Rebecca Miller; Mary-Louise Parker; David Mamet; Wes Anderson; Nicholas Hytner; Adam Duritz; Sam and Ellen Newhouse; Lincoln Center Theaters; and the Classic Stage Company. Kahn has taught at Yale University where he held a Davenport Chair Professorship. He received a Masters in Architecture from Yale University.

THE FILM FOUNDATION
The Film Foundation, the leading nonprofit organization dedicated to film preservation, was created to address the need for a single influential entity to take the lead in advocating and supporting the preservation of our collective cinematic heritage. The organization was founded in 1990 by Martin Scorsese and a distinguished group of fellow filmmakers: Woody Allen, Robert Altman, Francis Ford Coppola, Clint Eastwood, Stanley Kubrick, George Lucas, Sydney Pollack, Robert Redford, and Steven Spielberg. In 2006, they were joined on the foundation's board of directors by Paul Thomas Anderson, Wes Anderson, Curtis Hanson, Peter Jackson, Ang Lee, and Alexander Payne.

Through partnerships with the nation's leading film archives—Academy Film Archive, George Eastman House, Library of Congress, Museum of Modern

Art, and UCLA Film & Television Archive—The Film
Foundation has funded the preservation and restoration
work of more than 475 films that might otherwise have
been lost. The foundation also supports the National
Film Preservation Foundation, which works with over
100 regional archives, libraries and historical societies. A
broad range of films has been saved, including studio and
independent features, avant-garde works, documentaries,
newsreels, home movies, and films from the silent era.

Additionally, The Film Foundation created *The Story
of Movies* project, the first integrated interdisciplinary
curriculum, in recognition of the importance of exposing
future generations to classic cinema. This educational
program has been distributed, free of charge, to more
than 25,000 middle school and high school teachers
across the country, reaching some 8 million students.
The films for study are Robert Mulligan's classic *To Kill
A Mockingbird* (1962), Frank Capra's *Mr. Smith Goes to
Washington* (1939), and Robert Wise's *The Day the Earth
Stood Still* (1951).

For more information, please visit www.film-foundation.org

*A portion of the proceeds from the sales of this book
will benefit The Film Foundation's film preservation and
educational programs.*

ACKNOWLEDGMENTS

This book owes its existence to our contributors, whose willingness to share their secret films was remarkable. A heartfelt thanks goes to them for their endless generosity, talent, and enthusiasm.

We are especially grateful to the esteemed Martin Scorsese, as well as Margaret Bodde, Allison Niedermeier, and Jennifer Ahn for their patience and support. We would also like to thank The Film Foundation for championing this project and for its dedication to the preservation of film.

And, finally, we would like to thank all those who made this book come to life, especially Charles Miers for his good judgment; Caitlin Leffel Ostroy for her guidance; Gregory Mosher for his advice; Jackie Sibblies for her editing skills; Suzanne Charlé for her expansive spirit; Ingrid Bromberg Kennedy for her design expertise; and Wes Anderson for his counsel and encouragement.

"Escape from the crowds and chaos can be a challenge in Rome, but help comes in the form of *City Secrets Rome*. Architect and former resident Robert Kahn has collected the wisdom of his artist and writer friends in a guide that peels back the layers of the city's charms."
—*Condé Nast Traveler*

"Architect Robert Kahn's *City Secrets Rome* and *City Secrets Florence, Venice and the Towns of Italy* are full of interesting finds, even for those who know Italy well."
—*Town & Country*

"City Secrets guides are unlike any others on the market . . . in this case, a formidable cross section of London's intelligentsia . . . share their inside information on the parts of London they know best, the sorts of places that they might reveal to visiting friends, the keys that might unlock some of the city's meaning."
—*The Sunday Times* (London)

"*City Secrets New York City*, the latest installment in architect Robert Kahn's invaluable series of insider guides for travelers, comprises recommendations from more than 300 writers, artists, historians, gourmands, and other notables . . . who live and work in New York. Entries in the form of personal vignettes explore everything from art to food, architecture to shopping, and music to landmarks, in all five boroughs."
—*New York Magazine*

"The future of guidebooks." — *Good Magazine*